# WINNING THE PRESIDENCY 2016

The presidential election of 2016 was unlike any in modern American history. Donald Trump, a successful businessman, well known reality television host and a political novice with no clear policy views or political attachments, ran for the presidency. His opponent was Hillary Clinton, a candidate with a long and impressive career in politics. She was the first woman nominee of a major political party and, should she have won, the first woman President of the United States. No one gave Trump much of a chance. Yet he won the election. How did he do it? What explains his political success? What can we expect from a Trump presidency? This book answers these questions. It presents a clear and definitive overview of his campaign, its controversies and setbacks, and its successes. *Winning the Presidency 2016* identifies who voted for Donald Trump and why. It explains why Hillary Clinton lost. This is essential reading for understanding a campaign with no precedents and a presidential election that could have seismic consequences for the conduct of American government.

**William J. Crotty** is Thomas P. O'Neill, Jr. Chair in Public Life and Emeritus Professor of Political Science at Northeastern University. He is a recipient of the Samuel J. Eldersveld Lifetime Achievement Award of the Political Organization and Parties Section of the American Political Science Association and the Hubert H. Humphrey Award of the Policy Studies Association. He has served as president of the Policy Studies Association, the Political Organizations and Parties Section of the American Political Science Association, and as president of the Midwest Political Science Association. Among other areas of interest, he has written on political ideology and its policy-relevant applications, democratic development, and he has conducted surveys of black communities and written on a changing black politics.

## Praise for *Winning the Presidency 2016*

William Crotty and his colleagues have given us a serious and informative book on the 2016 election, which will nourish both citizens and scholars. Both America and the rest of the world badly need it.

**Thomas Ferguson,** *University of Massachusetts-Boston, USA*

This is an excellent volume for courses on U.S. elections and the presidency. Nine highly distinguished political science scholars examine an election that was unconventional and divisive – or, in the case of the congressional elections, conventional and divisive – to explain why this election defied expectations, and to consider whether 2016 is the new normal.

**Christine L. Day,** *University of New Orleans, USA*

*Winning the Presidency 2016* is a very fine, sober, insightful, and literate analysis of a most shocking election. Through wise and deep analysis that will appeal to scholars, students, and political observers, the authors explain how it happened and what it means, weighing a wide variety of factors – American history, contemporary culture, the campaigns and vote counts, and the state of our democracy.

**James A. Morone,** *Brown University, USA*

William Crotty has organized eight excellent, penetrating studies of the 2016 presidential election, the most significant election in this century. Scholars and students alike will welcome this new collection.

**Kenneth J. Janda,** *Northwestern University, USA*

No eight mortals can be expected to explain the inexplicable, but William Crotty and his stellar cast have taken on the challenge and produced a set of insights well worth the read. It's an explanation of many parts: The roles of institutions, campaigns, candidates, voters, social media, meddling, and luck (good and bad) are all well-explored. In the process, and very importantly, the authors don't ignore the "normal" while highlighting the many unique features of the 2016 election. As for implications, the book offers not just a significant list of challenges, but also some reasons for hope.

**Robert Harmel,** *Texas A&M University, USA*

The 2016 US election season was like nothing we have seen before. Its centerpiece—the election of Donald J. Trump—has confounded (most) predictions and drawn US democracy into unchartered territory. This new study, edited by one of the founding fathers of the study of American party politics, William Crotty, provides a much-needed perspective on what happened, why it happened, and what it all means for politics and democracy in the US and the world over.

**David Farrell,** *University College Dublin, UK*

*Winning the Presidency* is a powerful, sobering analysis of the 2016 election. Outstanding contributors apply the best political science theories and data to determine what happened and, more importantly, what it foretells of our political future. The book asks and forcefully answers the question, Has our very democracy been undermined or is this only a political blip? *Winning the Presidency* should be read by every serious scholar, student, activist, and citizen.

**Dick Simpson,** *University of Illinois, USA*

William Crotty's *Winning the Presidency 2016* is a first-rate collection of essays explaining the exciting and wholly unexpected 2016 presidential race. The authors explain how, though at the start of the season it looked likely to be a replay of the Clinton-Bush dynasties, political novice Donald Trump emerged to win the White House. It's a whole new ballgame. This persuasive book forces us to reexamine our conventional thinking.

**Thomas R. Marshall,** *University of Texas-Arlington, USA*

*Winning the Presidency 2016* is a greatly useful and insightful book about a most unlikely election by nine of America's best political scientists. Impressive for its comprehensiveness, the book covers the political and cultural context, the nomination campaigns, the gender issue, the role of demography, the congressional elections, and the collapse of the establishment and political parties. A valuable review and assessment for students, political scientists, and a general audience.

**Bruce Caswell,** *Rowan University, USA*

The 2016 presidential election will probably go down in the annals of history as a realignment election. This book focuses on Donald Trump's surprising victory and Hillary Clinton's unusual loss. William Crotty and his collaborators give us an inside glimpse at both the Democratic and Republican parties in an attempt to determine how each failed to draw support from traditional voters. Contributors share fresh insights into the party decision-making processes and illustrate the growing disconnect between the party establishments and voters. Will the events of this election yield lessons, and will these lessons lead to changes to the electoral system? *Winning the Presidency 2016* is the definitive look at the election, and is an excellent resource on what can be done to bring American democracy into the 21st century.

**Guy Lachapelle,** *Concordia University, Canada*

Bill Crotty's timely, accessible book examines the dynamics behind the unexpected victory of Donald Trump in the 2016 election. Outstanding political scholars offer new insights on nomination fights, the nominees' perils and promises, conventional and unconventional campaign strategies, explanations for the vote, nuances of gender and Latino politics, dissimilarities between congressional and presidential elections, and potentially seismic consequences of the election for political parties, government institutions, and the country. This book is a valuable, rich resource for students and all citizens.

**Jonathan P. West,** *University of Miami, USA*

There was little conventional about the 2016 election, and many believe that it left our understanding of parties and elections in tatters. William Crotty has assembled a team of scholars uniquely qualified to cut through the tweets, hacks, and videotapes to explain this weird election. If you want to know which theories still help to understand the American electorate and which ones need serious re-examination, this volume offers a great place to start.

**John J. McGlennon,** *College of William & Mary, USA*

Donald Trump's ascension from real estate developer and reality TV personality to the most powerful position on Earth was met with shock and consternation by most every thoughtful American. Was race the deciding factor in this election? Or was it perhaps economic distress, cultural change, or immigration concerns that motivated the typical Trump voter? In this insightful and perceptive new book, renowned political scientist William Crotty offers one of the few scholarly, empirical explanations of this astounding political phenomenon. This collection will help readers more clearly comprehend the perplexing and complicated etiology of Trump's rise to power.

**Charles Bittner,** *St. John's University* and *The New Republic, USA*

*Winning the Presidency 2016* is an informative and timely work that provides keen insights into the forces at play in the 2016 presidential election. Scholars and laypeople will find this book to be an interesting analysis of not only the election but also its impact upon the immediate future of American politics.

**Scott Buchanan,** *The Citadel, USA*

William Crotty has collated a series of chapters that will appeal to the political observer and academic alike. The book analyses the reasons for, and repercussions of, Donald Trump's success, while at the same time introducing the reader to the complex nature of the American electoral and party system. While it will have an obvious appeal to an American audience, its significance will also resonate with readers in Europe and further afield.

**Karl O'Connor,** *University of Ulster, UK*

One of the many troubling questions to come out of the 2016 election is, "How do I explain this to my students?" Along comes *Winning the Presidency 2016*, providing the tool I need. It has become a commonplace to recognize the voter distrust and disgust that animated 2016, but William Crotty and the leading political scientists featured here dig up that perception and examine it root and branch. We'll be studying the 2016 election for decades to come; *Winning the Presidency 2016* is an essential starting point.

**Maurice T. Cunningham,** *University of Massachusetts-Boston, USA*

It will take years to fully comprehend Donald Trump's hostile takeover of the GOP and bewildering victory over Hillary Clinton. William Crotty has assembled a crack team of superstar political scientists and made the first and most significant evaluation to date of the evidence pouring in from Election 2016. Even more valuable is how each chapter takes a different vantage point interpreting the election and how the aftershocks will rattle various institutions – and indeed shake the very foundations of the republic – in defining the American ethos in the 21st century.

**Scott McLean,** *Quinnipiac University, USA*

If you wish to understand an "election like no other," it's all here: In *Winning the Presidency 2016*, contributors probe a unique mingling of personalities and events in an election where strategically located white working class voters and late deciders wanted change. Donald Trump personified change more convincingly than any major party nominee in memory, while Hillary Clinton seemed wedded to the status quo. The chapters on women and Latinos are especially insightful and revealing.

**Howard Cody,** *University of Maine, USA*

# WINNING THE PRESIDENCY 2016

*Edited by*
*William J. Crotty*

NEW YORK AND LONDON

Published 2018
by Routledge
711 Third Avenue, New York, NY 10017

and by Routledge
2 Park Square, Milton Park, Abingdon, Oxon, OX14 4RN

*Routledge is an imprint of the Taylor & Francis Group, an informa business*

© 2018 Taylor & Francis

The right of William J. Crotty to be identified as the author of the editorial material, and of the authors for their individual chapters, has been asserted by them in accordance with sections 77 and 78 of the Copyright, Designs and Patents Act 1988.

All rights reserved. No part of this book may be reprinted or reproduced or utilized in any form or by any electronic, mechanical, or other means, now known or hereafter invented, including photocopying and recording, or in any information storage or retrieval system, without permission in writing from the publishers.

*Trademark notice*: Product or corporate names may be trademarks or registered trademarks, and are used only for identification and explanation without intent to infringe.

*Library of Congress Cataloging-in-Publication Data*
Names: Crotty, William J., editor.
Title: Winning the presidency 2016 / [edited by] William J. Crotty, Northeastern University.
Other titles: Winning the presidency two thousand sixteen
Description: New York, NY : Routledge, [2018] | Includes bibliographical references and index.
Identifiers: LCCN 2017008029 | ISBN 9781138654358 (hbk) | ISBN 9781138654365 (pbk) | ISBN 9781315623290 (ebk)
Subjects: LCSH: Presidents—United States—Election—2016.
Classification: LCC JK526 2016 .W56 2018 | DDC 324.973/0932—dc23
LC record available at https://lccn.loc.gov/2017008029

ISBN: 978-1-138-65435-8 (hbk)
ISBN: 978-1-138-65436-5 (pbk)
ISBN: 978-1-315-62329-0 (ebk)

Typeset in Sabon
by Apex CoVantage, LLC

# CONTENTS

| | |
|---|---|
| *List of Tables and Figures* | ix |
| *Acknowledgments* | xi |
| *Contributor Biographies* | xii |
| *Introduction to the Chapters* | xiv |

1  Not an Ordinary Election: The Presidential
   Race of 2016                                         1
   *William J. Crotty*

2  The Conventional Versus the Unconventional:
   Presidential Nominations in 2016                    34
   *Barbara Norrander*

3  The Presidential Election: A Troubled Democracy    57
   *Gerald M. Pomper*

4  Explaining the Vote                                87
   *Charles L. Prysby*

5  The Races for Congress in 2016: A Tale of
   Two Elections                                      103
   *Paul S. Herrnson and Raymond J. La Raja*

6  Women and the 2016 Presidential Election:
   Unrealistic Expectations of Cohesiveness                 129
   *Susan A. MacManus*

7  Navigating through Turbulence and Troublesome
   Times: Latinos, Election 2016, Partisan Politics,
   and Salient Public Policies                              150
   *John A. Garcia*

8  The Election in Perspective                              174
   *John Kenneth White*

*Index*                                                     196

# TABLES AND FIGURES

## Tables

| | | |
|---|---|---|
| 1.1 | Demographics of the 2016 Presidential Vote | 22 |
| 1.2 | Congressional Vote 2016 | 23 |
| 1.3 | Party Control of State Legislatures | 24 |
| 2.1 | Candidate Vote Percentages and Delegates per State in Republican Primaries and Caucuses | 44 |
| 2.2 | Candidate Vote Percentages and Delegates per State in Democratic Primaries and Caucuses | 48 |
| 3.1 | The 2016 Presidential Vote | 59 |
| 3.2 | Effects of the Electoral College | 64 |
| 3.3 | Demography of the Vote in 2016 and 2012 | 66 |
| 3.4 | Influences on the 2016 Presidential Vote | 80 |
| 4.1 | Voter Evaluations of the Presidential Candidates on Public Policy Issues | 94 |
| 4.2 | Voter Assessments of the Presidential Candidates on Character Traits | 97 |
| 5.1 | Top Congressional Races for Spending | 114 |
| 6.1 | National Election Results Mask Vastly Different Female Voting Patterns in States | 132 |
| 7.1 | Hispanics Will Continue to Account for Over 50% of Future U.S. Population Growth | 153 |
| 7.2 | Party Affiliation, by Group | 158 |
| 7.3 | Youth and Naturalizations Are the Main Sources of Eligible Hispanic Voter Growth | 169 |
| 8.1 | A Rising American Electorate: Obama and Clinton Compared | 183 |

## Figures

| | | |
|---|---|---|
| 1.1 | Presidential Election Results | 13 |
| 2.1 | Democratic Delegate Totals | 50 |
| 3.1 | Shifting Odds in 2016 Campaign | 70 |
| 5.1 | House Candidates: Outsiders | 110 |
| 5.2 | House Candidates: Women | 111 |
| 5.3 | Spending in Congressional Races | 113 |
| 5.4 | Fundraising for the House: Insiders vs. Outsiders, 2014 & 2016 | 115 |
| 5.5 | Fundraising for the House: Men vs. Women, 2014 & 2016 | 115 |
| 5.6 | House Elections: Women | 118 |
| 5.7 | House Success Rates | 119 |
| 6.1 | National Exit Poll Results: Gender Differences | 144 |
| 7.1 | Turnout Levels Among Eligible Latino Voters, 1986–2012 | 156 |
| 7.2 | Latinos' Views of Major Parties and Their Concerns for Latinos | 157 |
| 7.3 | Trump's Impact on Latinos' Views of Republican Party | 162 |

# ACKNOWLEDGMENTS

A number of people contributed to the publication of this book.

I would like to thank in particular Jennifer Knerr, Senior Editor for Politics at Routledge, a knowledgeable and highly professional editor and a pleasure to work with. Thanks also to Ze'ev Sudry and Amy Vanderzee, Autumn Spalding and Apex CoVantage, and my entire team at Routledge. Christopher Doucette of Fusion Design and Scott Kebschull's technical assistance was greatly appreciated.

I would also like to thank my wife, Mary Hauch Crotty, whose legal training proved invaluable while contributing as an editor and research analyst to the development of this book.

William J. Crotty

# CONTRIBUTOR BIOGRAPHIES

**John A. Garcia** is Research Professor Emeritus at the Inter-University Consortium for Political and Social Research at the University of Michigan, as well as Faculty Associate in the Center for Political Studies (ISR-Michigan), and is an expert on minority group politics, especially Latinos, and on political behavior.

**Paul S. Herrnson** is a Professor of Political Science at the University of Connecticut. His expertise includes political parties and elections; money and politics; and voting technology, ballot design and election administration. He has published numerous articles and books, including *Congressional Elections: Campaigning at Home and in Washington* (2016); *Voting Technology: The Not-So-Simple Act of Casting a Ballot* (2008, co-authored); and *Interest Groups Unleashed* (2014). He has advised Congress, the Connecticut General Assembly, the Maryland General Assembly, the Election Assistance Commission, and numerous other governmental agencies and nongovernmental organizations on matters pertaining to political campaigns and election reform.

**Raymond J. La Raja** is Professor of Political Science at the University of Massachusetts-Amherst and Associate Director of the UMass Poll, which conducts Internet-based surveys of voters nationally, and is an expert on campaign finance, public financing of elections, reforms to improve voter turnout, and factors that encourage or discourage women to run for office.

**Susan A. MacManus** is Distinguished University Professor in the Department of Government and International Affairs, University of South Florida, Director of the USF-Nielsen Sunshine State Survey, and a widely followed political news analyst. She recently co-authored *Politics in States and Communities*, 15th ed., with Thomas R. Dye (2015).

**Barbara Norrander** is a professor in the School of Government and Public Policy at the University of Arizona. Her expertise is American politics, elections, and the gender gap in partisanship and issue positions. She is author of *The Imperfect Primary: Oddities, Biases, and Strengths of U.S. Presidential Nomination Politics*, 2nd edition (2015).

**Gerald M. Pomper** is Board of Governors Professor of Political Science (Emeritus) at Rutgers University. Writing occasional blog posts on "Politics and All That," he is the author of *The New York Times on Critical Elections* (2010) and *Ordinary Heroes and American Democracy* (2004, 2007) which was nominated for a Pulitzer Prize.

**Charles L. Prysby** is Professor of Political Science at the University of North Carolina at Greensboro. His research interests include elections, voting behavior, political parties, and southern politics. He is the coauthor of the Voting Behavior SETUPS computer-based instructional packages. His most recent book, coauthored with David Holian, is *Candidate Character Traits in Presidential Elections* (2015).

**John Kenneth White** is Professor of Political Science at the Catholic University of America. He has written extensively on religion and politics, the American party system and the U.S. presidency. His most recent book is *What Happened to the Republican Party?: And What It Means for American Presidential Politics* (2016).

# INTRODUCTION TO THE CHAPTERS

Chapter 1, "Not an Ordinary Election: The Presidential Race of 2016," by William J. Crotty introduces the context of the 2016 presidential election and the evolution of the campaign from the emergence of the candidates in the prenomination phase, and notably Donald J. Trump for the Republicans and—after an unexpected battle with latecomer Bernie Sanders—Hillary Clinton for the Democrats, up to and through the general election. The controversies that marked the campaign are examined. These range from the late controversies over Trump's taxes and a video sex tape to a reopened FBI investigation into Clinton's use of a private email server as Secretary of State and its impact on the race. The final vote for President as well as for the Congress and the state races, the role of the Electoral College and, in a postscript, the recount effort are reviewed. The chapter ends with a discussion of the consequences of a contentious and potentially system-challenging election. The themes of the campaign and their development in this chapter represent a foundation for the analyses to come.

Chapter 2, "The Conventional Versus the Unconventional: Presidential Nominations in 2016," by Barbara Norrander provides an analysis of the prenomination battles in both parties, arguably the most important phase of the campaign. Few survive the demands made by the election process. Most are weeded out in the primaries and, to a lesser extent, caucuses that determine the final two party nominees. In this earlier phase, the voters who chose to participate can be faced with a variety of candidates and policy views, the limits of which are defined only by the party's historical ideological commitments. This was the case in the Republican party. Seventeen "serious" candidates contested for the nomination. When the projected frontrunners, Jeb Bush and Chris Christie, withdrew, the nomination was thrown open. For one reason or another, prospective candidates such as Marco Rubio, Ted Cruz, John Kasich, and the others failed to catch on. Donald Trump, a political novice, television celebrity and real estate billionaire, in time, came to the front of the field and, unexpectedly, went on to win the party's nomination, promising to "Make America Great Again." For the Democrats, Hillary Clinton was the established frontrunner, projected to win both the nomination and–in the early going–the general election. She had the name recognition, political financing, superior ground organization, and experience that appeared to ensure that she would do well. Belatedly, Bernie Sanders, a senator from Vermont, little known nationally and a self-proclaimed "Democratic Socialist," announced his candidacy. He represented a liberal challenge to Clinton with a campaign that stressed a populist message of economic equalization. His campaign proved more of a challenge than anticipated, appealing to liberals and Millennials. Clinton, of course, eventually won and—in an appeal to Sanders' supporters—adopted some of his liberal economic positions. It was an exciting and unpredictable period, captured and analyzed expertly in this chapter.

Chapter 3, "The Presidential Election: A Troubled Democracy," by Gerald M. Pomper analyzes the surprising electoral success of Donald Trump, a candidate with no governmental or previous campaign experience at any level and a shallow appreciation of the issues of the campaign and the problems of government. It is a curious story. Hillary Clinton ran a more traditional and recognizable campaign; Donald Trump, running as an outsider, went well beyond the bounds of previous campaigns. He relied on personal attacks and accusations as to his opponent's behavior. He appealed to the anger and frustrations of working-class whites. Trump had not been taken seriously initially in the nomination phase of the campaign and was not given much of a chance in the general election. In the campaign's initial stages Trump's erratic performance and the controversies associated with his candidacy appeared likely to derail his campaign. He managed to survive the controversies, turn attention to Clinton and her actions and views, and eventually win a narrow victory. Analyzing such an election is a challenge. The factors that dominated in the campaign provided a dynamic to the 2016 election that moved it beyond what had gone before. Trump presented himself as the only person capable of addressing the nation's problems and returning the United States to its former glory. "Critical markers" in the election are identified along with a sophisticated explanation for what occurred in the election that adds insight and clarity to our understanding of a most challenging election campaign, one that could represent a "sea change" in American politics. The chapter ends with caution as to what might be expected in the future.

Chapter 4, "Explaining the Vote," by Charles L. Prysby, isolates the factors that determined the final vote in one of the most perplexing and unpredictable elections of the modern age. These are placed within explanatory models that have been used to understand elections since World War II. Once the characteristics of greatest importance are identified and their association with the decision-making of voters established, the extent to which they fit a framework of what is known about presidential elections in previous years can be understood. Among the more stable and predictable forces in explaining voting behavior is party identification and political ideology. Election-specific attitudes—that is, those unique in importance to a specific election—complement the more traditional vote predictors. These include the candidates' personalities, the principal issues stressed in the campaign, and unanticipated developments that impact the vote. The 2016 presidential race had more than its share of unusual developments. Contemporary politics is characterized by a severe polarization of the parties and the electorate. The competing partisan divisions of voters held different world views as to who government should serve, tax and economic policies, the distribution of wealth in the society, the necessity of providing social services, relations with other nations, and any other perspectives of political relevance. These divisions peaked in 2016, adding a level of intensity and uncertainty to the race. Not surprisingly, given the level of divisiveness, just under 90 percent of identifiers voted for their party's nominee (a degree of loyalty for Republicans that Trump's actions had tested). Independently, once considered the key to electoral success, favored Trump by four points. Clinton, given her extensive service in government, was not seen as a candidate who would challenge the nation's political elite and bring fundamental change to Washington. Trump was seen as a transformative candidate. If nothing else, a vote for Trump would send a message to the ruling class dominant in the nation's affairs. It was this belief among the most decisive of Trump's appeals to voters bypassed by the economic gains of recent times. "Character" was a concern given particular attention in the race. Professor Prysby has been in the forefront of developing identifiable measures for a number of different qualities (leadership, judgment, morality, honesty, decisiveness, etc.) and identifies its importance for voters in addressing the candidates. There were other issues, less emphasized than in previous races, but still important in understanding Trump's victory. Jobs and the economy was such a consideration. Voters can misperceive both the candidates' policy commitments and the extent or consequences of the issues that divide the parties. This was particularly the case in 2016, making a definitive understanding of the policy consequences shaping the vote difficult. The election brought new meaning into what can be expected in future contests.

Chapter 5, "The Races for Congress in 2016: A Tale of Two Elections," by Paul S. Herrnson and Raymond J. La Raja examines the congressional races, their relationship to the presidential contest, the strategies of greatest importance in seeking office, the issues of greatest significance in these races, and the potential consequence of the results in which the Republican party retained control of both chambers of the Congress. Along with Trump's victory, this establishes a unitary government (one party control of three levels of office) that could facilitate the fundamental changes promised by Donald Trump in the campaign. Nonetheless Republican congressional candidates did not necessarily identify themselves with Trump's presidential campaign and its issues. Rather, these candidates tended to run on local issues and a more traditional Republican platform. This approach served them well. Democratic congressional candidates tied themselves more closely to the national Clinton campaign, a relationship that may not have helped them to the extent anticipated. The congressional as against presidential campaigns then led to the reference "a tale of two campaigns" which nicely summarizes what did happen.

Chapter 6, "Women and the 2016 Presidential Election: Unrealistic Expectations of Cohesiveness," by Susan A. MacManus explores the women's vote in the 2016 election, both within the context of the race itself and within the framework of expectations as to the women's vote in politics more generally. The two campaigns offered different focal points for women's concerns. The Trump campaign was marked by in a series of controversies that involved women. Trump himself was labelled a misogynist. Hillary Clinton, on the other hand, had a long record of championing women's and children's issues and she made these a focal point of her campaign. Additionally, Clinton, the first female nominee for President by a major party, would have been, had she won, the first woman elected to the presidency. The opportunity to "shatter the glass ceiling" presumably would motivate women across party lines to vote as a bloc for a woman candidate, as a number of analysts predicted. Politics is more complicated than such an approach, a point Professor MacManus makes in introducing an element of reality into gender-based assessments of party and candidate patterns of support. Women are a majority of the population, which in itself should introduce a challenge into any one-size-fits-all explanation of the vote. They cannot be subject to simplified gender-specific explanations as to their political behavior. Women are subjected to the cross-pressures that influence the decision-making of all voters, from party identification to economic and class factors, generational differences and the issues relevant to any presidential campaign, in addition to whatever pull gender solidarity may exert. Women are not unified in their beliefs, their support for candidates, or their reactions to campaigns. To assert otherwise is unrealistic. The differences are developed in the chapter with particular references to an emphasis on diversity. It is a welcome addition to an understanding of an election with a clear definition of candidates' approaches and appeals for women's support. It is also a politically sensitive reading of the real-world nature of a gender-based politics of relevance to all election campaigns.

Chapter 7, "Navigating through Turbulence and Troublesome Times: Latinos, Election 2016, Partisan Politics, and Salient Public Policies," by John A. Garcia, assesses the role and impact on elections of Latinos, as the fastest growing political community in the United States. Within a matter of decades, they will surpass blacks as the largest minority in the electorate. They formed a critical part of the Obama coalition that Hillary Clinton attempted to mobilize in 2016. The Latino vote was also targeted by Republican party strategists as the ethnic group the party needed to appeal to in order to revitalize its aging, predominantly white coalition, after the 2012 loss by Mitt Romney. Given this, the targeting of Latinos by the Republican candidate for President, Donald Trump, appears odd to incomprehensible. Trump called for a wall to be built across the border with Mexico, to be paid for by Mexico, to keep killers, rapists, and drug dealers out; threatened to return 11 million undocumented aliens (largely Latinos) to their home countries; and committed his administration to closing immigration into the country. The manner in which the Latino community in general and Latino voters responded to such attacks is the focal point of an analysis by Professor Garcia, one of the most accomplished scholars of Latino political behavior. He divides his analysis into an identification of the most pressing of the challenges facing the Latino community; a critique of Latino voters, their potential impact on American politics and the difficulties that needed to be overcome for their potential to be realized; the nature of political identification with the community and the relevance to the parties for meeting for future needs; and, specific to the 2016 election, Latinos' assessments of the principal candidates, Donald Trump and Hillary Clinton, and the impact these had on their vote. The election of 2016 saw Hispanic candidates, Marco Rubio and Ted Cruz, in contention for the Republican party's presidential nomination, one indicator of the growth and increasing importance of this group within an electorate in a nation on its way to becoming majority-minority dominant. This, in itself, was a source of concern for a white population facing a projected 17% decline in numbers during the period 2015–2060 (Latinos would account for 50% of the population growth during the same period). Over time, Latinos have voted primarily (although not exclusively) for Democratic presidential candidates and have identified primarily with the Democratic party. However, while registering at rates commensurate with other groups (whites, African Americans), they turn out to vote less. Polls show Latinos believe that both parties could do more to help their community. For Latinos, the importance of the 2016 election was in the ability to solidify and expand their political influence and advance their policy agenda. Latinos, like other voting blocs, are separated by a number of factors—nativity, gender, language, generation and education—yet in 2016 there was little difference in issue stands in relation to social, economic, and generational differences and country of origin. The Republican party had little appeal (65% had an unfavorable view of the party). The Democratic party, while receiving the majority of support, was not believed to be as accommodating to group interests as Latinos would like. Yet Latinos voted 70% for Clinton to 19% for Trump. How the Republican party chooses to develop its relationship is a question largely for the Trump administration. The Democratic party faces a similar concern, although significant defections in group support in the near future are not expected. Given the tenor and targeting of attacks by the Republican candidate in the 2016 race, an aggressive advocacy of the Latino agenda can be considered both a necessity and the greatest challenge the community will face.

Chapter 8, "The Election in Perspective," by John Kenneth White concludes the book by taking on the task of explaining what for some was the inexplicable: the victory of Donald Trump in the general election. His negatives were pronounced, highly visible in the debates and rallies, a source of constant entertainment or dread on national television, and repeatedly assessed and for the most part condemned in political discussion. It is difficult to think of a candidate with such a negative persona being taken as a serious contender for the presidency. Hillary Clinton, in contrast, while far from perfect herself, presented a sharp contrast with the Republican candidate. She had the training and necessary skills that should have resulted in her winning the presidency as virtually all analysts had predicted. Clinton also had the full support of her party. Trump could not make such a claim. Professor White identifies the sense of restlessness in the electorate, the belief in a need for a change of direction and the alienation and unease among sectors of the population who felt forgotten. Clinton's message, "Stronger Together," did little to indicate a concern with their problems of economic exclusion or to address their needs. Trump in turn did reach this disaffected group of largely white, less educated, and rural voters who would stand by him, regardless of his actions on the attacks on his behavior and character. The relative weakness of both political parties, more evident in the Republican party with the success of Trump, was alarming to those who believe a vital and representative party system was a necessity for a strong democracy. The "party of Trump" constituted a coalition quite different from those of the major parties. It was in a white underclass, attempting to survive in a nation where—for the first time in

American history—minorities, single women and the young constituted a majority of the electorate. Trump's core support in concert with the economic decline in the Rust Belt states, Clinton's failure to reach and address the concerns of what would normally be a Democratic constituency and the perception of Donald Trump as the engine for fundamental change combined to provide an answer to "Why Trump?" The Reagan coalition has reached its end. It did little for less educated, less-well-off working-class whites. The outline of future presidential elections can be found in the 2016 results.

# 1

## NOT AN ORDINARY ELECTION

### The Presidential Race of 2016

*William J. Crotty*

> *It is what it is.*
>
> — Bill Belichick

The election of 2016 has no precedent in modern American history. The meaning of an election for a restrained conception of democratic leadership, one equal to the task of leading the world's greatest power, constitutes the essence of a presidential race. Were the criteria met? It was a long and contentious campaign. The issues in the election ranged from domestic anger, alienation and political deadlock to international crises, fundamental concerns that will take insightful and experienced leadership.

The election, and more specifically the manner in which it was conducted, raises a number of questions. Among these, and among the more fundamental, is whether it is a blip, an aberration and exception in the long life of national elections, the manner in which they have been conducted and the underlying dynamics that have come to explain the past contests. Or, alternatively, 2016 could be an introduction to future such races, with political parties lacking influence of any magnitude and voter discontent turning to the more radical and unrestrained of candidate alternatives with consequences yet to be seen for the operation of a democratic state.

One thing is clear and that is considerable voter anger in both parties over the manner in which elected officials have largely ignored their real needs, and in particular those associated with the economic well-being of major segments of the population. The discrepancy between the promises and agendas of the candidates and parties over the last half century and the operations and priorities in office of those who would emerge as the winners in elections has much to do with the level of current discontent. The candidate races in both parties—in a strikingly different manner—serve to illustrate the point.

The outcome of the election was unexpected. It ranks as one of the major upsets in American history. Its full importance will not be known for years but it could have radical, even seismic, consequences for the future of the United States.

## The Candidates and Their Campaigns

The election pitted two candidates and parties, Donald Trump, the Republican party nominee, and Hillary Rodham Clinton, the Democratic nominee, with contrasting personalities, life experiences and personal values as well as polarized conceptions of what government should do and who it should represent.

### Donald Trump and His Campaign

First, there was the newcomer to politics representing the Republican party. Donald Trump was a political novice; he had never held office at any level or competed for office in a campaign. He was a New York real estate billionaire, with interests in casinos, apartment houses, office buildings, golf courses and other real estate ventures worldwide. Trump was a surprise winner of the Republican primaries which fielded a group of 17 candidates, mostly minor political figures with a sprinkling of newcomers added. None however had the party following, type of issue they could ride to victory, financing or organization needed to win. Most were also largely unknown. Trump was, among other things, a television personality, the host of a television reality show, "The Apprentice," where Trump became known for uttering the catch phrase "You're fired!" to contestants who failed at game tasks. The show had a wide familiarity among mass audiences.

Trump claimed to have the money needed to finance his own campaign, as opposed to creating Super Political Action Committees (Super PACs) or asking for donations. He was also at ease in front of large audiences, had a quick response to almost everything and knew how to package complex ideas in a few pointed, if often angry, words. He was not interested in the details of policy concerns, as such. What he did—through default or planning—was to appeal to white voters, less educated and generally less well-off than most, bypassed by the economic gains of recent decades. He managed to tap into their anger and frustration; their sense of being left behind as the rest of the country did increasingly better; their belief that minorities were getting preference for jobs at their expense; and their fear of multiculturalism, that the America they had known was passing. Above all was the sense of not being represented by the candidates for national office. They were isolated, ignored and exploited. Trump spoke to their concerns, acknowledged their alienation and gave voice to their frustrations. Given this, they proved willing in return to ignore or discount his excesses and failings in exchange for having someone finally speak for them in a national campaign.

Trump did not have much of a campaign organization at any level. He had few close advisors beyond the immediate members of his family. He depended on his own instincts and a sense of what would appeal to the voters who formed his constituency. At the same time, he showed an unusual disregard for the Republican party mainstream or the centrists/moderates believed to be the keys to an electoral victory. His freewheeling, tell-it-like-it-is style could, and did, get him into seemingly endless controversies. If nothing else, they kept Trump in the forefront of television news, fed the cable networks' insatiable demand for material and commanded seemingly endless social media attention.

Donald Trump is a skilled negotiator and a successful businessman who has built an international empire. He is a world-class salesman, a savvy student of a media he uses for his own purposes, and he loves success and the personal attention that comes with it. He has shown himself to be an entrepreneur few can match and one who likes to bet big. He prizes winners and, as he has said, hates losers. He has an unchallengeable faith in his own ability and he relies almost exclusively on his own judgment and instincts. These are qualities made clear in the campaign and likely will guide his domestic policymaking and his international dealings in the presidency.

## Hillary Clinton and Her Campaign

Hillary Rodham Clinton has had a long and impressive career in politics. She had been Secretary of State in the Obama administration (2009–2013); First Lady during her husband Bill Clinton's presidency; a U.S. Senator from New York (2001–2009); and a candidate for Democratic party nominee for President in 2008, losing a close battle to Barack Obama. In addition, she had been the First Lady of Arkansas during her husband's gubernatorial terms (1979–1981 and 1983–1992). The presidential election of 2016 was her second attempt to be the first woman to serve in the White House.

At each stop, she had compiled a list of accomplishments in advancing children's issues, women's rights and improvements in health care, as well as evidencing a commitment to service on an extensive number of legal commissions and committees reforming and modernizing the law and its application. After law school she worked with the Children's Defense Fund and as a staff member of the congressional committee establishing the groundwork for the impeachment of Richard M. Nixon. She ranked as one of the most experienced and best prepared of candidates to ever seek the presidency.

Bill Clinton won the presidency in 1992 with Hillary Clinton's help. Bill Clinton had been accused of a long-term sexual relationship by the woman involved, Gennifer Flowers. Hillary Clinton went on television to defend her husband and Bill Clinton survived the episode. The effort was to be made again when Bill Clinton was accused of having sex in the White House with an intern. He denied the accusation initially and she made an angry television appearance claiming it and a series of other attacks on their character were products of a concentrated right wing conspiracy. Bill Clinton later admitted in a brief televised address to an inappropriate relationship with the intern, publicly embarrassing his wife, among others. He was impeached by the House but acquitted by the Senate on the two articles of impeachment, perjury and obstruction of justice, allowing him to remain in office. The incident was believed to be the most critical point in a frequently contentious relationship between the Clintons. The controversies involving her husband and later those surrounding the funding and operations of the Clinton Foundation helped shape the image Hillary Clinton carried over in her presidential bid.

As First Lady, Hillary Clinton was an active advisor on a range of issues. She was given responsibility for developing a national health care plan. After two years of work, the proposed plan failed to win congressional approval. She blamed the defeat on the lobbying of health care corporations and the financial indebtedness of legislators to them.

In 2000, her career went in another direction. She was elected the first female senator from New York. Her years in the Senate were notable for her efforts to get $20 billion in federal health care and other aid for the police and service workers who responded to the 9/11 World Trade Center terrorist attacks, a determination to stimulate economic development in the poor and rural areas of New York state and her continued concern with children and women's issues (Borchers 2016). She was reelected in 2006 with 67% of the vote.

In 2008, she ran for President. In retrospect, she may have made the mistake of continuing to serve as Senator from New York, a position she worked on virtually full time, while also attempting to run for the Democratic party's nomination for President. Her campaign concentrated power in a competing circle of advisors. They did not get along with each other and had different strategies for the campaign. Between them, they managed to use most of her political financing before the delegate selection process began. Consequently, she was relatively underfunded compared with her adversary, Barack Obama. Her campaign underestimated the strength of the Obama challenge and never quite overcame its initial mistakes. She ended up losing a race in which she had been the heavy favorite. After the election, surprising many, she agreed to serve as Obama's Secretary of State.

In her 2016 race, Clinton constantly contrasted her record and experience in government with Trump's lack of it, his business ventures and his focus on a television reality show. In an election with the need for change as the undercurrent, her years of experience may actually not have helped. She could be seen, as Trump claimed, as part of the problem, a representative of the status quo. It may well have played to his self-designated role as the outsider and agent for change.

Careers, personalities, backgrounds, values, ideologies, the temperaments of the candidates, all came to shape the race for the presidency to an extent that went well beyond the ordinary. The nominees were unlike in everything from gender to their belief as to what American government stood for and what its role and mission should be. All of this would come to mark the highly unusual campaign that followed.

One final thing about the candidates: neither Hillary Clinton nor Donald Trump were trusted by large numbers of the American public. Taken together, they may well have been the two most unpopular candidates to run in a presidential election since the polls measured such things (Chozick and Thee-Brenan 2016). Gallup polling conducted October 31-November 5, 2016 showed Clinton at 57% unfavorable and Trump 62% unfavorable (Gallup 2016).

## The Nomination Phase

The race to select the parties' nominees, like the general election to come, established basic constraints in approach. With no incumbent of either party seeking reelection, it was an open race. These usually draw a large number of prospective nominees. Such was the case with the Republicans. The Democratic party appeared to have its candidate decided as early as two years before the election. Hillary Clinton, the loser in a close primary fight to Barack Obama in 2008, appeared to have the Democratic party's full support.

### *The Democrats*

Clinton had left her position as Secretary of State in the Obama administration to run for President. She had a well-funded campaign in place, led by a Super PAC that began early to build a financial base for her run and, not incidentally, to scare off other prospective opponents who might have considered running. She had a professional organization in place, with a formidable ground organization both in the nomination and general election races; she had national name recognition and an impressive political résumé; she could count on the support of the Democratic party activists who decide such outcomes; and she was popular with the party's base. Clinton would also be the first female presidential nominee of a major party and, if elected, the first woman President—as she put it: breaking the glass ceiling. Everything, it would seem, was in order. She was seen as the presumptive nominee and projected to go on to win the presidency.

Clinton had no serious opposition within the party for its nomination, or so it would appear. Unexpectedly, Bernie Sanders, a U.S. Senator from Vermont, little known nationally, and in fact calling himself an Independent (actually a "Democratic Socialist") decided to oppose Clinton and bring a new and more progressive message to the campaign. He met with the Democratic party caucus in the Senate and normally voted with the Democratic party. Sanders was 74 years old, had no national reputation in any particular policy area; and was not organized or funded at the beginning of his campaign. In declaring his intention to contest Clinton for the party's nomination, Sanders was to put forth a decidedly more liberal policy agenda in an effort to begin what he referred to as a "political revolution." In reality, his program was closer to an updated New Deal/Great Society agenda. It was one the Democratic party had moved away from. This occurred most significantly during the Bill Clinton presidency and his administrative embrace of a more business-friendly, Wall Street economic approach in his efforts to push the Democratic party in a new direction.

A year before the election, Sanders was undecided as to if he would run, announcing late. He was given no chance to win the Democratic nomination. It was unclear even after he began campaigning and he started to bring in large crowds to his rallies if he really wanted to be President. He said that his objective was to end economic polarization and the accumulation of the nation's wealth in the hands of a small number of billionaires; and better equalize the income distribution and reward the working classes left out of the economic recovery that followed the 2007–2008 Great Recession. In addition, he proposed to cut college costs for students, which appealed to the Millennials who formed a base for his campaign; fight the abuses of globalization most evident in the international trade agreements supported by both Republicans and Democrats (including Barack Obama and Hillary Clinton) that had moved jobs out of the country and penalized both the working class and labor unions; and speak for those ignored by the political class that ruled Washington. These were issues he had concerned himself with since his early days growing up in Brooklyn, as mayor of Burlington, Vermont, and as a U.S. Congressman and Senator.

Sanders' message was popular with Democrats, especially liberals and the young Millennials, who believed themselves unrepresented by the Clinton campaign. They were suspicious of her ties to Wall Street and the financial industry. She had received $675,000 for three speeches from

Goldman Sachs alone. Estimations were that the Clintons taken together had made $125 million from talks they gave since Bill Clinton had left office in 2001. It was to become a campaign issue.

Sanders began to attract large crowds, turned out to be an effective speaker with an ability to draw in his listeners and to motivate them; and, in a short period of time, became an unexpected sensation among sectors of the Democratic coalition dissatisfied with both economic conditions in a class-biased system and the records of previous Democratic presidents, notably Bill Clinton and Barack Obama, in these regards. Sanders' message had some relation to what Trump was saying, but his appeal was centered within more traditional groups of Democratic party identifiers.

Clinton was slow to recognize the potential seriousness of the Sanders campaign, much as she had been slow to recognize the threat of the Obama challenge in 2008. Nonetheless, she had the funding, professional organization and intra-party support needed to win the nomination. She also had the support of the controversial "super delegates" (awarded national convention seats based on their elective or party position) who did not have to compete for their seats in the primaries and caucuses. Virtually all had committed to Clinton.

Sanders did raise money for his campaign, amounting to over $236 million. It was less than half that raised by the Clinton campaign (Federal Election Commission 2016). Throughout his campaign Sanders claimed that his average donation was small, $27. He was to win 23 states and Democrats Abroad, for a total of 1,865 delegates and 43.1% of the pre-nomination vote. Clinton won 34 states and territories, and 2,842 of the total 4,763 delegate votes (or 55.2%).

Martin O'Malley, a former governor of Maryland, had also run for the nomination. He participated in the primary debates but received little support. Among other potential candidates who did not run, most notable was Vice President Joe Biden. He was still grieving the death of his son in May of 2015. While Biden would have presented the most serious challenge to Clinton, they had often been on opposing sides of domestic and foreign policy issues, including the invasion of Libya, in the Obama administration. It is uncertain whether he could have beaten her formidable advantages in financing and organization.

## *The Republicans*

The Republican field included 17 "serious" candidates. There was no acknowledged frontrunner. In the year prior to the election, Chris Christie, governor of a "blue state," New Jersey, and believed to have mainstream party support as well as potentially cross-party appeal among disaffected Democrats, was considered a frontrunner. Additionally Jeb Bush, the brother of one President and the son of another as well as a former governor of Florida, was expected to seek the nomination. Given his network of funders, party officials, policy experts and consultants, he also was considered to be a mainstream contender and by many the potential nominee, posing a "clash of dynasties," Bushes and Clintons, for the presidency. While Christie and Bush did run unsuccessfully, Mitt Romney, the 2012 Republican nominee, considered to be another potential candidate, declined. Romney did come to severely criticize the eventual nominee, Donald Trump, in a number of talks throughout the campaign period.

Christie withdrew from the race on February 10, 2016, a day after an embarrassing sixth place finish in the New Hampshire primary. He received only 7% of the vote and won no delegates. He was also the subject of a criminal investigation into a massive five-day traffic tie-up on the George Washington Bridge, known as "Bridgegate." It had been created by Christie's office in retribution to the mayor of Fort Lee, NJ, the town that bore the brunt of the traffic jam, who had refused to support Christie's reelection. Jeb Bush did announce on June 15, 2015. He came to be seen as an ineffective campaigner and was the butt of Trump barbs as to his "low energy" campaign. He had no message that distinguished his candidacy and before withdrawing had his mother and brother campaign for him. Their involvement in his campaign may have sent a mixed message. His mother had warned early on that Jeb Bush's seeking the Republican nomination may be one Bush too many. His brother, George W. Bush, had initiated the war against Saddam Hussein and Iraq in 2003 and presided over the economic collapse of 2007–2008. He ended his presidency as one of the most disliked in the post-World War II period.

With Christie and Bush removing themselves from the race, the field was wide open. The race then came to focus on Senator Ted Cruz of Texas, elected as a Tea Party candidate in 2012, an evangelical and strong conservative, who was to offer the most consistent threat to Trump. He suspended his campaign on May 3 after losing the Indiana primary to Trump. Additionally, John Kasich, governor of Ohio, a critical state in the election, a conservative/centrist with mainstream backing, also remained unofficially in the race until the national convention although he had suspended his campaign on May 4. He won his home state of Ohio but little else.

Other aspirants for the nomination:

- Mike Huckabee, evangelical preacher, Fox News commentator, former Arkansas governor and a previous candidate for the nomination with a down-home demeanor;
- Senator Rand Paul (KY), a libertarian and surgeon whose father Rep. Ron Paul of Texas had sought the Republican nomination in earlier races;
- Rick Perry, governor of Texas, a conservative who had run previously for the nomination and a proponent of oil, gas and coal interests;

- Senator Marco Rubio (FL), a Latino candidate, elected as a Tea Party member with a Tea Party agenda in 2010 to the Senate and a former Speaker of the House in the Florida legislature. He presented himself as a less controversial, more mainstream alternative to Trump. He made little note of his earlier agenda, instead emphasizing God, the Constitution, Second Amendment rights (gun ownership) and family in his rallies. He also had the worst attendance record in the Senate, which became an issue. His response was that it was not worth his time. Trump ridiculed him as "Little Marco" and questioned in the Fox News debates what he had done to qualify as a presidential candidate. Christie, a former prosecutor, in a withering attack, mocked Rubio's carefully prepared responses to questions and their lack of content, in both YouTube satirical videos as well as during the February 6 debate. The attacks unsettled Rubio. Once considered a potential frontrunner by the Clinton campaign and by the media, he began to robotically repeat himself in the debate. He removed himself from the race after losing his home state Florida's primary to Trump on March 15. He was to be reelected, however, to the Senate in 2016.
- Scott Walker, governor of Wisconsin, a conservative and favorite of the wealthy industrialist brothers Charles and David Koch who had funded his state campaigns. In return he championed their state legislative initiatives (American Legislative Exchange Council, or ALEC) and anti-union policies. He promised to build a wall along the Canadian border to keep immigrants out;
- Rick Santorum, a former U.S. Senator from Pennsylvania and presidential candidate, representing a moral (Roman Catholic) social conservative point of view;
- Carly Fiorina, former CEO of Hewlett Packard and unsuccessful 2010 candidate for the U.S. Senate from California, the only woman in the Republican race;
- Dr. Ben Carson, a retired neurosurgeon with no political experience. When asked in the first Fox News debate his qualifications for the presidency he said he was the only candidate who had separated twins conjoined at the head;
- Bobby Jindal, former conservative governor of Louisiana, who had inherited a state with billions of dollars surplus in the treasury. He left it bankrupt while cutting health, education, emergency funds and other services;
- George Pataki, a former governor of New York state with little name recognition, even in the Republican party;
- Senator Lindsay Graham of South Carolina, an experienced senator knowledgeable on foreign policy and a committed conservative, little known outside of Washington; and
- Jim Gilmore, a former governor of Virginia and the only candidate with military experience.

Declining to run, in addition to Romney, the 2012 Republican candidate, was Mike Pence, governor of Indiana, an evangelical and anti-abortion, anti-gay advocate. Later he was to be named as Trump's running mate and after a stoic appearance in the vice presidential debate was projected by a number of analysts to be a frontrunner for the Republican nomination in 2020 (Trump at this point in the campaign was believed to be losing). Also declining to run was Speaker of the House Paul Ryan (Wisconsin), the highest-ranking Republican in the country, the party's vice presidential nominee in 2012, and a conservative budget specialist; as well as other lesser known possibilities.

A number of the Republican candidates (including Rubio, Cruz and Walker) sought financing for their campaigns from billionaires with the money and motivation to invest. The consequences of the Supreme Court's decision in *Citizens United* (2010) came into play in the 2016 presidential race. The Koch brothers alone promised to invest $889 million, a sum on par with that to be spent by each of the major political parties, in such contests. Apparently, with Trump's nomination, his command of television and his personal wealth, the Kochs placed their money primarily in state and local races.

Such financing, when given, would be earned. The candidates chosen would be expected to advance their benefactors' conservative economic agenda and immediate business interests. For those billionaires who felt strongly on the issue, support for Benjamin Netanyahu and his conservative Likud party agenda in Israel was demanded. One of Trump's campaign pledges that proved effective was that since he himself was a billionaire, unlike the others he could finance his own campaign and could not be bought. Another was that in relation to Washington and officials of government, he vowed to "drain the swamp."

The Republican nomination process received extensive media coverage, especially through a series of early debates that took place in the year before the formal selection process began. Fox News, with a reputation as the conservative news source, sponsored the debates. Given the size of the field, the network designated an "A" list and a "B" list of contenders. The "A" list appeared on the evening debates and therefore drew the greatest number of viewers. The "B" list debate took place earlier in the day and drew considerably fewer viewers and less media coverage. Fox News decided the division based on poll results as to who would appear in the evening debates. Those candidates polling lower numbers (mostly 1–2% or so) appeared in the earlier program. In effect, and responding to levels of name recognition in the earliest going, Fox News placed itself in the position of choosing, and then promoting, the candidacy of those it selected.

The television exposure particularly suited Trump. He was a veteran TV performer, at ease in front of the camera. Given such a venue, he excelled and with the televised debates, his constant Tweets, the leverage of social media and free media coverage his campaign received he in time came to the front of the field. Initially dismissed by forecasters, media analysts and the Clinton campaign itself, he had been given no chance. He won by rewriting the rules. He invested little in paid television until well into the general election campaign and given his television appeal and his unpredictability (making for good TV), managed to effectively counter both his primary competitors and in the general election Clinton's funding advantage and solid ground organization.

The Democrats held three debates between Sanders and Clinton. These were scheduled by the Democratic National Committee. Sanders' people complained that the number was kept deliberately low and the scheduling less than ideal in order to promote Clinton's candidacy and limit Sanders' opportunities to get his message across. The chair of the Democratic National Committee (DNC), Debbie Wasserman Schultz, was a Clinton supporter, as was the man who appointed her, Barack Obama.

There were other quarrels with the DNC and its chair over access to voting and election data meant to be available to all candidates. It was shut off to the Sanders campaign at one point, but given the controversy that ensued was quickly restored. Leaked emails released by WikiLeaks appeared to support claims of bias on the part of the DNC. The claim was made with a "high degree" of certainty by the government and its national security agencies that Russia was behind the leaks. The charges as to the manipulation were never fully investigated during the campaign; the charges as to Russian attempts to influence the race, allegedly against Clinton and in favor of Trump, while never proven during the campaign, received the major share of media attention. After the election, the Clinton campaign argued the FBI should have focused on the hacking and charges of Russian interference in the election rather than on her use of a private email server while in office, which it considered a minor matter and a political distraction.

## The National Conventions

The Democratic National Convention was a sophisticated, Hollywood-style spectacle, held July 25–28, 2016 in Philadelphia. It ran smoothly and the tone was upbeat and positive. It provided both entertainment and speeches in carefully moderated doses in a fast-moving, made-for-television show. Local and state politicians and office-seekers were given their brief moments; high-profile celebrities, actors and entertainers were slotted at set intervals; and political figures, from members of Congress to governors and past candidates for office, made appearances. The speakers emphasized Clinton's qualifications and the "temperamental unsuitability" of Donald Trump for the office of President and the position of Commander-in-Chief with his finger on the nuclear button. It was a theme pushed hard in the early stages of the campaign by Clinton and her surrogates. All in all, it was a well-conceived and expertly executed convention that stood in contrast to the less synchronized, lower wattage Republican effort.

To win the nomination, Clinton needed 2,382 delegates of the 4,763 certified for the roll call vote on July 26. She received 2,842. She had incorporated into the party platform the agreements on international trade; plans to reduce college costs, including free tuition at public universities; and her programs to revise tax and budgetary policy to ensure a greater equalization of wealth in the society; as well as a promise to oppose international trade agreements (once supported) to protect worker and union rights. All were pledges made to Bernie Sanders and his supporters. The platform was seen to be the most progressive in the Democratic party's history. The Democrats left the convention unified and enthused and, while expecting a close fight, believing they held the upper hand.

The Republican National Convention took place July 18–21 in Cleveland. It came across as a disorganized affair with few recognizable participants and the speeches mostly by a series of largely unknown figures. Vice presidential nominee Mike Pence made a presentation, as did a number of military leaders later to appear as Cabinet nominees or aspirants. Trump's daughter Ivanka and wife Melania, and other family members, made appearances. Melania Trump's speech caused a minor media sensation when she adopted phrases from Michelle Obama's talk at the 2008 Democratic National Convention without acknowledging the source (she later said it was unintentional).

The Republican platform received little attention, which was a mistake. It was a Far Right road map, largely a reincorporation of Reagan neoliberal economic policies and commitments. Trump did make made clear in his campaign his commitment to a heavy investment in military defense and nuclear weaponry and to institute an aggressive foreign policy. The outlines of the Trump presidency to come could be found in this document (Republican Platform 2016).

## The General Election

There is a structure to presidential elections not found in the primaries or in state or local races, the Electoral College. It is a constitutional process that awards a state's general election vote to candidates largely but not totally on a winner-take-all basis (there are variations in several states). Each state is allocated the same vote in the Electoral College as it has total representatives in the Congress. The intention of the Founders was to ensure state representation in the selection process and to moderate a direct vote for President. The result has been a skewing of the national vote to over-represent the smaller states at the expense of the larger ones.

There is no guarantee that a candidate who wins a majority of the votes cast will win a majority of the Electoral College delegates. In fact, quite the opposite. In 2016, Clinton became the second Democratic candidate this century, and the fifth since the country was founded (if you count Andrew Jackson who founded the Democratic party as a result of this issue) to win the popular vote but lose the Electoral College vote and the presidency.

The Electoral College, whatever its faults, does impose a structure on presidential campaign that is all but immutable. The Democratic party's strength in election after election is found on the East Coast—New England, New York, New Jersey, Maryland, Washington, D.C. and normally Pennsylvania—and on the West Coast—Washington state, Oregon, California and in 2016 Nevada. The Democrats in 2016 also took New Mexico and Colorado. An area of strength normally is the industrial states of the Midwest, but Clinton won only Minnesota and Illinois, losing the Rust Belt states of Michigan, Wisconsin, Iowa, Indiana and Ohio to Trump. Several other states can be in play in the South and border states, including Florida, depending on economic conditions, the candidates and their appeal and the major concerns of the time. Mostly these states and the rest of the country are Republican strongholds. The design of the Electoral College over-rewards the Republican candidate. The electoral map for 2016, given the selective nature of the Democratic appeal in major population centers, looks like a GOP landslide (Figure 1.1).

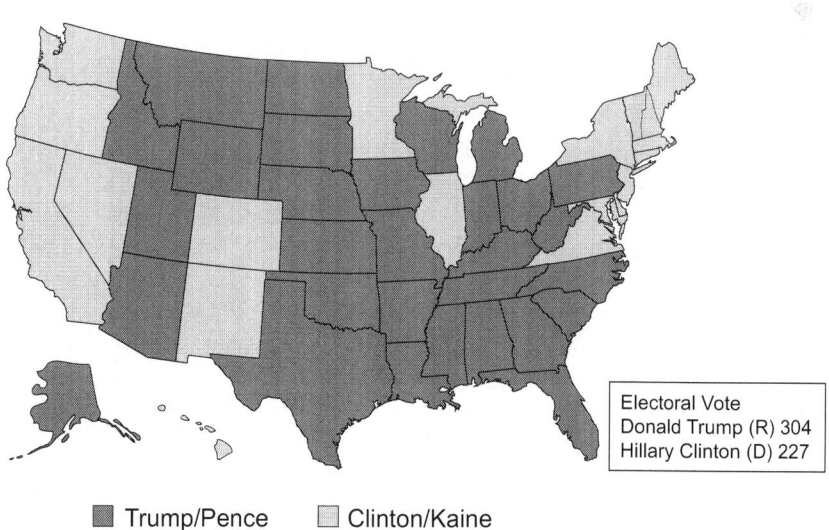

FIGURE 1.1  Presidential Election Results

Given this alignment, the two parties' strategies are clear. They determine the states to be cultivated as the core of the campaign, the states considered to be potentially winnable (if longshots) and those to be essentially conceded to the opposition. There are always several surprises but the overall outline and strategic focus remains much the same over time, as it did in the 2016 race. Within this dictated electoral structure, the personal campaign appeal of the candidates (both unpopular) and their campaign skills predicted a tight campaign and a close final vote.

Both candidates had their liabilities. Among Clinton's were her ties to the Clinton Foundation, headed by her daughter Chelsea Clinton, which Democratic party leaders attempted unsuccessfully to have her end. The WikiLeaks (allegedly Russian) release of emails showed donors to the foundation requested meetings with Clinton while Secretary of State which were granted. Clinton also had voted for the war in Iraq in 2003 while in the Senate. Trump used this against her and claimed he had opposed the war from the beginning, charging it was a terrible mistake (others claimed he initially supported it and later changed his mind). The issue of the war in Iraq continued to divide voters, given that it had fed into other conflicts, including that in Afghanistan, the longest war in U.S. history. Trump and other Republicans also held Clinton personally responsible for advising the President to attack Libya and the chaos and terrorism (especially that involving ISIS) that followed. Clinton was held responsible for providing the poor security that led to the death of four state department officials in Benghazi, Libya (her response, which received little media attention, was that a Republican Congress would not fund security). She was also severely criticized for her use of a private mail server while Secretary of State. While not illegal at the time, the argument was that she might have made classified information available to an enemy. This was never shown despite a number of congressional committee investigations by a Republican Congress, plus one 11-hour session by Clinton before an intelligence committee of the Congress. An FBI investigation initially found no laws broken. The Director of the FBI in the press conference at the time did criticize her for "extremely careless" behavior, an unusual addition to the normal termination of an FBI inquiry. The report was released in July, 2016. Seemingly this should have ended the matter, but it did not. The issue was used against Clinton throughout the campaign and was given new life in the final days of electioneering when the FBI announced it was reopening its email investigation.

Both candidates campaigned relentlessly. Clinton had a ground organization that Trump did not come close to matching. She also had ample financing and bought heavily in major television markets. Trump did employ a strategy of selectively buying television time late in the campaign but did not have the funds available (he did little fundraising and largely depended on the Republican National Committee to raise what financing he needed). He received free—if often critical—television and print exposure that had the effect of making an invaluable contribution to his election effort. His outgoing personality, impetuous nature and lack of restraint as to who he would attack or how made for exciting television, if not in the traditional manner of former candidates.

## The Debates

An essential part of the campaign was the televised debates. Hillary Clinton had a reputation for thorough preparation, in addition to a clear and well developed appreciation of the policy agenda of the campaign. She demonstrated this in the debates. Her biggest negative in this context was her delivery. While professional, it lacked the charisma and drama associated with Trump. His behavior in the debates and elsewhere and his willingness to attack, create controversy and unnerve opponents was an approach that had been honed in the primary debates and then carried over into the general election.

There was one other aspect of the Trump approach that directly influenced his debate performance. He did not like to prepare and went out of his way, despite consistent efforts by his campaign staff, to avoid pre-debate practice sessions. Beginning a debate, he could be calm and seem presidential for brief periods of time but would soon revert back to the form that had served him well. He depended primarily on instinct and his perception of events and his evaluation of his opponents and what he believed to be their weaknesses. It was a carry-over from his business negotiations, and he was very good at it. He directed accusations and personal comments at his opponents. These were intended to both rattle them, elicit a response (none could compete with him effectively in such exchanges) and move the debate to a format he both felt more comfortable in dealing with and excelled at.

Along his positions during the campaign and the debates, Trump promised he would build a wall across the Mexican border to keep rapists and killers out of the United States and that the cost would be paid by Mexico. The idea was to appeal to Trump supporters, anxious to decrease violence in cities and, again, fearful of losing jobs and of the multicultural nation America was becoming. Trump also promised to reinstate "stop and frisk" police procedures in cities. His argument was they had worked in New York City in the 1990s under Mayor Rudolph Giuliani, a vocal Trump supporter, and they would work again. Such practices are heavily discriminatory against blacks and other minorities. That practice as conducted in New York had been declared unconstitutional by a federal judge in 2013 in terms of its application. Trump also lashed out against a Muslim American lawyer, Khizr Khan, and his wife Ghazala. The Khans were a "Gold Star" family, having lost a son in the war in Iraq. This also caused a sensation, although Khan had spoken out against Trump at the Democratic National Convention nominating Hillary Clinton and also in campaign rallies.

Given all of this, the first presidential debate on September 26, 2016 was much anticipated. Trump demonstrated the characteristics that defined his campaign. He appeared unprepared and spent his time on angry attacks against his opponent and conditions in the country in general. He had little new to offer in terms of policy concerns and largely avoided such issues. Clinton was more reserved and her demeanor more recognizable from the debates in other presidential years. She emphasized her issue positions to the extent she could while directing her own criticisms at Trump. One barb that struck home concerned Trump's past criticisms of a former Miss Universe's weight (he owned the Miss Universe pageant at the time). He had gone so far as to take the woman to a gym to work out with the media invited to watch (Johnson 2016).

During the campaign, the woman supported Clinton and accused Trump of having called her "Miss Piggy" and "Miss Housekeeping," among other things. The surfacing of this story appeared to infuriate Trump and he found it difficult to move off of the topic. Megyn Kelly, a Fox News commentator and host of one of the early pre-nomination debates, had attacked him during the debate, and Trump later responded saying "There was blood coming out of her eyes, blood coming out of her wherever." It was a strange episode that led to much criticism. Trump was accused of being a misogynist with frequent statements about women's looks and dress, and a known history of occasionally ranking them on a 1-to-10 scale in media interviews. A few days after the debate, Trump sent out a series of tweets in the middle of the night again criticizing the Miss Universe winner and, as he was often to do, expressing unedited views on whatever concerned him. The attacks were used by the media and Clinton as an example of his disdain for women more generally.

Clinton won the debate in the polls overwhelmingly. The size of the television audience, 84 million, set a new record for presidential debate viewership. Several million additional viewers followed the exchanges on social media. The three presidential debates and one vice presidential debate taken as a whole reached an estimated 259 million viewers according to Nielson Media Research, a new record.

On October 2, just prior to the second debate scheduled for October 4, the *New York Times* released a story on Trump's business failures and tax problems (Barstow, Craig, Buettner and Twohey 2016). It would cause a major sensation in the campaign. The newspaper reported that it had received a copy of Trump's tax returns for 1995 which showed he had declared a $916 million business loss for the year. The *Times* reported that this discovery meant Trump could legally avoid paying federal taxes based on this loss for 18 years, assuming a write-off on an income of $50 million per year over that time period. Trump had refused to release his tax returns, saying that they were under audit (although this by itself would not stop their release). For several decades, presidents and other presidential candidates had customarily made their tax returns (all or in part) public.

The *Times* reported that Trump had experienced severe financial difficulties in the 1980s and early 1990s. Further he lost other real estate properties and reportedly sought Chapter 11 bankruptcy protection for various of his business operations on a number of occasions. He himself did not lose money.

After extensive consideration, the banks, pension funds, hedge funds and investment corporations that had put money into Trump's businesses decided to keep Trump on a retainer. He would not own the companies, casinos, hotels or real estate with the Trump name on them, but he would be given a sum for the use of his name and he would manage some of them. They believed they would benefit more from using the Trump name for marketing purposes than engaging in an extensive legal effort to recoup their money (Buettner and Bagli 2016).

Also in regard to the $918 million in tax deferments for his losses, Trump's argument was that "crooked Hillary" or "corrupt Hillary" had been in government and in Congress for six years and should have changed the tax laws and that he was simply taking advantage of the law as it was.

Trump had built his appeal for "Making America Great Again" on the basis of his widespread business success. His argument was that he had the skills to negotiate with China and Russia as well as the North Atlantic Treaty Organization (NATO) to get better deals for America. He contended that international trade agreements, such as the North American Free Trade Agreement (NAFTA) and the Trans-Pacific Partnership (TPP) that President Obama had negotiated and was trying to have adopted, hurt the working man. These, he (and Bernie Sanders) said, took jobs away from Americans and cut workers out of the economic benefits that came to favor others. It was a powerful argument and it appealed to the constituency Trump had targeted.

His business failures struck at the very heart of his appeal as a wealthy and successful billionaire with the knowledge and skills to reshape the American economy; reward those at the lower levels of the economic hierarchy, ignored and exploited over the decades; and, as a consequence, return the United States to its former greatness.

As it turned out, Trump continued to manage his business interests while he was running for President. After the election, he indicated also that he would continue as an executive producer of the NBC reality TV show, "Celebrity Apprentice."

If this was not enough, a few days later, the *Washington Post* released a video tape of Trump a decade earlier at a planned taping of a segment for a Hollywood program in which Trump had agreed to appear (Fahrenthold 2016). In talking to a television personality accompanying him he is quoted as using vulgar language, saying he is "automatically attracted to beautiful [sic]—I just start kissing them. It's like a magnet. . . . And when you are a star, they let you do it. . . . You can do anything. . . . Grab them by the p—y." He also recounted how he took a married woman shopping for furniture because he wanted to make advances to her.

The video caused a sensation, the biggest controversy the campaign was to experience and the most difficult single episode Trump had to deal with. His response was that the tape was just "locker room talk," was old (over a decade or so) and did not represent who he was now. By mid-October, a dozen women had come forth to claim Trump had sexually harassed or groped them at various times or in different situations (Helderman 2016).

Trump's behavior was severely criticized and the question was raised as to whether he would withdraw from the race. The Republican party was in turmoil, a "civil war" as it was called, with some members withdrawing their support for his candidacy and others questioning the impact his behavior would have on congressional and state races.

Trump's response was to say, as he had in the debate, that rather than withdraw he would make an issue of Bill Clinton's sexual behavior, which he argued was much worse than anything he might have done. This he did. He held a press conference immediately before the second debate featuring four women, three of whom reported they had sexual encounters with the former President and one who said she had been raped as a child by a man Hillary Clinton had defended in a legal action (a *pro bono* case assigned Clinton by an Arkansas judge). Trump then had them seated in the audience for the debate after a squabble was resolved over Trump's original plan to seat them in the VIP box near Bill Clinton.

The format of the second debate was a town hall-style meeting with questions from the audience. Trump walked around the stage, often standing directly behind Clinton, hovering as she spoke in what was interpreted as "uncomfortable," even threatening posturing. He engaged in a series of personal attacks and accusations, this time more effective in disrupting Clinton's issue focus. As for her husband's sexual history, now a campaign issue, she refused to defend or discuss it.

That left the third and final debate of the campaign. The first two had been explosive, and for the media involved, theatrical. More of the same was expected. Trump was again the focal point of attention. He began in a more subdued manner, appearing to read most of his answers, an uncomfortable position for him. After a short interlude, Trump, Clinton and their interaction in the debate returned to the more familiar arguments and personal exchanges, with some effort to contrast what were quite different issue positions thrown in, that had characterized the earlier session and the campaign as a whole. Among the most controversial things Trump had to say during the campaign was that should he win, he would put "crooked," "lying" Hillary in jail. In this same category, he called for a special prosecutor to investigate her for alleged missteps while Secretary of State (Stevenson 2016). This was a promise he made in the debate, and had repeated a number of times and at rallies, as his supporters chanted "Lock her up." Also in the last presidential debate and afterwards he refused to commit to accepting the final election results. He added the country would have to wait to learn his decision until the election had taken place. He did add the proviso he would accept the vote count if he won (Rappeport and Burns 2016).

This was widely condemned as behavior more befitting for a third-world dictatorship than America's advanced democratic state—though as before, it did not appear to drive away voters committed to his candidacy.

The reality, however, was that those Trump spoke to and for proved willing to overlook his personal frailties as well as his serial involvement in controversies in exchange for having someone on the national stage who gave voice to their interests. The consequence was that whatever immediate problem came up, while it led to criticisms and occasional defections by other Republicans running for office, and while Trump and his campaign were attacked by prominent mainstream Republicans and by the media, among others, these had little impact on his core supporters. The election would remain close to the very end.

Trump, of course, did win the election so any potential constitutional crisis over a candidate's refusing to accept the results of the race was avoided. Also, after the election in speaking to the editorial board of the *New York Times*, he relented on the threat to jail Clinton. "I don't want to hurt the Clintons, I really don't. She went through a lot and suffered greatly in many different ways." He also added: "The campaign was vicious." Many would agree (Davis and Shear 2016).

The range of issues in the three debates touched on—if not developed in any depth—was extensive. These were Syria, terrorism, Russia (and Trump's relationship with Russian President Vladimir Putin), immigration, job creation, Trump's tax and business history, Trump's sexual advances to women, Clinton's emails, nuclear weapons, a "rigged election," abortion, guns, energy, "birtherism" (a movement Trump had informally led for five years that questioned if Barack Obama had been born in the United

States), cyberterrorism, Muslim prejudice, the operations of the Clinton and Trump foundations, Clinton's speeches to Wall Street and the pay she received, Trump's tweets, Clinton's "basket of deplorables" (remarks she made in referring to Trump supporters; she said she was trying to show empathy) and, not to be ignored, the Affordable Care Act and its replacement. It was in truth a broad spectrum and stood to illustrate a certain lack of focus, a problem for both campaigns and one dictated by the type of exchanges that dominated the contest. The inability to identify a handful of core concerns and develop these in depth and the reliance by both Clinton and Trump throughout the campaign and their media buys on "character," a distraction from what voters were most concerned about (jobs and terrorism) made for a campaign that while it covered much ground lacked a clear focus on the issues that voters wanted discussed. One major issue that stood out to many, particularly Millennials, for its absence from the debate was any mention of climate change.

Seemingly what was left was to complete the state-level campaigning and move on to Election Day. Such a prosaic ending to the campaign was not to be. On October 28, 12 days before the vote, came another unpredictable development. It was one that both sides would come to feel influenced the final vote, benefitting Trump and Republicans at all levels of races and hurting Clinton, Democratic congressional candidates and those running for state offices. The Clinton campaign, feeling good about their projections, had begun to campaign more forcefully in solid Republican states and to concentrate more attention on Senate and House candidates.

This all came to an abrupt halt. The campaign was forced to return to the basic swing states it believed it had largely won, drop their more aggressive campaigning in Republican areas, and do their best to counter the new revelations. Trump and Republicans returned to an issue that had plagued her campaign throughout the election and one that had shown itself to be her biggest political liability.

In a letter to Congress dated October 28, the FBI said it had come across a new batch of Clinton emails that had been found on the computer belonging to Anthony Weiner, the estranged husband of a top Clinton aide. To add to the drama, if needed, Weiner was a former U.S. Congressman from New York forced to resign after admitting he had sent sexually explicit photos of himself to various women on the social media platform Twitter, behavior he had repeated until it was revealed publicly in late August 2016. The FBI Director said in its October letter the newly found emails could be pertinent to their investigation of Clinton's email issues. He also wrote in the letter that the agency could not assess whether the material would be significant and he could not say how long the review would take. It involved just under 650,000 communications. This was 12 days before the vote. On the Sunday just two days before the election, the FBI released another letter saying nothing incriminating involving Clinton had been found and the FBI had not changed its earlier conclusion (Comey 2016a, 2016b).

Clinton was furious. She demanded to see what the FBI Director was talking about and that "the FBI release all the information that it has" and that it do so immediately. She went on to say that: "It's pretty strange to put something like that out with such little information right before an election" . . . In fact, it's not just strange; it's unprecedented and it is deeply troubling."

It was an odd development, the FBI publicly reopening an investigation previously terminated and doing it during a close election and immediately prior to Election Day. It also went against FBI policy to avoid involvement in elections. Additionally, the FBI Director had been advised by the Attorney General and others in the Justice Department not to release the letter at that stage of the campaign. Nonetheless, FBI Director James Comey's announcement changed the dynamic of the campaign. Trump and Republicans at all levels hit on the development to attack Clinton. She and her advisors were forced to revamp their campaign strategy. The revised strategy was to focus on efforts to hold states earlier believed to be in the Clinton column (among these: Michigan, Wisconsin, Pennsylvania and, in a tight race, Ohio, as well as several southern border states). Most critically in the election, she was to lose Rust Belt Midwestern industrial states by exceptionally narrow margins. These were to determine the outcome of a very close contest.

Clinton believed it was an effort to undermine her campaign. Postelection she, along with others, would claim that the extraordinary action by the FBI immediately prior to the vote determined the election's outcome. She may have been right, given the sensation caused by the announcement, its lack of substance, its immediate incorporation into the election debate, its potential to hurt one side and help the other, and the number of latedeciders in what was seen as a close race. There was nothing to rival such an incident in earlier campaigns. Whatever the motive or naïveté or impolitic nature of the FBI in announcing a new facet of a revived investigation, there was nothing that could be done about it or to the FBI or to counter the political impact of the action.

An ABC/*Washington Post* poll released November 1 in the wake of the FBI release showed essentially a tie between the Clinton and Trump, 46% to 45%, adding to the tension and the controversy over what affected the final vote (Langer 2016; Healy and Martin 2016; Apuzzo, Goldman, Schmidt and Rashbaum 2016; Goldman, Rappeport, Schmidt and Apuzzo 2016).

## Conclusion: A Red Nation?

The electoral map (Figure 1.1) made it appear Donald Trump had won a landslide. In the Electoral College, there was some support for this interpretation. The Electoral College breakdown was 306 (56.9%) for Trump against 232 (43.1%) for Hillary Clinton, an unexpectedly large margin for a candidate not projected to win the race.[1] Trump carried 31 states, Clinton 19 and the District of Columbia. Clinton however won the popular vote by 48.2% to Trump's 46.1%, a difference of almost 3 million votes, winning more votes than any losing presidential candidate in U.S. history (*New York Times*, December 20, 2016). Her vote margin was the third largest for any losing U.S. presidential candidate, topped only by the elections of 1824 and 1876. Clinton had won California alone, her best showing, by more than 3 million votes (61.5% to Trump's 32.9%) (Krieg 2016; Porter 2016).

As indicated, the Electoral College is a product of another age and its thinking as to strategies of representation. It was a constitutional experiment designed at a time when there were no models in other countries to follow by Founders suspicious of a direct vote and the potential for mob rule. It has continued to have its problems over the years.

There has been a sense of bewilderment as to why it has lasted so long, and there have been calls for a direct popular vote in line with other democratic nations. Changing or replacing the Electoral College, however, would be extremely difficult. This would involve either a constitutional convention called for such a purpose (used only once, in the adoption of the 21st Amendment on Prohibition) plus passage by three-fourths of the states, or passage of a constitutional amendment by a two-thirds vote of both houses of the Congress and by three-fourths of the states. Given the advantage by the less populous states enjoy, change is not likely.

In relation to the group vote, the differences in the candidate coalitions comes across clearly (Table 1.1). Trump did best among men, white (70% of the electorate), older voters and the less educated. Clinton did well among women, blacks and Latinos (although the turnout of these groups was lower than expected), the young and both college-educated and non-college non-white voters. As for issues, the economy was far and

**TABLE 1.1** Demographics of the 2016 Presidential Vote

|  | *Voter Breakdown* | *Clinton* | *Trump* |
|---|---|---|---|
| **Sex** | | | |
| Men | 48% | 41% | 53% |
| Women | 52 | 54 | 42 |
| **Race** | | | |
| White | 70 | 37 | 58 |
| Black | 12 | 88 | 8 |
| Hispanic | 11 | 65 | 29 |
| Asian | 4 | 65 | 29 |
| Other | 3 | 57 | 37 |

|  | Voter Breakdown | Clinton | Trump |
|---|---|---|---|
| **Age** | | | |
| 18–29 | 19 | 54 | 37 |
| 30–44 | 25 | 50 | 42 |
| 45–64 | 40 | 44 | 53 |
| 65+ | 16 | 45 | 52 |
| **Household Income** | | | |
| <$50,000/year | 36 | 52 | 41 |
| $50,000+/year | 64 | 47 | 49 |
| **Education by Race** | | | |
| White/College Grad | 37 | 45 | 49 |
| White/Non-College | 34 | 28 | 67 |
| Nonwhite/College Grad | 13 | 71 | 23 |
| Nonwhite/Non-College | 16 | 75 | 20 |
| **Most Important Issue** | | | |
| Economy | 52 | 52 | 42 |
| Foreign policy | 13 | 60 | 34 |
| Immigration | 13 | 33 | 64 |
| Terrorism | 18 | 39 | 57 |

Source: Data from "How You Voted in the 2016 Election." *Boston Globe*. November 9, 2016. P. A18.

away the most important of voter concerns. Terrorism and immigration, both Trump strong points, came in as far less significant.

The congressional results, once expected to show significant gains for the Democrats, resulted in continued Republican majorities in both houses of the Congress (Table 1.2). This gave the Republicans control of all three branches of government.

The results:

**TABLE 1.2** Congressional Vote 2016

|  | House | | Senate | |
|---|---|---|---|---|
|  | Democrats | Republicans | Democrats | Republicans |
| 2017: | 194 | 241 | 48* | 52 |
| 2016: | 186 | 246 (3 seats vacant) | 46* | 54 |

*Includes 2 Independents who caucus with the Democrats.
Source: Data from Ballotpedia, *https://ballotpedia.org/United_States_Congress_elections,_2016*.

The Democrats did gain two seats in the Senate and increased their House representation by six seats. The Republicans maintained a solid majority in both houses of the Congress. In one indication of both how polarized the parties have become and how gerrymandered the congressional districts are, only 21 states had at least one battleground race in either the House or Senate. The rest were largely uncompetitive.

On the state level, gubernatorial elections were also held in 12 states. The Republican party gained two governorships and increased the total number of Republican governors to 33, the highest number seen since 1922. The Democrats lost two governorships, resulting in a total of 16 states (one state, Alaska, had an independent governor who had won office in 2014).

As for state legislative elections, beginning in the post-World War II years and continuing through to the 2008 election, the political party of an outgoing, two-term President, or consecutive one-party presidencies, lost an average of 450 state legislative seats. During Barack Obama's years in office the total doubled to a net party loss of 958 seats ("Changes in State Legislative Seats During the Obama Presidency" 2016). Obama, the putative leader of the party, had little interest in intra-party affairs, leading to the results indicated.

This level of losses should have indicated to national party leaders the neglect of the party at the local level. It also should have told Democratic party strategists that the party's message, essentially a cultural, identity-based emphasis during the Obama presidency and as reflected in Hillary Clinton's choice of a campaign slogan "Stronger Together" (replacing the earlier slogan emphasizing the economy) had little appeal to grassroots voters and especially those concerned with economic conditions. Such historic losses in state legislative races should have provided warning signs that a return to more traditional party concerns directed to working and middle class voters and dealing with jobs and economic conditions needed emphasis in the 2016 presidential campaign. Considerably more Republican seats were at risk and the Democrats should have done well, as they were expected to do. They did not. It was the Republican party that continued its mastery of state legislative races (Table 1.3).

The results:

**TABLE 1.3** Party Control of State Legislatures

| Legislative Chamber | 2016 Democratic | 2016 Republican | 2017 Democratic | 2017 Republican |
| --- | --- | --- | --- | --- |
| State Senates | 14 | 36 | 13 | 37 |
| State Houses | 16 | 33 | 18 | 31 |
| Total | 30 | 69 | 31 | 68 |

*Source*: Data from Ballotpedia, https://ballotpedia.org/State_legislative_elections,_2016.

One further note: As of 2017, the Republican party controlled the governorships and both houses of the state legislature in 25 states to six states for the Democrats. The significance is to add importance to the 2018 and 2020 state races in preparation for the congressional redistricting to come after the decennial Census. Congressional district lines as presently drawn are gerrymandered to substantially benefit the Republican party, leading to popular vote majorities nationwide for Democrats and congressional party dominance for Republicans. The battle over the drawing of district lines will resume after the 2020 races.

## *Recap*

The conditions that gave rise to a Trump victory in actuality had been long in the making. These could be found in the restructuring of the nation's economic system, in line with neoliberal assumptions that began in earnest during the Reagan years and carried through later presidencies, most notably those of George W. Bush and Bill Clinton as the ideology proved to be bipartisan. A second major contributor was the racial realignment of working-class white voters after the Voting Rights Act of 1965. The realignment began in the South and later spread to the rest of the country. It was spearheaded by Alabama Gov. George C. Wallace and co-opted by President Richard M. Nixon, who repackaged Wallace's extremist message into more acceptable mainstream appeal. In addition, the increasing lack of relevance of the nation's political parties, their inability to adapt to the changing tides of history or to stay in touch with their constituent bases and adequately represent their interests contributed to what was to come in 2016 and potentially thereafter.

The consequences could be predicted. In fact, a now-deceased philosopher of pragmatism in 1998 did that in a strikingly relevant projection of events to come. Richard Rorty wrote:

> [M]embers of labor unions, and unorganized unskilled workers, will sooner or later realize that their government is not even trying to prevent wages from sinking or to prevent jobs from being exported. Around the same time, they will realize that suburban white-collar workers—themselves desperately afraid of being downsized—are not going to let themselves be taxed to provide social benefits for anyone else.
>
> At that point, something will crack. The non-suburban electorate will decide that the system has failed and start looking around for a strongman to vote for—someone willing to assure them that, once he is elected, the smug bureaucrats, tricky lawyers, overpaid bond salesmen, and postmodernist professors will no longer be calling the shots. . . .

One thing that is very likely to happen is that the gains made in the past 40 years by black and brown Americans, and by homosexuals, will be wiped out. Jocular contempt for women will come back into fashion. . . . All the resentment which badly educated Americans feel about having their manners dictated to them by college graduates will find an outlet.

(qtd. in Senior 2016)

A harsh assessment of contemporary American politics perhaps, but one that would find echoes in the 2016 election. Ross Douthat, a conservative/centrist columnist for the *New York Times*, writing shortly before the vote projected as to what a Trump or Clinton presidency might look like. He characterized the broad outlines of the election race, as seen from the perspective of the Clinton campaign, as a choice of extremes:

A vote for Hillary Clinton over Donald Trump, the Clinton campaign has suggested in broad ways and subtle tones, isn't just a vote for a Democrat over a Republican: It's a vote for safety over risk, steady competence over boastful recklessness, psychological stability in the White House over ungovernable passions.

In regards to each of the campaigns, should Trump win:

The perils of a Trump presidency are as distinctive as the candidate himself, and a vote for Trump makes a long list of worst cases—the Western alliance system's unraveling, a cycle of domestic radicalization, an accidental economic meltdown, a civilian-military crisis—more likely than with any normal administration.

Indeed, Trump and his supporters almost admit as much. 'We've tried sane, now let's try crazy,' is basically his campaign's working motto. The promise to be a bull in a china shop is part of his demagogue's appeal. Some of his more eloquent supporters have analogized a vote for Trump to storming the cockpit of a hijacked place, with the likelihood of a plane crash entirely factored in.

And for a Clinton victory, the outlook was bleak also:

The dangers of a Hillary Clinton presidency are more familiar than Trump's authoritarian unknowns, because we live with them in our politics already. They're the dangers of elite groupthink, of Beltway power worship, of a cult of presidential action in the service of dubious ideals. They're the dangers of a recklessness and radicalism that doesn't recognize itself as either, because it's convinced that if an idea is mainstream and commonplace among the great and good then it cannot possibly be folly.

Almost every crisis that has come upon the West in the last 15 years has its roots in this establishmentarian type of folly.

*(Douthat 2016)*

In this account, Clinton, then projected to win the election, represented the continuation of a politics, unaware of its faults and failures, condemning the nation to more of the same. Whether Douthat captured the essence of the concerns about a projected Clinton presidency as felt by Trump supporters can only be speculated on. Still, the Washington consensus, group-think mentality and the status-quo continuation of economic imbalances, military misadventures and terrorist threats and corresponding rise of a national security state may well have provided the foundations of the essential distrust encountered by the Clinton candidacy and the appeal of Donald Trump and his message of change.

One of the oddities of an election full of them was the failure of the Clinton campaign to focus on the economy. It had improved under the Obama administration, although not to the extent some would like and not reaching all levels of the society. Limited evidence of an upturn was enough to get Obama reelected in 2012. After that election, the economic upswing gained momentum. A total of 15.6 million private sector jobs had been added since 2010 and the unemployment rate had been reduced to 4.9% by Election Day. Consumer confidence had approached its highest level in a decade. Economic improvements had begun appearing nationwide and while not dramatic (or for that matter, not evenly distributed in the society) should have given the Democrats a cutting issue entering the campaign (Sachs 2016).

Most presidential elections are tied to the state of the economy. In 2016 it was seen by most voters as strong. A Clinton focus on this growth, a promise to continue it and a pledge to bring it home to the largely rural white sectors of the country that constituted Trump's base of support, would have had a strong appeal. It was an appeal with a proven track record of success.

Clinton as a senator had concentrated on stimulating economic development in white, rural areas of upstate New York badly in need of it. She had experienced a degree of success and did well in these areas (and the rest of New York) winning reelection with two-thirds of the vote. Clinton also did have a series of economic proposals buried in her platform, ones she had difficulty in summarizing and presenting in the abbreviated form necessitated by campaign rallies and debates. Trump in turn had a brief and effective message to the effect his supporters were left out of any recovery and that he, and only be, could and would change this.

When questioned in the debates as to jobs and her economic policy, Clinton continually repeated she would put her husband, Bill Clinton, in charge of the economy. It is difficult to know if she was serious but it did send a mixed message to viewers. It appeared, and for no understandable reason, that a candidate conversant with the need for targeted economic development and with a record of attention to the problem in less well-off areas while in the Senate preferred not to deal with it in the campaign. As for entrusting Bill Clinton with the responsibility for the economy, his administration did experience a spike in employment before he left office that approached full employment. It was mostly in low-wage jobs at McDonald's, Starbucks and the like, and did not last. At another level, Clinton's actions as President had helped bring about the economic collapse of 2007–2008. He had embraced Republican deregulation positions and his association with and advancement of the interests of Wall Street and the financial industry did not turn out well. Hillary Clinton's refusal to prioritize jobs, a traditional Democratic message, in turn left Trump free to appeal to voters through vague promises with little substantive content and, equally important, to project a symbolic personal identification with economic out-groups to gain their support.

The election was won and lost here. Exceptionally close wins in the Upper Midwest, normally Democratic and labor union strongholds, gave Trump his edge in the Electoral College. Additionally six states Barack Obama had won would all end in Trump's column (Cohen 2016).

Post-election, local and state party officials in Michigan, Ohio and other struggling Rust Belt areas claimed they had made repeated efforts to send a message to the Clinton campaign that a "one-size-fits-all strategy" was not working with their voters. To appeal to union workers and working-class voters, the campaign needed to address issues of job growth and economic development in detail. Clinton's campaign manager later was to say the fight over campaign tactics in the economically depressed regions of the country never reached his desk.

It may be that a number of conditions contributed to the Clinton loss and the economy (as is usual in a presidential contest) was among the most decisive. The problems experienced in reaching voters in these areas may suggest another explanation for the outcome.

> Clinton's loss could be attributed to any number of factors—FBI Director . . . Comey's letter shifting late deciders, the lack of a compelling economic message, the apparent Russian hacking. But heartbroken and frustrated in-state battleground operatives worry that a lesson being missed is a simple one: Get the basics of campaigning right.
>
> *(Dovere 2016)*

It was an angry and unrelentingly contentious campaign. As indicated earlier, both candidates were unpopular and distrusted by large segments of the population (Sachs 2016; Martin, Sussman and Thee-Brenan 2016). Given this, and the entirely unexpected victory of a political novice with a questionable business and personal background and a disregard for restraint or civility, the anger of his opponents at the results should have been predictable. These critiques ranged in intensity and alarm depending on how each individual viewed the result. David Remnick presents his take on the outcome. It is unforgiving, and in his eyes "a tragedy for the American republic."

> There are, inevitably, miseries to come: an increasingly reactionary Supreme Court; an emboldened right-wing Congress; a President whose disdain for women and minorities, civil liberties and scientific fact, to say nothing of simple decency, has been repeatedly demonstrated. Trump is vulgarity unbounded, a knowledge-free national leader who will not only set markets tumbling but will strike fear into the hearts of the vulnerable, the weak, and, above all, the many varieties of Other whom he has so deeply insulted. The African-American Other. The Hispanic Other. The female Other. The Jewish and Muslim Other. The most hopeful way to look at this grievous event—and it's a stretch—is that this election and the years to follow will be a test of the strength, or the fragility, of American institutions. It will be a test of our seriousness and resolve.
>
> (Remnick 2016)

Trump's early appointments of Wall Street insiders to the top economic posts and military generals to positions in national security and defense did little to calm those who questioned his commitments and/or feared his presidency.

Whatever the nature of the presidency to come, Hillary Clinton's concession speech offers a contrast to what had gone before. It did include veiled references to points raised in the campaign exchanges but in overall terms took a positive approach. While acknowledging that "the loss hurts," she went on to say "Please never stop believing that fighting for what's right is worth it." As for her opponent, she indicated her hope that Trump would be "a successful President for all Americans" and would defend "the rule of law; the principle we are all equal in rights and dignity; freedom of worship and expression." As she said: "We owe him an open mind and a chance to lead. Our constitutional democracy enshrines the peaceful transfer of power. And we don't just respect that. We cherish it." (Clinton 2016).

It may be best to remember that the nation has survived crises that provided severe threats to its unity, its equality and its ability to preserve the values that made it great. American government has proven flexible and adaptive to change. The likelihood is that however mild or extreme the challenge to come, it should continue to do so.

## The Recount

American elections are normally well run, although of course errors can occur. Historically, fraud at the individual voter level has been infinitesimal. No change in the vote count sufficient to overturn the final results in a recount was to be expected.

Why then seek a recount? Clinton had been presented with evidence from election experts that her vote totals in counties using electronic voting machines was 7% lower than those using hand-counted paper ballots and optical scan voting systems, both considered more precise and reliable. The figures would provide a grounds for the recount in the targeted states.

There was another issue. The Russians had been accused during the campaign of hacking the Democratic National Committee email and then releasing the findings through WikiLeaks to the public in an effort to advance a Trump presidency (Trump had stated his admiration for Vladimir Putin, the Russian president, repeatedly during the campaign.) It turned out the accusations as to Russian hacking had merit but there was nothing to indicate they had done so in the states chosen for a recount (Lipton, Sanger and Shane 2016).

The Clinton camp decided not to seek a recount (although they later associated themselves with the effort). Dr. Jill Stein, the Green Party's presidential candidate, decided at that point she would file for recounts in three industrial states with strong union movements that went for Trump. The three states in question—Wisconsin, Michigan and Pennsylvania—were chosen since they were critical in determining the election's outcome. Trump's margin of victory in each was minuscule (less than 1%). Trump had won Wisconsin by 27,257 votes (0.7%); Michigan by 10,704 (0.2%); and Pennsylvania by 49,543 (0.8%). Should the vote results after a recount have favored Clinton in each, she would have gained 46 electoral votes, changing Trump's total from 306 to 260 and hers from 232 to 278. This would have been enough to meet and exceed the 270 needed for victory.[1]

States and localities do not want to engage in recounts and do everything they legally can to avoid them. They are expensive and time-consuming, and normally amount to little. There is an additional problem in terms of time constraints; the states' electoral vote count was due by December 19, a difficult deadline to meet should a recount take place. Consequently, the states establish a series of arcane standards and financial requirements that need to be met to engage in such a challenge. Also the courts are historically unfriendly to recounts as well.

Challenges by Trump and by the state Republican parties led to court actions that effectively killed the recount efforts in Pennsylvania and Michigan. Wisconsin was the only state to complete the process and it only slightly changed the final vote count, although not the results.

This then finally ended a long, angry and—for many—dispiriting campaign.

## Note

1 In the December 19, 2016 official vote of the Electoral College, there were seven defectors (or "faithless electors"), who declined to vote for their party's nominee. Trump received 304 electoral votes to Hillary Clinton's 227, still surpassing the 270 needed for Trump to be the election victor.

## Bibliography

Apuzzo, Matt, Adam Goldman, Michael S. Schmidt and William K. Rashbaum. 2016. "Justice Dept. Warned F.B.I. About Timing." *New York Times*, October 30. P. A1. www.nytimes.com/2016/10/30/us/politics/comey-clinton-email-justice.html (accessed December 19).

Barstow, David, Susanne Craig, Russ Buettner and Megan Twohey. 2016. "Trump's 1995 Tax Records Claim $916 Million Loss." *New York Times*, October 2. P. A1. www.nytimes.com/2016/10/02/us/politics/donald-trump-taxes.html?_r=0 (accessed November 20).

Borchers, Callum. 2016. "How the Media Covered Hillary Clinton and Donald Trump After 9/11." Washington Post, September 11. www.washingtonpost.com/news/the-fix/wp/2016/09/11/how-the-media-covered-hillary-clinton-and-donald-trump-after-911/?utm_term=.e35f0ee00779 (accessed December 10).

Buettner, Russ and Charles V. Bagli. 2016. "Business Decisions in '80s Nearly Led Trump to Ruin." *New York Times*, October 4. P. A1. www.nytimes.com/2016/10/04/nyregion/donald-trump-taxes-debt.html?_r=0 (accessed November 25).

"Changes in State Legislative Seats During the Obama Presidency." 2016. *Ballotpedia*. https://ballotpedia.org/Changes_in_state_legislative_seats_during_the_Obama_presidency (accessed December 20).

Chozick, Amy and Megan Thee-Brenan. 2016. "Poll Finds Voters in Both Parties Unhappy With Their Candidates." *New York Times*, July 14. www.nytimes.com/2016/07/15/us/politics/hillary-clinton-donald-trump-poll.html?_r=0 (accessed December 7).

*Citizens United vs. Federal Election Commission* 558 U.S. 310 (2010). https://supreme.justia.com/cases/federal/us/558/08-205/opinion.html (accessed December 10, 2016).

Clinton, Hillary. 2016. Concession Speech. *Vox*, November 9. www.vox.com/2016/11/9/13570328/hillary-clinton-concession-speech-full-transcript-2016-presidential-election (accessed December 12).

Cohen, Patricia. 2016. "Obama's Gift to Successor: The Economy." *New York Times*, December 3. P. A1. www.nytimes.com/2016/12/02/business/economy/jobs-report.html (accessed December 20, 2016).

Comey, James B. 2016a. "FBI Director James B. Comey Letter to Congressional Leaders." October 28. https://assets.documentcloud.org/documents/3197546/October-28-Letter-2.pdf (accessed December 10).

———. 2016b. "FBI Director James B. Comey Letter to Congressional Leaders." November 6. https://assets.documentcloud.org/documents/3214831/Fbiletter.pdf (accessed December 10).

Davis, Julie Hirschfeld and Michael D. Shear. 2016. "Trump Pulls Back But Still Defies the Conventions." *New York Times*, November 23. P. A1. www.nytimes.com/2016/11/22/us/politics/donald-trump-hillary-clinton-investigation.html-?action=click&contentCollection=Politics&module=RelatedCoverage &region=Marginalia&pgtype=article (accessed December 10).

Douthat, Ross. 2016. "The Dangers of Hillary Clinton." *New York Times*, October 23. P. SR11. http://nyti.ms/2erOQTQ (accessed online December 12).

Dovere, Edward-Isaac. 2016. "How Clinton Won Michigan—and Blew the Election." *Politico*, December 14. www.politico.com/story/2016/12/michigan-hillary-clinton-trump-232547 (accessed December 21).

Fahrenthold, David. A. 2016. "Trump Recorded Having Extremely Lewd Conversation About Women in 2005." *Washington Post*, October 8. www.washingtonpost.com/politics/trump-recorded-having-extremely-lewd-conversation-about-women-in-2005/2016/10/07/3b9ce776-8cb4-11e6-bf8a-3d26847eeed4_story.html?utm_term=.10993c6b21e2 (accessed December 10).

Federal Election Commission, Campaign Finance Data. 2016. https://beta.fec.gov/data/candidates/president/?election_year=2016&cycle=2016&election_full=true (accessed December 11).

"Gallup Presidential Election 2016: Key Indicators." www.gallup.com/poll/189299/presidential-election-2016-key-indicators.aspx?version=print (accessed November 9).

Goldman, Adam, Alan Rappeport, Michael S. Schmidt and Matt Apuzzo. 2016. "New Emails Jolt Clinton Campaign in Race's Last Days." *New York Times*, October 29. P. A1. www.nytimes.com/2016/10/29/us/politics/fbi-hillary-clinton-email.html (accessed December 19).

Healy, Patrick and Jonathan Martin. 2016. "Clinton Shifts to Attack Mode on Email Issue." *New York Times*, October 30. P. A1 www.nytimes.com/2016/10/30/us/politics/hillary-clinton-emails-fbi-anthony-weiner.html (accessed December 19).

Helderman, Rosalind S. 2016. "The Growing List of Women Who Have Stepped Forward to Accuse Trump of Touching Them Inappropriately." *Washington Post*, October 22. www.washingtonpost.com/politics/the-growing-list-of-women-who-have-stepped-forward-to-accuse-trump-of-touching-them-inappropriately/2016/10/15/a65ddf1c-92df-11e6-9c85-ac42097b8cc0_story.html?utm_term=.8447c9d06001 (accessed December 10).

Johnson, Jenna. 2016. "Trump Attacks Former Miss Universe Who 'Gained a Massive Amount of Weight' and Had 'Attitude'." *Washington Post*, September 27. www.washingtonpost.com/news/post-politics/wp/2016/09/27/trump-attacks-former-miss-universe-who-gained-a-massive-amount-of-weight-and-had-attitude/?utm_term=.3c38203cd4d0 (accessed December 10).

Krieg, Gregory. 2016. "It's Official: Clinton Swamps Trump in Popular Vote." *CNN*, December 21. www.cnn.com/2016/12/21/politics/donald-trump-hillary-clinton-popular-vote-final-count/index.html citing Dave Leip, *U.S. Elections Atlas*. http://uselectionatlas.org/RESULTS/ (accessed December 21).

Langer, Gary. 2016. "Clinton, Trump All But Tied as Enthusiasm Dips for Democratic Candidate." *ABC News/Washington Post* tracking poll produced by Langer Research Associates. http://abcnews.go.com/Politics/clinton-trump-tied-democratic-enthusiasm-dips/story?id=43199459 (accessed December 19).

Lipton, Eric, David E. Sanger and Scott Shane. 2016. "Hacking the Democrats." *New York Times*, December 14. P. A1. www.nytimes.com/2016/12/13/us/politics/russia-hack-election-dnc.html?hp=undefined&action=click&pgtype=Homepage&clickSource=story-heading&module=photo-spot-region&region=top-news&WT.nav=top-news&_r=0 (accessed December 14).

Martin, Jonathan, Dalia Sussman and Megan Thee-Brenan. 2016. "In Poll, Voters Express Disgust in U.S. Politics." *New York Times*, November 4. P. A1. www.nytimes.com/2016/11/04/us/politics/hillary-clinton-donald-trump-poll.html?_r=0 (accessed December 21).

Porter, Steven. 2016. *The Christian Science Monitor*, December 22. www.csmonitor.com/USA/Politics/2016/1222/Clinton-wins-US-popular-vote-by-widest-margin-of-any-losing-presidential-candidate

"Presidential Election Results: Donald J. Trump Wins." 2016. *New York Times*, December 20. www.nytimes.com/elections/results/president (accessed December 20).

Rappeport, Alan and Alexander Burns. 2016. "Trump Stays Firm on Having Option to Dispute Vote." *New York Times*, October 21. P. A1. www.nytimes.com/2016/10/21/us/politics/campaign-election-trump-clinton.html?_r=0 (accessed December 10).

Remnick, David. 2016. "An American Tragedy." *The New Yorker*, November 9.

Republican Platform. 2016. https://prod-cdn-static.gop.com/media/documents/DRAFT_12_FINAL[1]-ben_1468872234.pdf (accessed December 11).

Sachs, Jeffrey D. 2016. "Restoring Civic Virtue in America." *Boston Globe*, December 4. www.bostonglobe.com/opinion/2016/12/04/restoring-civic-virtue-america/p0bBJhr9R0qHPOLOsDvH5K/story.html?event=event12 (accessed December19).

Senior, Jennifer. 2016. "A Book From 1998 Envisioned 2016 Election." *New York Times*, November 21. P. C1. www.nytimes.com/2016/11/21/books/richard-rortys-1998-book-suggested-election-2016-was-coming.html?_r=0 (accessed December 12).

Stevenson, Peter W. 2016. "A Brief History of the 'Lock Her Up!' Chant by Trump Supporters Against Clinton." *Washington Post*, November 22. www.washingtonpost.com/news/the-fix/wp/2016/11/22/a-brief-history-of-the-lock-her-up-chant-as-it-looks-like-trump-might-not-even-try/?utm_term=.772944b770c9 (accessed December 10).

# 2

# THE CONVENTIONAL VERSUS THE UNCONVENTIONAL

Presidential Nominations in 2016

Barbara Norrander

> *In politics . . . never retreat, never retreat . . . never admit a mistake.*
> — Napoleon Bonaparte

The 2016 Republican nomination was truly unconventional. The nominee chosen was a businessman who never held public office, the first time this occurred since 1952 when Republicans nominated World War II general Dwight Eisenhower. Donald Trump employed unconventional campaign techniques, as well. His campaign relied on social media, especially Twitter, and domination of media coverage rather than traditional methods of advertising and direct voter contact. Trump won over a field cluttered by 16 other opponents. Most of Trump's competitors left the race in 2015 or after the first few primaries and caucuses in 2016. The field quickly dwindled to four candidates: Trump, Ted Cruz, Marco Rubio and John Kasich. Trump was the anti-establishment candidate who struck a chord with Republican voters angry over the economy and cultural changes. With the other three candidates splitting the remaining vote, none would catch up to Trump, and all three left the race before the last votes were cast.

The 2016 Democratic nomination followed a more traditional pattern. Hillary Clinton established herself as the frontrunner in the years leading up to the election. She was well ahead in the public opinion polls. The party's elected officials rallied around her candidacy as well, with most Democratic governors and members of Congress endorsing Clinton. Clinton also used the pre-election season to court key constituency groups and raise funds. By the summer of 2015, she had campaign offices across all 50 states to help locate activists and volunteers who would spread the campaign's message and get people to the polls (Terkel 2015). Clinton's strong pre-election position dissuaded most potential challengers. Only Senator Bernie Sanders of Vermont challenged Clinton, though he turned out to be a tougher than expected challenger. Courting young supporters and with a focus on economic inequality, Sanders attempted to move the Democratic party to the left. Nevertheless, Clinton's groundwork paid off. She developed a lead in pledged delegates after the March 1 Super Tuesday, a day on which 17 primaries or caucuses were held. Sanders would never catch up.

While the two parties' paths to their presidential nominations were dissimilar, both were structured by components in place since the last quarter of the 20th century. Each party establishes rules for its nominations. States, too, play a role by choosing between a primary or caucus and selecting the date for their nominating events. Candidates raise funds under strict national rules, but recent changes in campaign finance allows outside groups to raise and spend money freely. Finally, the nomination process is split into different phases: a preseason (in the year or two before the election), the main event of primaries and caucuses in 2016, and the national conventions, where official nominations are bestowed.

## The Rules

The purpose of primaries and caucuses is to select each state's delegates to attend the Democratic or Republican national convention. Each national convention retains the legal authority to pick its party's presidential nominee. A candidate needs the support of 50 percent of convention delegates to win the nomination. Since the last quarter of the 20th century, most states opt to hold primaries. In 2016, three-quarters of the states did so. Unlike presidential elections, residents of U.S. territories also participate in the presidential nominations and mostly select their delegates through caucuses.

In primary elections, voters cast ballots for candidates, which subsequently determines the number of delegates sent to the national conventions in support of that candidate. This is similar to the two-step process in the Electoral College, where the popular vote determines whether the Democratic or Republican slate of electors is chosen. Convention delegates are typically selected in party meetings (either before or after the primary), and with tightening of Republican rules in 2016, Republican and Democratic delegates are almost always bound to support a specific candidate. Still, Republican delegate selection rules would be a source of controversy when in April it appeared a contested convention might be possible. In such case, if no candidate won on the first ballot, many Republican delegates would be free to vote for any candidate on the second ballot. Ted

Cruz hoped that previously bound Trump delegates would support him on the second ballot, while Trump decried this possibility as part of a rigged system.

Caucuses are a bit more elaborate. The public attends a local caucus, which is a party meeting held in each voting precinct. Attendees gather at a local school, church or other location on a specific day and time. In Republican caucuses candidate support is typically measured by an entrance poll, which determines the allocation of delegates among the candidates. Democratic caucus rules are more elaborate, and two rounds of voting might occur before delegate slots are distributed across candidates' supporters. The local caucus is just the first step. Delegates chosen from the caucus attend a subsequent meeting, typically a county convention, where the delegate selection process occurs again to select people to attend congressional district conventions and ultimately a state convention. Most delegates to the national convention are chosen from these last two events. This multistep process unfolds over several months. For example, in 2016 the Iowa caucuses were held on February 1, county conventions took place on March 12, congressional district conventions followed on April 9 and the state convention ended the process on May 21. Caucus critics focus on low turnout rates (typically less than 5 percent), while caucus defenders point to them as the epitome of grassroots democracy. Sanders, with his ardent group of supporters, tended to win in Democratic caucuses. Cruz won half of the Republican caucuses.

The two parties use different rules to translate votes from primaries or caucuses into delegates. Since the 1990s, all Democratic delegates are awarded proportionately. If a candidate wins 40 percent of the vote, that candidate is awarded 40 percent of the delegate slots. A candidate needs to win a minimum of 15 percent of the vote in order to be awarded any delegate. The Republican party allows states to select a variety of rules. Among the 36 Republican primaries in 2016, eight used proportional representation rules and eight others used a simple, statewide winner-take-all in which the first-place candidate is awarded all of the state's delegates. Most of the other Republican primaries were a variant on winner-take-all. Some states required a candidate to win an absolute majority of the primary vote before a candidate would be awarded all of the state's delegates. Other states separated the vote at the state level and the congressional district and awarded votes on a winner-take-all provision at both levels. The remainder used winner-take-all at one level and other allocation rules, such as proportional representation, at the other level. In West Virginia, Republican voters cast votes directly for delegates rather than the presidential candidates (Republican Delegate Allocation Rules 2016).

Who can vote in a primary election or a caucus is determined by state law. Participation in closed primaries is limited to those who designated that party on their voter registration forms. Semi-closed primaries allow registered independents to select either of the party primaries. Open primary states do not have party registration, and voters select a party's primary ballot at the polls. Bernie Sanders, who did better among independents, argued that all states should hold open primaries. However, political science research shows these primary participation rules have far fewer effects on the composition of the electorate than generally presumed (Norrander and Wendland 2016).

Over the past few election cycles, the Democratic and Republican parties agreed on a common calendar. Iowa, New Hampshire, South Carolina and Nevada go first with contests scheduled for February. The remaining states choose dates between March and June. In 2008 and 2012, a few states violated the designated calendar and were punished by losing delegates. In 2016, no state violated the calendar rules. Still, the ordering of the states across the election year matters. In 2016, many southern states held early contests, which helped Clinton establish her delegate lead. In many years, the nomination race is over by the middle of the election calendar, before all of the states have voted. The 2016 Republican race ended after Trump's victory in the May 3 Indiana primary, which led Cruz and Kasich to withdraw. Nine states had not yet voted. The Democratic contest, however, extended to the last round of primaries held in June, repeating the pattern of 2008.

## The Republican Candidates

When a party does not control the presidency, typically five to 10 candidates may run to be that party's presidential nominee. In 2016, the Republican party had 17 declared candidates! Voters faced a hefty task trying to sort through so many options. Most Republican candidates mirrored past presidential nominees by being current or former governors and senators. Among the senators running for the 2016 Republican nomination were Ted Cruz (TX), Lindsey Graham (SC), Rand Paul (KY), Marco Rubio (FL) and Rick Santorum (PA). From the ranks of governors came Jeb Bush (FL), Chris Christie (NJ), Jim Gilmore (VA), Mike Huckabee (AR), Bobby Jindal (LA), John Kasich (OH), George Pataki (NY), Rick Perry (TX) and Scott Walker (WI). Senators and governors possess the political experience that makes them viable presidential candidates. They have political and government experience, and they have run successful statewide campaigns. A few candidates come from outside the political world. Three of the 2016 Republican candidates fit this mode: Ben Carson, a retired pediatric neurosurgeon; Carly Fiorina, former head of Hewlett-Packard who had lost her bid for the U.S. Senate seat in California in 2010; and Donald Trump, a real estate mogul and reality TV star. Such outside candidates often do not fare well, as they are inexperienced campaigners which tends to lead to missteps.

In most election cycles, a few candidates drop out before the first votes are cast, because they fail to make traction in public opinion polls or raise insufficient funds. Republican candidates dropping out in 2015 were Walker, Perry, Jindal, Graham and Pataki. Seven more candidates (Paul, Huckabee, Santorum, Fiorina, Christie, Gilmore and Bush) would be out after the first four events of 2016. Carson withdrew after the first week in March, faring poorly on Super Tuesday. This left a final group of four Republican candidates: Trump, Rubio, Cruz and Kasich.

These four main Republican candidates aimed to establish support among a core group of voters before expanding their appeal to win the nomination. Cruz ran as a true conservative hoping to gain support from religiously conservative Republicans and Tea party supporters who viewed the federal government as too large and intrusive. Rubio aimed to be the candidate with electability—the candidate who could win the general election. Kasich ran as the moderate alternative and also as someone who could take away votes from the Democratic nominee in the fall.

Donald Trump built upon the frustrations of voters who saw good working-class jobs disappear in the face of global competition and increased immigration, and who felt slighted for their cultural values. Such sentiments reflect a populist appeal to voters who felt government programs no longer served their interests and that the political elite was out of touch with the average voter. The appeal of a populist campaign was not unique to Trump's campaign, with a recent rise in populist-based parties in European democracies, as well. Trump employed unusual tactics. He downplayed typical strategies such as advertisements, recruiting and organizing activists, and direct voter contacting. Instead, Trump relied on large rallies, frequent Twitter messages and extensive media coverage. In the debates and at his rallies, Trump eschewed political correctness and belittled his opponents as weak, liars or little. Trump's campaign slogan, "Make American Great Again," was emblazoned on signs and the ubiquitous baseball caps he wore at his rallies.

## The Democratic Candidates

Sometimes who doesn't run is as important as who does. That was true for the 2016 Democratic contest. In October 2015, Vice President Joe Biden indicated he would not run, saying it was too soon after the death of his son. This eliminated any challenge to Hillary Clinton from the Democratic party mainstream. As former Secretary of State, former U.S. Senator from New York, and former First Lady, Hillary Clinton had a long political career and ties to a variety of Democratic constituencies. It also would be her second attempt at winning the Democratic presidential nomination, as she narrowly lost to Barack Obama in 2008. Challenging

Clinton from the left was Vermont's Bernie Sanders, someone who was not well known and only recently a Democrat, as he was elected to the U.S. Senate (and previously to the U.S. House) as an independent. Three other candidates, who quickly left the contest, included former Maryland governor Martin O'Malley; Lincoln Chafee, former governor and senator from Rhode Island who previously had been both a Republican and an independent prior to becoming a Democrat; and Jim Webb, former senator from Virginia. Chafee and Webb dropped out of the race in 2015, while O'Malley exited after failing to garner support in the Iowa caucuses. The Democratic field quickly became a two-person race between Clinton and Sanders.

The main focus of Sanders's campaign was economic inequality and the corrupting influence of money in elections. Sanders offered bold policy proposals including a call for a single-payer health insurance plan, in which the government, rather than private insurance companies, pays health costs. Sanders also advocated for tuition-free college for all. He criticized Clinton for her Senate vote to support the war in Iraq and for her paid speeches before corporations. Sanders's campaign effectively used social media to garner large, passionate crowds for his campaign speeches and rallies. His fundraising also relied on a large number of small donations.

Clinton tied herself to Obama's record. She maintained support for the Affordable Care Act, commonly called Obamacare—in which the government provides subsidies to people to buy private insurance—along with an expansion of the Medicaid program for the poor (in those states that adopted that element). Clinton supported broader gun control, such as expanding background checks to include those sold at gun shows. In her 2008 bid for the Democratic nomination, Clinton downplayed gender to overcome a bias against a female Commander-in-Chief. In 2016, Clinton stressed issues that would appeal to women—equal pay, paid family leave and tax subsidies for child care. Clinton preferred meeting with voters in smaller settings to holding large rallies.

Two controversies plagued Clinton's presidential bid. One was questioning by a congressional committee about whether her policy decisions as Secretary of State contributed to the loss of life by the U.S. ambassador and three others in the September 2012 attack in Benghazi, Libya. The second controversy involved questions about her use of a private email server when she served as Secretary of State. The congressional inquiry into Benghazi made its report on June 28, 2016 rebuking the State Department for failing to protect its diplomats before and during the attack. On July 5, FBI Director James Comey indicated that Clinton's email practices did not violate the law, but in his statement Comey criticized Clinton and her staff for being "extremely careless" in their handling of sensitive government information.

## The Preseason: 2015

In the year (or two) before the election, candidates prepare for the primaries and caucuses to come by gathering resources. These resources include raising funds, hiring a staff and recruiting volunteers. Candidates travel around the country, with a strong emphasis on visiting states with early contests such as Iowa and New Hampshire. Candidates seek out endorsements from national and local party leaders. In recent years, a series of candidate debates in the pre-election year also can be used by candidates to make their name.

### *Raising Money*

Raising money is a major task during the preseason as well as the election year. Almost all the money given directly to candidates are contributions from individual U.S. citizens or immigrants with "green cards." In 2016, individuals could contribute a maximum of $2,700 to a candidate. Typically less than 5 percent of the money comes from traditional political action committees (PACs), which can contribute a maximum of $5,000. Candidates may spend unlimited amounts of their own money on their campaigns. In 2008, Mitt Romney spent $35 million of his own money on an unsuccessful bid for the Republican nomination. In 2016, Trump supported his campaign with $46 million, three-quarters of the money spent on his primary campaign. Trump claimed his reliance on self-funding would mean he would not be beholden to special interests.

Candidates are not the only ones gearing up in the preseason. Super PACs and other groups independent of the candidates raise money, typically to support one of the candidates. In 2012 super PACs played a dominate role by running advertisements. Most super PAC ads are negative, criticizing opponents of their preferred candidate. Super PACs are legally separate from the candidates, but they often devise complementary strategies. In 2015–2016, the role of super PACs expanded beyond advertising to developing voter and fundraising lists, providing support for candidate appearances, and engaging in get-out-the-vote efforts (Corasaniti and Flegenheimer 2015). However, super PAC money alone cannot help a candidate win if the message does not resonate with voters, as Jeb Bush soon found out. Even with the support of $120 million in outside money, Bush did not win the hearts of Republican voters.

Among the four main Republican candidates, Cruz raised the most money by the end of May 2016, at $92 million. Rubio followed with $52 million, while Kasich only raised $19 million. All three of these candidates accrued more money in large contributions (over $200) than in smaller ones. Cruz and Rubio each were supported by more than $60 million from outside groups. Along with Kasich's own meager campaign funds, he was backed by only $15 million in outside money. Trump is distinctive for the amount of his personal money spent on the campaign and the scant amount of support from outside groups. Clinton and Sanders amassed approximately the same amount of money, around $225 million. Their campaigns differed in proportions that came from small donations versus larger sums. Sixty percent of Sanders's money came from small donations, while 71 percent of Clinton's support came in large donations. Sanders shunned outside support, while Clinton benefited from $84 million in outside spending (Center for Responsive Politics 2016).

## Debates and Media Coverage

Republican party leaders believed that the 2012 debates hurt their eventual nominee, Mitt Romney, as Democrats could repeat criticisms originally lodged against him by the other Republican contenders. Some also reasoned that the debates allowed eloquent but electorally weak candidates to shine while potentially stronger candidates floundered in these appearances. To limit damage in 2016, the Republican party restricted the number of debates to 12, seven scheduled to be held before the Iowa caucuses. With so many candidates, those participating in the early debates were split into two groups based on candidates' average standings in public opinion polls. The 2016 Republican debates were even more dramatic than those of 2012 and drew a wide television audience. Donald Trump frequently dominated the stage, but most of the candidates traded barbs about issues, past histories and personal characteristics. Trump called Cruz a liar, labeled Bush as having low energy and referred to Rubio as "little Marco." Trump attacked Fox News anchor Megyn Kelly after she asked him about his portrayal of women at the August 6, 2015 debate, saying that Kelly had "blood coming out of her eyes. Blood coming out of her wherever" (Rucker 2016).

Trump dominated outside the debate forum, as well. His campaign benefited from extensive, and mostly positive, media coverage. A study by mediaQuant of traditional and social media calculated that the coverage Trump received from the media through February 2016 was the equivalent of $1.9 billion spent on campaign advertisements. Cruz had the second highest total at the equivalent of $313 million, while Bush and Rubio garnered the equivalent of $200 million (Confessore and Yourish 2016). Early media coverage is often determined by public opinion poll standings or measures of a candidate's strength, such as money raised. Neither of these factors explains the level of coverage for Trump in early 2015. Rather the media saw Trump as a news story that would draw in a big audience. Not only was Trump's media coverage extensive, it also was mostly positive or neutral rather than negative. Horse-race stories about Trump's rise in the polls and his campaign activities outweighed criticisms of his policy positions (Patterson 2016).

Early media coverage of Sanders and Clinton was less extensive than that of the Republicans. Not until Sanders began to climb in the public opinion polls did the media become interested in the Democratic race. When Sanders did receive coverage, it was mostly positive. In fact, his coverage was the most positive of any candidate in 2015. While Clinton received more coverage in the early stages of the campaign, it was mostly negative. Frontrunners often receive more harsh assessments in the media, and Clinton also faced continuing stories about the Benghazi attack and the email scandal. Attacks by Republicans on Clinton also accounted for her negative news coverage. While the high level of positive coverage of Trump aided his campaign, the more negative coverage of Clinton made her quest for the nomination harder (Patterson 2016).

### Elite Endorsements and Public Opinion Poll Standings

Political scientists often describe political parties as having three components: the party in the electorate (e.g. voters), the formal party organization (staffed foremost by local volunteers) and the party in government (e.g. members of Congress who are Democrats or Republicans). Elite endorsements represent the opinion of the last two components of the party: elected officeholders and party officials. Political scientists Marty Cohen, David Karol, Hans Noel and John Zaller wrote in their book, *The Party Decides*, how party leaders at national, state and local levels still shape presidential nominations (Cohen, Karol, Noel and Zaller 2008). When most of these leaders support a single candidate, this sends a strong signal about the strength of that candidate. This candidate also benefits from campaign knowledge that senators and governors have of their states' electorate.

In 2015, Democratic party leaders decided on their candidate. By the end of 2015, Hillary Clinton was endorsed by 12 governors, 38 senators and 142 members of the U.S. House. In 2016, she would receive endorsements from 32 additional top Democrats, for a total of 224 endorsements. Bernie Sanders throughout his campaign received only nine endorsements, one from a senator and the rest from members of the House (Bycoffe 2016). The Democratic party elite sent a clear signal as to their preference. No such consensus existed among the Republican party elite. Even by the end of the primaries in 2016, Trump had only 15 major endorsements. Rubio garnered the most at 67, followed by 44 for Cruz, 31 for Bush and 13 for Kasich.

The early voice of the public is gauged by pre-election year polls. At the beginning of the preseason, support for Republican candidates was mixed. Through mid-July 2015, Bush, Walker, and Rubio lead at various points in time. After that, Trump swiftly moved to the top of the rankings. By September, 32 percent of Republicans supported Trump with Ben Carson in second place at 15 percent. Carson's support peaked at 21 percent in late October, while Trump's support held steady. By the end of December, the Republican numbers broke down as Trump with 37 percent, Cruz at 17 and Rubio with 11 percent. On the Democratic side, Clinton was the clear frontrunner in early polling. Sanders started out as a relative unknown, with less than 5 percent support in early 2015. Meanwhile, Clinton's support stood at 60 percent. Sanders's popularity rose throughout 2015, ending in December at 33 percent to Clinton's 55 percent (*Pollster* 2016a, 2016b).

## The Main Events: 2016 Primaries and Caucuses

### On the Republican Side

Iowa's February 1 caucuses led off the 2016 Republican contest. In the days and months before the caucuses, Iowans experience the "retail politics" of frequent candidate visits, phone calls, social media posts, and door-to-door campaigning, coupled with $40 million of television commercials. Cruz ran an extensive ground game, visiting all 99 counties and employing mailers and other get-out-the vote tactics. Trump held rallies in Iowa but banked more on his national popularity. Trump, sensing Cruz as his main opponent in Iowa, questioned whether Cruz's Canadian birth disqualified him from being President and asserted that Cruz was unpopular in the Senate because he was "a very nasty guy" (Savransky 2016; McLaughlin 2016). Meanwhile, the super PAC, Right to Rise, spent nearly $15 million in support of Jeb Bush's campaign—mostly on attack ads against his competitors. On caucus night, turnout was high. Religiously conservative voters are a strong contingent of the Iowa Republican party, and they helped Cruz win the Iowa caucuses with 28 percent of the vote. Trump and Rubio were close behind. A top tier of candidates was quickly emerging, as none of the other candidates polled more than 10 percent of the vote.

The New Hampshire primary was just as negative, with $30 million spent on advertising. Bush's ads criticized Rubio for skipping congressional votes and Kasich for using the Obamacare provision of expanding Medicaid eligibility in Ohio. Rubio's media message attacked Cruz for flip-flopping on issues and Christie for being close to Obama. Trump focused on Cruz, calling him weak on immigration, while Cruz in turn criticized Rubio's position on immigration as weak. Kasich's campaign bucked the trend and ran mostly positive ads (Corasaniti and Parlapiano 2016). Trump got his first victory in New Hampshire, winning with one-third of the vote. Kasich, who banked on support from the state's more moderate voters, finished second trailing Trump by 16 percentage points. Rubio's weak performance in the debate held on the Saturday before the primary probably contributed to his fourth-place finish. Table 2.1 lists results for all of the Republican primaries and caucuses.

**TABLE 2.1** Candidate Vote Percentages and Delegates per State in Republican Primaries and Caucuses

| Date | State | Format | Trump | Cruz | Kasich | Rubio | Delegates |
|---|---|---|---|---|---|---|---|
| February 1 | Iowa | Caucus | 24.3 | 27.6 | 1.9 | 23.1 | 30 |
| February 9 | New Hampshire | Primary | 35.6 | 11.7 | 15.9 | 10.6 | 23 |
| February 20 | South Carolina | Primary | 32.5 | 22.3 | 7.6 | 22.5 | 50 |
| February 23 | Nevada | Caucus | 45.9 | 21.4 | 3.6 | 23.9 | 30 |
| March 1 | Alabama | Primary | 43.4 | 21.1 | 4.4 | 18.7 | 50 |
| | Alaska | Caucus | 33.6 | 36.4 | 4.0 | 15.2 | 28 |
| | Arkansas | Primary | 32.8 | 30.5 | 3.7 | 24.8 | 40 |
| | Georgia | Primary | 38.8 | 23.6 | 5.6 | 24.4 | 76 |
| | Massachusetts | Primary | 49.0 | 9.5 | 17.9 | 17.7 | 42 |
| | Minnesota | Caucus | 21.4 | 29.0 | 5.7 | 36.2 | 38 |
| | Oklahoma | Primary | 28.3 | 34.4 | 3.6 | 26.0 | 43 |
| | Tennessee | Primary | 38.9 | 24.7 | 5.3 | 21.2 | 58 |
| | Texas | Primary | 26.8 | 43.8 | 4.2 | 17.7 | 155 |
| | Vermont | Primary | 32.5 | 9.7 | 30.2 | 19.2 | 16 |
| | Virginia | Primary | 34.8 | 16.7 | 9.5 | 32.0 | 49 |
| March 5 | Kansas | Caucus | 23.4 | 47.5 | 11.1 | 16.8 | 40 |
| | Kentucky | Caucus | 35.9 | 31.6 | 14.4 | 16.4 | 46 |
| | Louisiana | Primary | 41.4 | 37.8 | 6.4 | 11.2 | 46 |
| | Maine | Caucus | 32.6 | 45.9 | 12.2 | 8.0 | 23 |
| March 6 | Puerto Rico | Primary | 13.8 | 9.1 | 1.5 | 72.9 | 23 |
| March 8 | Michigan | Primary | 36.5 | 24.7 | 24.3 | 9.3 | 59 |
| | Mississippi | Primary | 47.3 | 36.3 | 8.8 | 5.1 | 40 |
| | Idaho | Primary | 28.1 | 45.4 | 7.4 | 15.9 | 32 |
| | Hawaii | Caucus | 43.4 | 32.3 | 10.0 | 13.2 | 19 |
| March 10 | Virgin Islands | Caucus | 6.4 | 11.7 | 0.0 | 9.9 | 9 |
| March 12 | Washington, D.C. | Convention | 13.8 | 12.4 | 35.5 | 37.3 | 19 |
| | Wyoming | County convention | 7.4 | 65.4 | 0.0 | 20.0 | 29 |
| March 14 | Florida | Primary | 45.7 | 17.1 | 6.8 | 27.0* | 99 |
| | North Carolina | Primary | 40.2 | 36.8 | 12.7 | 7.7 | 72 |

| Date | State | Type | | | | |
|---|---|---|---|---|---|---|
| | Ohio | Primary | 35.6 | 13.1 | 46.8 | 2.9 | 66 |
| | Illinois | Primary | 38.8 | 30.2 | 19.7 | 8.7 | 69 |
| | Missouri | Primary | 40.8 | 40.6 | 10.1 | 6.1 | 52 |
| March 22 | Northern Mariana Islands | Caucus | 72.8 | 24.0 | 2.1 | 1.1 | 9 |
| | Arizona | Primary | 45.9 | 27.6 | 10.6 | 11.6 | 58 |
| | Utah | Caucus | 13.8 | 69.5 | 16.7 | 0.0 | 40 |
| April 1 | North Dakota | Convention | 75.0 | 21.4 | 0.0 | 0.0 | 28 |
| April 5 | Wisconsin | Primary | 35.0 | 48.2 | 14.1 | 1.0 | 42 |
| April 19 | New York | Primary | 60.2 | 14.8 | 25.1 | 0.0 | 95 |
| April 26 | Connecticut | Primary | 57.9 | 11.7 | 28.3 | 0.0 | 28 |
| | Delaware | Primary | 60.8 | 15.9 | 20.4 | 0.9 | 16 |
| | Maryland | Primary | 54.1 | 19.0 | 23.2 | 0.7 | 38 |
| | Pennsylvania | Primary | 56.6 | 21.7 | 19.4 | 0.7 | 71 |
| | Rhode Island | Primary | 63.7 | 10.4 | 24.3 | 0.6 | 19 |
| May 3 | Indiana | Primary | 53.3 | 36.6* | 7.6* | 0.5 | 57 |
| May 10 | Nebraska | Primary | 61.5 | 18.4 | 11.4 | 3.6 | 36 |
| | West Virginia | Primary | 77.1 | 9.0 | 6.7 | 1.4 | 34 |
| May 17 | Oregon | Primary | 64.2 | 16.6 | 15.8 | 0.0 | 28 |
| May 24 | Washington | Primary | 75.5 | 10.8 | 9.8 | 0.0 | 44 |
| June 7 | California | Primary | 74.8 | 9.5 | 11.3 | 0.0 | 172 |
| | Montana | Primary | 73.7 | 9.4 | 6.9 | 3.3 | 27 |
| | New Jersey | Primary | 80.4 | 6.2 | 13.4 | 0.0 | 51 |
| | New Mexico | Primary | 70.6 | 13.3 | 7.6 | 0.0 | 24 |
| | South Dakota | Primary | 67.1 | 17.0 | 15.9 | 0.0 | 29 |

*Notes:* Colorado held caucuses on March 1, but these were not connected to delegate selection. Colorado's 37 delegates were chosen in April at congressional district conventions (Cruz won 17 delegates with four unpledged) and the state convention (Cruz won 13 delegates with three unpledged). Guam (March 12, nine delegates) and American Samoa (March 22, nine delegates) held conventions with delegates selected as unpledged to any candidate.

\* = candidate dropped out after this contest

*Sources:* Compiled by the author from state election websites and The Green Papers, www.thegreenpapers.com.

South Carolina came third on the schedule, and is frequently a critical primary in sorting out the Republican field. It did so once again in 2016. Bush and his allies pulled out all the stops in a last-ditch effort to remain a credible candidate, but his fourth-place finish led him to withdraw from the race. Rubio rebounded and appeared to have claimed the support of traditional Republican voters. Meanwhile, Cruz faltered as he was not able to solidify the support from the state's conservative religious voters. The big winner was Trump, and his South Carolina victory established him as the party's frontrunner. Trump also won the last of the front-four events with a strong first-place finish in Nevada.

The March schedule included a mostly southern states Super Tuesday on March 1, caucuses and a few primaries over the next week, a second Super Tuesday of southern and Midwestern states on March 15, and a wrap up with the Arizona primary and another round of caucuses near the end of the month. Trump confirmed his frontrunner status with the March 1 primaries, winning seven of the nine primaries. Cruz won his home-state primary in Texas and in the next-door state of Oklahoma. Rubio's sole victory was in the Minnesota caucuses. The following week, Trump and Cruz competed for Michigan's disaffected working-class voters, but Trump claimed the victory in the March 8 primary. Trump also won in Mississippi, while Cruz claimed victory in Idaho. Trump's string of primary victories put pressure on the other three candidates to score decisive wins to stay in the race and to halt Trump's path to the nomination. Rubio, however, was soon out of the race after his loss in his home state of Florida on March 15. On the same day, Kasich won his home state of Ohio, but this would be his only primary victory.

Trump continued to dominate in April. The one exception was Cruz's victory in the April 5 Wisconsin primary. Neither Cruz nor Kasich was making a strong foothold as they seemingly split the opposition vote. The media began to talk about a contested convention, where Trump would not have the necessary 50 percent of the vote needed for a first-round victory. Under such a scenario, most Republican delegates would be free to change their votes on a second-round vote, and Cruz and Kasich each hoped that they could gain support in any subsequent votes. May brought last-ditch efforts by Cruz and Kasich to stop Trump. Cruz and Kasich announced an alliance such that Cruz would concentrate on Indiana while Kasich would try to win in Oregon and New Mexico. The alliance quickly fell apart. Cruz tried one final tactic, selecting Carly Fiorina as his vice-presidential running mate. Such announcements typically come from a presumptive nominee in the week before the national convention. This tactic also had little effect. After Trump's lopsided victory in Indiana's primary, Cruz and Kasich withdrew from the race. At this point, Trump had support from 1,147 of the 1,237 delegates needed for the nomination. Without any remaining opposition, Trump secured the needed 50 percent of delegates by the end of May.

## On the Democratic Side

The Iowa caucuses were a crucial first battle on the Democratic side, as well. Bernie Sanders banked on a large turnout among his enthusiastic supporters. Hillary Clinton's strategy focused on a strong ground organization to help locate supporters and get them to the caucuses. On caucus night, Clinton and Sanders supporters gathered on different sides of the room. Supporters of Martin O'Malley and voters who were uncommitted also had their spots. As Democratic party rules require a minimal support of 15 percent before any delegates are awarded, people who initially supported O'Malley or were uncommitted had a second chance to change their minds and move to another candidate. After this point, delegates would be awarded proportionally to the candidates based on the number of their supporters. The result was a razor-thin margin with Clinton edging out Sanders 49.9 percent to 49.6 percent. Due to his dismal performance in Iowa, O'Malley suspended his campaign.

The next round went to Sanders. He won New Hampshire's primary by a comfortable margin of 23 percentage points: 61 percent to 38 percent. Sanders was expected to do well as he hailed from the next-door state of Vermont. That left two more of the front four events to determine the flow of the early contests. In Nevada's caucuses, Clinton came up the winner by 6 percentage points: 53 percent to 47 percent. By winning two of the first three events, Clinton demonstrated her electability, and prevented Sanders from gaining early momentum.

The fourth contest moved into the south, a region of the country where Clinton would continually outperform Sanders. South Carolina was Clinton's first big victory: 73 percent to 26 percent. Even with proportional representation, such a lopsided victory meant that Clinton picked up 39 delegates to Sanders's 14. Clinton won in South Carolina, and in other southern states, due to her strong support from minority voters. Clinton laid the groundwork for these victories by courting African American voters and leaders in the southern states. She did especially well among African American women, who voted in large numbers and overwhelmingly supported Clinton.

Super Tuesday, on March 1, saw a large number of southern states holding their primaries. Of the nine states holding primaries, seven were southern or border states. Clinton won by lopsided margins (29 percentage points or more) in six of the southern states, with Sanders winning the primary in Arkansas plus securing a lopsided victory in his home state of Vermont. Sanders also won caucuses in Minnesota and Colorado. Table 2.2 shows vote percentages for all the Democratic contests. With Clinton's large victories in the southern states, she picked up 569 pledged delegates on Super Tuesday compared to Sanders' 335. Clinton established a lead in pledged delegates that Sanders would not be able to narrow.

TABLE 2.2 Candidate Vote Percentages and Delegates per State in Democratic Primaries and Caucuses

| Date | State | Format | Clinton | Sanders | Pledged Delegates | Super Delegates |
|---|---|---|---|---|---|---|
| February 1 | Iowa | Caucus | 49.8 | 49.6 | 44 | 7 |
| February 9 | New Hampshire | Primary | 38.2 | 61.0 | 24 | 8 |
| February 20 | Nevada | Caucus | 52.6 | 47.3 | 35 | 8 |
| February 27 | South Carolina | Primary | 73.4 | 26.0 | 53 | 6 |
| March 1 | Alabama | Primary | 77.9 | 19.2 | 53 | 7 |
| | American Samoa | Caucus | 68.4 | 25.7 | 6 | 5 |
| | Arkansas | Primary | 66.1 | 30.0 | 32 | 5 |
| | Colorado | Caucus | 40.3 | 59.0 | 66 | 12 |
| | Georgia | Primary | 71.3 | 28.2 | 102 | 15 |
| | Massachusetts | Primary | 49.7 | 48.3 | 91 | 24 |
| | Minnesota | Caucus | 38.1 | 61.2 | 77 | 16 |
| | Oklahoma | Primary | 41.5 | 51.9 | 38 | 4 |
| | Tennessee | Primary | 66.1 | 32.5 | 67 | 8 |
| | Texas | Primary | 65.2 | 33.2 | 222 | 29 |
| | Vermont | Primary | 13.6 | 86.0 | 16 | 10 |
| | Virginia | Primary | 64.3 | 35.2 | 95 | 13 |
| March 5 | Kansas | Caucus | 32.3 | 67.7 | 33 | 4 |
| | Louisiana | Primary | 71.1 | 23.2 | 51 | 8 |
| | Nebraska | Caucus | 42.9 | 57.1 | 25 | 5 |
| March 6 | Maine | Caucus | 35.5 | 64.3 | 25 | 5 |
| March 8 | Mississippi | Primary | 82.6 | 16.5 | 36 | 5 |
| | Michigan | Primary | 48.3 | 49.7 | 130 | 17 |
| March 12 | Northern Mariana Islands | Convention | 54.0 | 34.4 | 6 | 5 |
| March 15 | Florida | Primary | 64.4 | 33.3 | 214 | 32 |
| | North Carolina | Primary | 54.5 | 40.9 | 107 | 13 |
| | Ohio | Primary | 56.5 | 42.7 | 143 | 17 |
| | Illinois | Primary | 50.6 | 48.6 | 156 | 27 |
| | Missouri | Primary | 49.6 | 49.4 | 71 | 13 |

| Date | State | Type | | | | |
|---|---|---|---|---|---|---|
| March 21 | Democrats Abroad | Primary | 30.9 | 68.8 | 13 | 4 |
| | Arizona | Primary | 56.3 | 41.4 | 75 | 10 |
| | Idaho | Caucus | 21.2 | 78.0 | 23 | 4 |
| | Utah | Caucus | 19.8 | 77.2 | 33 | 4 |
| March 26 | Alaska | Caucus | 20.2 | 79.6 | 16 | 4 |
| | Hawaii | Caucus | 30.0 | 69.7 | 25 | 9 |
| | Washington | Caucus | 27.1 | 72.7 | 101 | 17 |
| April 5 | Wisconsin | Primary | 43.0 | 56.6 | 86 | 10 |
| April 9 | Wyoming | Caucus | 44.3 | 55.7 | 14 | 4 |
| April 19 | New York | Primary | 58.0 | 42.0 | 247 | 44 |
| April 26 | Connecticut | Primary | 51.8 | 46.4 | 55 | 16 |
| | Delaware | Primary | 59.8 | 39.2 | 21 | 11 |
| | Maryland | Primary | 62.5 | 33.8 | 95 | 25 |
| | Pennsylvania | Primary | 55.6 | 43.5 | 189 | 19 |
| | Rhode Island | Primary | 43.1 | 54.7 | 24 | 9 |
| May 3 | Indiana | Primary | 47.5 | 52.5 | 83 | 9 |
| May 7 | Guam | Caucus | 59.5 | 40.5 | 7 | 5 |
| May 10 | West Virginia | Primary | 35.8 | 51.4 | 29 | 8 |
| May 17 | Kentucky | Primary | 46.8 | 46.3 | 55 | 5 |
| | Oregon | Primary | 42.1 | 56.2 | 61 | 13 |
| June 4 | Virgin Islands | Caucus | 87.1 | 12.9 | 7 | 5 |
| June 5 | Puerto Rico | Primary | 61.5 | 38.1 | 60 | 7 |
| June 7 | California | Primary | 53.1 | 46.0 | 475 | 76 |
| | Montana | Primary | 44.2 | 51.6 | 21 | 6 |
| | New Jersey | Primary | 63.3 | 36.7 | 126 | 16 |
| | New Mexico | Primary | 51.5 | 48.5 | 34 | 9 |
| | North Dakota | Caucus | 25.6 | 64.2 | 18 | 5 |
| | South Dakota | Primary | 51.0 | 49.0 | 20 | 5 |
| June 14 | Washington, D.C. | Primary | 78.5 | 20.8 | 20 | 24 |

*Note*: One additional super delegate slot was unassigned to any state.

*Sources*: Compiled by the author from state election websites and The Green Papers, www.thegreenpapers.com.

Figure 2.1 illustrates how these victories established Clinton's delegate lead. From the beginning, Clinton had more support from the party's super delegates, who are party leaders and elected Democrats free to support any candidate. Clinton started out with support from 388 super delegates and would end the primary season with support from 604. Sanders only received the backing of 47 super delegates. The 712 super delegates are 15 percent of the Democratic delegates, while 4,051 pledged delegates are selected on the basis of votes in primaries and caucuses. Clinton's pledged delegate numbers jumped with her early March victories. At this point, Clinton led in both pledged delegates and super delegates, and hence, her total delegate count exceeded that of Sanders. Since Sanders had so few super delegates, only his total delegates (super and pledged combined) are shown in Figure 2.1.

Sanders's upset victory in Michigan on March 8, gave his campaign a needed boost and a rationale for staying in the race. He could argue that Clinton's nomination was not inevitable and that many Democrats supported his more progressive agenda. Yet the next round of events went back to Clinton, with a second Super Tuesday on March 15. Clinton won all of these primaries. She won overwhelmingly in Florida and handily in

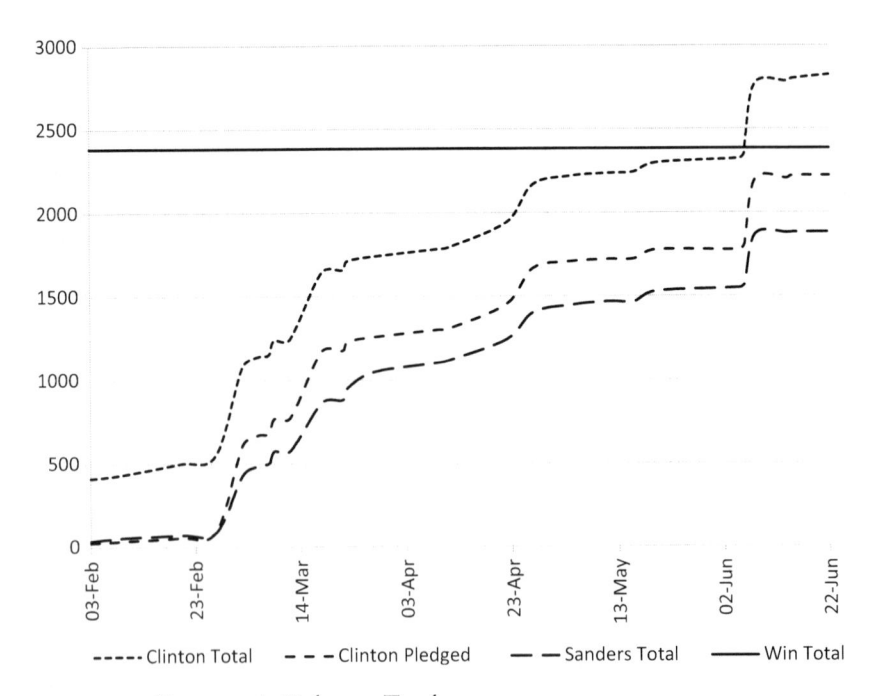

**FIGURE 2.1** Democratic Delegate Totals

*Source*: Compiled by the author from delegate totals as posted on CNN webpages throughout the primary season, www.cnn.com/election/primaries/parties/democrat.

North Carolina and Ohio. She eked out victories in Illinois and Missouri. Momentum shifted back in Sanders's favor in the last half of March and early April. During this time period, six states held caucuses and Sanders won all of them. Clinton won Arizona's primary on March 21, while Sanders took Wisconsin's primary on April 5. Even though Sanders did well during this time period, his delegate gains were not enough to catch up to Clinton's lead.

At the end of April, the calendar again turned to mostly primaries. Clinton would win in New York, Pennsylvania and three other states in late April to Sanders's victory in Rhode Island. May saw few events and resulted in a split in wins for both candidates. That left the final big event: June 7. Five primaries and one caucus would be held. Early polls showed Clinton ahead in New Jersey, so both campaigns focused on California with its 475 pledged delegates at stake. Sanders campaigned more heavily in the state, but Clinton led in the pre-election polls and had won California's primary in 2008. Election-night totals showed Clinton winning by more than 10 percentage points, but the vote count in California would be slow. Most Californians vote by mail and ballots postmarked by Election Day would be counted even though they arrived later. Sanders's supporters hoped that these late arriving ballots would split his way, but they did not. In the final, official vote, Clinton won California 53 percent to 46 percent.

With Clinton's victory on June 7, she added to her pledged delegate lead, ending the primary season with a 387 edge over Sanders in pledged delegates. Combined with her substantial advantage among super delegates, Clinton actually had the support of 50 percent of the convention delegates on the day before the June 7 primaries, when the media called the race for her. In the end, Clinton won 55 percent of the pledged delegates and 84 percent of the super delegates for a combined total of 59 percent of all delegates. She won 28 primaries to Sanders's 10, and her primary vote total was 16.7 million to Sanders' 12.3 million. Sanders bested Clinton in 12 of the 14 caucus states, but these states selected only 13 percent of the pledged delegates.

Sanders and his supporters claimed that Democratic party rules were biased against his campaign. One of their concerns was with the super delegates, who overwhelmingly supported Clinton. However, as Clinton won a majority of the pledged delegates, she still would have won the nomination if there were no super delegates. Sanders also did better in open primaries and believed that closed primaries hurt his campaign. Yet an analysis by Harry Enten and Nate Silver revealed that Clinton would still have won if all primaries had been open to independent voters (Enten and Silver 2016). Sanders did better in caucuses, and only under the implausible scenario that all states held open caucuses would Sanders have won the nomination. Presidential primaries have a 100-year history in the United States and became the most common way to select convention delegates in the 1970s. A return to caucuses would not be a popular option. One bias in the Democratic rules did help Sanders. Sanders won in smaller population states, and Democratic rules that distribute delegate totals across the states have a small state bias (Norrander 2010). This is due to these allocation rules being partly based on each state's Electoral College vote, which also is biased toward smaller states as each state, regardless of population, receives two electors to reflect their equal representation in the U.S. Senate. All election rules are biased, but those used by the Democrats in the 2016 nomination did not unduly affect the fate of the Sanders campaign.

## On to the Conventions

Typically nomination battles are settled after the last presidential primaries in early June (or earlier), but that was not the case in 2016. Sanders did not immediately concede the nomination to Clinton, as Clinton had done in 2008 within a week of losing the delegate race to Obama. Sanders at times hinted he wanted to take the race to the Democratic convention, perhaps by convincing super delegates to change their minds or by gaining extra pledged delegates as final vote totals were calculated. Meanwhile, President Barack Obama, Vice President Joe Biden and Senator Elizabeth Warren of Massachusetts each endorsed Clinton on June 9. After Washington, DC's June 14 primary, Clinton and Sanders met, but he declined to endorse her. On June 22, Sanders acknowledged in an interview that he was not going to be the nominee, and two days later he indicated that he would vote for Clinton for President. Clinton faced two other challenges at this time. The U.S. House Benghazi report was issued on June 28, and results of the FBI investigation into her use of a private email server during her tenure as Secretary of State were released on July 5.

Donald Trump faced his own intraparty skirmishes in June and July. A "never-Trump" faction of the Republican party tested various tactics to deny Trump the nomination at the Republican convention. In Virginia, a successful lawsuit allowed its delegates to switch support away from Trump. Notable party figures, including senators and past Republican presidential nominees, announced that they would not attend the convention. The never-Trump faction tried to convince the Republican Rules Committee to change convention rules to allow delegates to vote their conscious rather than being bound by the primary or caucus results. This attempt failed. The first day of the Republican convention saw one last attempt by the never-Trump faction to get a roll call vote on the convention floor to demonstrate their concern over Trump's impending nomination. Instead, the convention chair ruled that a voice vote confirmed the preexisting rules for the convention.

National party conventions have developed a rhythm over past decades. The goal is to highlight the assets of the party's nominee and demonstrate party unity. A variety of speeches are given by party luminaries, such as governors and senators. Average Americans take the podium to relate personal stories about party issues or the candidate, and a few celebrities are thrown into the mix for added pizazz. Video presentations highlight party issues and candidate testimonials.

The Republican party's national convention met on July 18–21. The mix of speakers at the Republican convention was more unconventional, with fewer party dignitaries participating. Trump's wife, Melania, spoke on the first day of the convention. While her speech was well received on the floor of the convention, controversy developed afterwards as it was discovered that a small portion of her speech borrowed words from Michelle Obama's 2008 convention address. The second day included the formal roll call of states to determine the official nomination. In the final count, Donald Trump garnered the support of 1,725 of the 2,472 delegates for 70 percent of the total. Among the speakers on the third day was Ted Cruz, who received boos from the floor when he failed to endorse Trump. Vice Presidential nominee Mike Pence, governor of Indiana, also gave his speech on the third day. Saved for the last day of the convention is the speech by the presidential nominee. Trump's speech depicted America as plagued by a host of problems and asserted that only a Trump presidency would cure these ailments. While Trump's speech was well received on the convention floor, most media reports painted his speech as dark. Still, many public opinion polls showed Trump gaining a convention bounce, with a slight uptick in his support.

The Democratic convention met from July 25–28. The Democrats, too, had some internal battles over potential rule changes. The Rules Committee, after some haggling, agreed to create a post-convention commission to investigate issues such as super delegates and caucuses. One other event marred the start of the Democratic convention. On the Sunday before the convention opened, WikiLeaks released hacked emails from the Democratic National Committee that showed some departures from the traditional candidate neutrality prior to the official nomination. During the first hours of the convention on Monday, Sanders's delegates chanted and booed during the initial speeches. The Sanders and Clinton teams, however, worked together to quell the dissent, and Sanders urged his followers to avoid disrupting the proceedings, though there continued to be some booing at various points throughout the convention.

The Democratic convention, however, was mostly a well-orchestrated public relations event. Well-received speeches were made by Michelle Obama, Elizabeth Warren, Bernie Sanders, Barack Obama and Bill Clinton. The roll call of states produced a final delegate count of 2,842 for Clinton and 1,865 for Sanders. A moving speech by Khizr Khan, the father of a fallen soldier, challenged Trump's knowledge of the Constitution and whether Trump had made any sacrifices for the country. Trump's retorts through the media were seen as harming his campaign. The Democratic convention ended with Hillary Clinton's speech as she reached out to Bernie Sanders's supporters, criticized Trump and portrayed herself as a fighter for the interests of women, children, the poor and the middle class. The traditional balloon drop followed. Clinton, too, received a post-convention bounce in the polls.

A final question for the fall campaign was if a third-party candidate might steal more votes from Trump or Clinton to alter the outcome. The two candidates most likely to do so were the nominees of the Libertarian and Green parties. The Libertarian party held its nominating convention on May 27–30 in Orlando, Florida. Gary Johnson, former governor of New Mexico, was renominated as the presidential nominee, something he had been in 2008. William Weld, former governor of Massachusetts and viewed as an electable candidate, became the vice presidential nominee. Opponents to Weld viewed his late conversion to the Libertarian party as indicating he did not fully support the party's positions. Two ballots were needed for both the presidential and vice presidential nominations, as both candidates fell a few votes short of the required 50 percent on the first ballot. The Green party easily renominated its 2008 presidential candidate, Jill Stein, at its convention in Houston on August 4–7. Human rights scholar and activist Ajamu Baraka was selected as her running mate.

## Conclusion

The Republican party ended up with an unconventional nominee in 2016. Donald Trump is a businessman and reality-show star, not an elected official or politician. He used unusual campaign tactics, issuing frequent tweets and attracting high levels of media coverage. He beat out 16 other contenders. In the process, the tenor of the campaign reached new lows, with candidates trading frequent barbs and even innuendos about the meaning of men's hand sizes. Yet, the dynamics of the Republican race followed a traditional pattern. Most candidates quickly left the race, leaving a four-candidate race during the middle phase of the campaign. A multi-candidate contest ends when all but one candidate leaves the race. Trump captured his niche of the Republican party early, while the other candidates competed with one another for their piece of the pie. In the end, Trump won the title of the Republican party's presumptive nominee at the beginning of May when Cruz and Kasich dropped out. After a few more skirmishes, he officially became the party's nominee at the Republican convention in July.

The Democratic race was a classic two-person battle. Momentum passed back and forth as Clinton and Sanders traded primary victories. Clinton opened a lead in pledged delegates with lopsided victories in early March primaries. Sanders remained in the race due to ample fundraising, committed supporters, and victories in some primaries and most of the caucuses. Still,

Sanders would not catch up to Clinton's delegate lead, and each new primary added to her total whether she won (and gain more delegates than Sanders) or lost (but still won delegates under proportional representation rules). With the last round of primaries, Clinton secured the necessary delegate total. Clinton won by establishing herself as the early frontrunner, in part by building support among the party's elite, activists, and important constituency groups. Once the primaries commenced in 2016, her well-run campaign calculated the best strategy for winning the maximum number of delegates in each state. Clinton had a traditional political background and ran a traditional campaign, but in the end, she would be an unconventional nominee, too. She is the first woman nominated for President by a major political party.

## Bibliography

Bycoffe, Aaron. 2016. "The Endorsement Primary." *FiveThirtyEight*, June 7. http://projects.fivethirtyeight.com/2016-endorsement-primary/.

Center for Responsive Politics. 2016. "Money Raised Through May 2016." www.opensecrets.org

Cohen, Marty, David Karol, Hans Noel and John Zaller. 2008. *The Party Decides: Presidential Nominations Before and After Reform*. Chicago: University of Chicago Press.

Confessore, Nicholas and Karen Yourish. 2016. "$2 Billion Worth of Free Media for Donald Trump." *New York Times*, March 15. https://www.nytimes.com/2016/03/16/upshot/measuring-donald-trumps-mammoth-advantage-in-free-media.html.

Corasaniti, Nick and Matt Flegenheimer. 2015. "As TV Ad Rates Soar, 'Super PACs' Pivot to Core Campaign Work." *New York Times*, December 22. www.nytimes.com/2015/12/23/us/politics/as-tv-ad-rates-soar-super-pacs-pivot-to-core-campaign-work.html.

Corasaniti, Nick and Alicia Parlapiano. 2016. "Republicans Trade Attack Ads in New Hampshire." *New York Times*, February 8. www.nytimes.com/interactive/2016/02/08/us/politics/republican-presidential-candidates-attacks-new-hampshire.html.

Enten, Harry and Nate Silver. 2016. "The System Isn't 'Rigged' Against Sanders." *FiveThirtyEight*, May 26. http://fivethirtyeight.com/features/the-system-isnt-rigged-against-sanders/.

McLaughlin, Seth. 2016. "Senators Deny That 'Everybody Hates' Cruz, But None Have Endorsed Him." *Washington Times*, January 20. www.washingtontimes.com/news/2016/jan/20/ted-cruzs-senate-colleagues-reject-donald-trumps-n/

Norrander, Barbara. 2010. *The Imperfect Primary*. New York: Routledge. Pp. 72–77.

Norrander, Barbara and Jay Wendland. 2016. "Open Versus Closed Primaries and the Ideological Composition of Presidential Primary Electorates." *Electoral Studies* 42. Pp. 229–236.

Patterson, Thomas E. 2016. "Pre-Primary News Coverage of the 2016 Presidential Race: Trump's Rise, Sanders' Emergence, Clinton's Struggle." Shorenstein Center on Media, Politics and Public Policy, Harvard Kennedy School. http://shorensteincenter.org/pre-primary-news-coverage-2016-trump-clinton-sanders/.

Pollster. 2016a. "2016 National Republican Primary." Polling Averages published on *Huffington Post*. http://elections.huffingtonpost.com/pollster/2016-national-gop-primary

———. 2016b. "2016 National Democratic Primary." Polling Averages published on *Huffington Post*. http://elections.huffingtonpost.com/pollster/2016-national-democratic-primary.

Republican Delegate Allocation Rules as Given on The Green Papers website, "Republican Delegate Selection and Voter Eligibility." 2016. *Green Papers*. www.thegreenpapers.com/P16/R-DSVE.phtml (accessed June 20).

Rucker, Philip. 2016. "Trump Says Fox's Megyn Kelly Had 'Blood Coming Out of Her Wherever'." *Washington Post*, August 8. www.washingtonpost.com/news/post-politics/wp/2015/08/07/trump-says-foxs-megyn-kelly-had-blood-coming-out-of-her-wherever/?utm_term=.38fcbf4743d2

Savransky, Rebecca. 2016. "Trump on Cruz: 'He Was Born in Canada'." *The Hill* blog, May 1. http://thehill.com/blogs/ballot-box/presidential-races/278328-trump-on-cruz-he-was-born-in-canada

Terkel, Amanda. 2015. "Hillary Clinton Campaign Launches Grassroots Organizing Program in All 50 States." *Huffington Post*, April 22. www.huffingtonpost.com/2015/04/22/hillary-clinton-grassroots_n_7117884.html.

# 3

# THE PRESIDENTIAL ELECTION

## A Troubled Democracy

Gerald M. Pomper*

> *Upon what meat doth this our Caesar feed,*
> *That he is grown so great? Age, thou art shamed!*
> *Rome, thou hast lost the breed of noble bloods!*
> — William Shakespeare, *Julius Caesar*, I:2:148

The oldest democracy in the world set off on a fearful new course in the election of 2016.

For its 45th President, the United States chose a man without experience in government, a man regarded as unqualified for the office by a large majority of the voters, a man who rejected many of the country's established public policies. But, in Donald Trump, the voters elected a man with distinct insight into the deep discontent of the population and with unique abilities to exploit that anger to win ultimate power.

Trump's success was impressive in political terms, achieved even in the face of the voters' rising approval of retiring incumbent President Barack Obama, and even without a majority of the popular vote. The Republican real estate developer gained his party's nomination over the opposition of its established leaders and sixteen opponents. The nominee went on to win nearly half of the total popular vote for the two major parties and, against three principal opponents, 46% of the total 137 million ballots cast. He masterfully threaded a narrow path across the country, carried thirty of the fifty states, and accumulated 306 of the nation's 538 electoral votes.

Trump will have an immediate impact on the nation and the world because of the distinctive and often contradictory policies he has pledged and the distinctive and often threatening character he has revealed. The greater long-term impact of this contest, however, comes from the campaign he waged against his defeated Democratic opponent, Hillary Rodham Clinton. That campaign shaped a new politics that is likely to bear even greater consequences than the different experiential background of the new chief executive.

America was transformed, in the election of 2016—and possibly as greatly damaged—as the model republic of ancient Rome was destroyed by the assassination of Julius Caesar. Shakespeare warned of that earlier magnetic politician: "Why, man, he doth bestride the narrow world like a Colossus." We may need to heed the Bard's fears lest "we petty men walk under his huge legs and peep about to find ourselves dishonorable graves." (Shakespeare, *Julius Caesar*, I:2:135).

## The Presidential Vote

### The Electoral Map

Geographically, as seen in the map of the United States (Figure 1.1), Donald Trump carried the states of the greatest land area, giving a visual impression of dominance throughout the country. The Republican candidate won all of the southern Confederacy, all but three of the inland states from the Mississippi River west across the Plains and Mountain states, and—critically—most of the Midwest (Table 3.1 shows the full results).[1]

Clinton's reach was far more limited. She achieved pluralities in only twenty states and the District of Columbia. Seemingly, her campaign usually required ocean water to succeed, carrying most of the Atlantic Northeast and all but Alaska on the Pacific coast, but only two states in the former Democratic stronghold of the Midwest and three newer friendly territories in the Rocky Mountains.

Clinton ran—and lost—as the heir of President Obama, her loss continuing the historical tradition that a party is unlikely to win three consecutive terms. In American history only Martin Van Buren and George H. W. Bush had succeeded to the White House after two full terms of their party's predecessor.[2] Compared to Obama, Clinton performed badly in the Electoral College. Six states—all but one with large bundles of electoral votes—which switched from Obama to Trump, a total and decisive decline of 100 electoral votes. Two others, Indiana and North Carolina, had defected from the original Obama coalition in 2012.

The geographical pattern of the 2016 vote showed both continuity and change from previous elections. In the last six contests from 1992–2012, the Democrats had seemingly erected a "blue firewall"—eighteen states (and the District of Columbia) that had consistently supported the party's

**TABLE 3.1** The 2016 Presidential Vote

| State | Electoral Vote Clinton | Electoral Vote Trump | Popular Vote (1,000s) Clinton | Popular Vote (1,000s) Trump | 2-party vote %, 2016 Clinton | 2-party vote %, 2016 Trump | Other Vote % of Total | 2-party vote % 2012 Obama | 2-party vote % 2012 Romney | Democratic % Change 2012–2016 |
|---|---|---|---|---|---|---|---|---|---|---|
| Alabama | 0 | 9 | 730 | 1,318 | 35.6 | 64.4 | 3.6 | 38.8 | 61.2 | -3.2 |
| Alaska | 0 | 3 | 116 | 163 | 41.6 | 58.4 | 12.2 | 42.7 | 57.3 | -1.1 |
| Arizona | 0 | 11 | 1,161 | 1,252 | 48.1 | 51.9 | 7.3 | 45.4 | 54.6 | 2.7 |
| Arkansas | 0 | 6 | 380 | 685 | 35.7 | 64.3 | 5.8 | 37.8 | 62.2 | -2.1 |
| California | 55 | 0 | 8,581 | 4,393 | 66.1 | 33.9 | 6.5 | 61.9 | 38.1 | 4.3 |
| Colorado | 9 | 0 | 1,339 | 1,202 | 52.7 | 47.3 | 8.6 | 52.8 | 47.2 | -0.1 |
| Connecticut | 7 | 0 | 898 | 673 | 57.1 | 42.9 | 4.5 | 58.8 | 41.2 | -1.6 |
| Delaware | 3 | 0 | 236 | 185 | 56.0 | 44.0 | 4.7 | 59.6 | 40.4 | -3.6 |
| Dist. Columbia | 3 | 0 | 283 | 13 | 95.7 | 4.3 | 5.0 | 92.7 | 7.3 | 3.0 |
| Florida | 0 | 29 | 4,505 | 4,618 | 49.4 | 50.6 | 3.9 | 50.4 | 49.6 | -1.1 |
| Georgia | 0 | 16 | 1,878 | 2,089 | 47.3 | 52.7 | 4.1 | 46.0 | 54.0 | 1.3 |
| Hawaii | 4 | 0 | 267 | 129 | 67.4 | 32.6 | 7.7 | 71.7 | 28.3 | -4.3 |
| Idaho | 0 | 4 | 190 | 409 | 31.7 | 68.3 | 13.3 | 33.6 | 66.4 | -1.9 |
| Illinois | 20 | 0 | 3,084 | 2,141 | 59.0 | 41.0 | 6.0 | 58.6 | 41.4 | 0.4 |
| Indiana | 0 | 11 | 1,039 | 1,557 | 40.0 | 60.0 | 5.3 | 44.8 | 55.2 | -4.8 |
| Iowa | 0 | 6 | 654 | 801 | 44.9 | 55.1 | 7.1 | 53.0 | 47.0 | -8.0 |
| Kansas | 0 | 6 | 427 | 671 | 38.9 | 61.1 | 7.3 | 38.9 | 61.1 | 0.0 |
| Kentucky | 0 | 8 | 629 | 1,203 | 34.3 | 65.7 | 4.8 | 38.4 | 61.6 | -4.1 |
| Louisiana | 0 | 8 | 780 | 1,179 | 39.8 | 60.2 | 3.5 | 41.3 | 58.7 | -1.4 |
| Maine | 3 | 1 | 352 | 333 | 51.5 | 48.5 | 7.0 | 57.9 | 42.1 | -6.4 |
| Maryland | 10 | 0 | 1,678 | 943 | 64.0 | 36.0 | 5.7 | 63.3 | 36.7 | 0.7 |
| Massachusetts | 11 | 0 | 1,995 | 1,091 | 64.7 | 35.3 | 7.2 | 61.8 | 38.2 | 2.9 |

(Continued)

TABLE 3.1 (Continued)

| State | Electoral Vote Clinton | Electoral Vote Trump | Popular Vote (1,000s) Clinton | Popular Vote (1,000s) Trump | 2-party vote %, 2016 Clinton | 2-party vote %, 2016 Trump | Other Vote % of Total | 2-party vote %, 2012 Obama | 2-party vote %, 2012 Romney | Democratic % Change 2012–2016 |
|---|---|---|---|---|---|---|---|---|---|---|
| Michigan | 0 | 16 | 2,269 | 2,280 | 49.9 | 50.1 | 5.2 | 54.8 | 45.2 | -4.9 |
| Minnesota | 10 | 0 | 1,368 | 1,323 | 50.8 | 49.2 | 8.6 | 53.9 | 46.1 | -3.1 |
| Mississippi | 0 | 6 | 484 | 700 | 40.9 | 59.1 | 2.1 | 44.2 | 55.8 | -3.3 |
| Missouri | 0 | 10 | 1,055 | 1,586 | 39.9 | 60.1 | 4.9 | 45.2 | 54.8 | -5.3 |
| Montana | 0 | 3 | 178 | 279 | 38.9 | 61.1 | 7.6 | 43.0 | 57.0 | -4.1 |
| Nebraska | 0 | 5 | 283 | 495 | 36.4 | 63.6 | 5.7 | 38.9 | 61.1 | -2.5 |
| Nevada | 6 | 0 | 539 | 512 | 51.3 | 48.7 | 6.6 | 53.4 | 46.6 | -2.1 |
| New Hampshire | 4 | 0 | 349 | 346 | 50.2 | 49.8 | 6.7 | 52.9 | 47.1 | -2.7 |
| New Jersey | 14 | 0 | 2,144 | 1,600 | 57.3 | 42.7 | 4.0 | 59.0 | 41.0 | -1.7 |
| New Mexico | 5 | 0 | 385 | 320 | 54.7 | 45.3 | 11.7 | 55.3 | 44.7 | -0.6 |
| New York | 29 | 0 | 4,159 | 2,645 | 61.1 | 38.9 | 4.5 | 64.3 | 35.7 | -3.2 |
| North Carolina | 0 | 15 | 2,189 | 2,363 | 48.1 | 51.9 | 4.0 | 49.0 | 51.0 | -0.9 |
| North Dakota | 0 | 3 | 94 | 217 | 30.2 | 69.8 | 9.8 | 39.9 | 60.1 | -9.7 |
| Ohio | 0 | 18 | 2,394 | 2,841 | 45.7 | 54.3 | 5.4 | 51.5 | 48.5 | -5.8 |
| Oklahoma | 0 | 7 | 420 | 949 | 30.7 | 69.3 | 5.7 | 33.3 | 66.7 | -2.6 |
| Oregon | 7 | 0 | 1,000 | 781 | 56.1 | 43.9 | 12.0 | 56.3 | 43.7 | -0.1 |
| Pennsylvania | 0 | 20 | 2,916 | 2,963 | 49.6 | 50.4 | 4.3 | 52.7 | 47.3 | -3.1 |
| Rhode Island | 4 | 0 | 253 | 181 | 58.3 | 41.7 | 6.7 | 64.1 | 35.9 | -5.8 |
| South Carolina | 0 | 9 | 855 | 1,155 | 42.5 | 57.5 | 4.4 | 44.7 | 55.3 | -2.1 |
| South Dakota | 0 | 3 | 117 | 228 | 34.0 | 66.0 | 6.7 | 40.7 | 59.3 | -6.7 |
| Tennessee | 0 | 11 | 869 | 1,521 | 36.4 | 63.6 | 4.0 | 39.7 | 60.3 | -3.3 |

| | | | | | | | | |
|---|---|---|---|---|---|---|---|---|
| Texas | 0 | 38 | 3,878 | 4,685 | 45.3 | 54.7 | 4.5 | 42.0 | 58.0 | 3.3 |
| Utah | 0 | 6 | 311 | 515 | 37.6 | 62.4 | 27.6 | 25.4 | 74.6 | 12.2 |
| Vermont | 3 | 0 | 179 | 95 | 65.2 | 34.8 | 13.1 | 68.2 | 31.8 | -3.0 |
| Virginia | 13 | 0 | 1,981 | 1,769 | 52.8 | 47.2 | 5.8 | 52.0 | 48.0 | 0.9 |
| Washington | 12 | 0 | 1,743 | 1,222 | 58.8 | 41.2 | 10.0 | 57.6 | 42.4 | 1.2 |
| West Virginia | 0 | 5 | 189 | 489 | 27.8 | 72.2 | 6.0 | 36.3 | 63.7 | -8.4 |
| Wisconsin | 0 | 10 | 1,382 | 1,404 | 49.6 | 50.4 | 6.4 | 53.5 | 46.5 | -3.9 |
| Wyoming | 0 | 3 | 56 | 174 | 24.3 | 75.7 | 10.0 | 28.8 | 71.3 | -4.5 |
| Totals | 232 | 306 | 65,240 | 62,687 | 51.0 | 49.0 | 5.9 | 52.0 | 48.0 | -1.0 |
| Linear correlation 2012–16 | | | | | | | 0.96 | | | |
| Median | | | | | 48.1 | 51.9 | 6.0 | 51.5 | 48.5 | -2.5 |
| Standard deviation | | | | | 12.8 | | | 12.0 | | 3.7 |

*Note*: 5.9% of the total national vote went to third-party candidates, including Gary Johnson (Libertarian), 3.3%, Jill Stein (Green), and other candidates, 2.6%.

*Sources*: Data from Leip (2016)

candidates. These areas totaled 242 electoral votes, close to assuring the party a majority of 270 in the Electoral College.

The firewall was decisively breached in 2016, with pivotal losses in three industrial states, as well as Ohio and other battlegrounds. However, party alignments did show continuity, statistically measured by a correlation of 0.96 between the state-by-state outcomes in 2012 and 2016. In effect, the combat lines of party foxholes between the parties remained, but the demarcations had moved a small but determining margin to the right.

Focusing on the direct confrontations of Republicans and Democrats (two-party vote) in the individual states, the predominant pattern showed shifts away from Obama and toward Trump. Clinton did better than Obama in eleven constituencies, but none switched their party allegiance. Trump was more successful—even where the Republican vote share dropped, Trump still held every state his party won in 2012. Overall, the nation showed a change of 2.5% in the average (median) state. West Virginia, once the epitome of working-class Democratic loyalty, led the shift to Trump and became the second most Republican state in the nation; Utah, the embodiment of religious conservatism, decreased its Republican vote by 12 percentage points, but still gave Trump "only" five of every eight votes.

The Electoral College provided a clear Republican victory. But the result was only a limited triumph. The underlying mass base for this official result was a severely divided electorate. Clinton actually won more popular votes than Trump, leading him by nearly three million tallies and two percentage points in the individual count. She won more votes than any candidate in American history other than Obama. She lost only a fractional share of the vote compared to her predecessor, a 1% shift in the two-party balloting. In a different scenario, she would have won the presidency, too, if she could have added as few as eighty thousand votes in three states.

In the real world, however, Trump clearly won. He lacked a popular lead, and gained only a narrow electoral majority, among the least convincing in the historical record. But he did get 100% of the Presidency. The election of 2016 was a one-performance spectacular; there would be no rerun.

### Effect of the Electoral College

These results were created by 137 million individual voters, casting their votes separately by states, with each unit's electoral vote determined by its own popular plurality (except in Maine, where division by congressional district gave one electoral vote to Trump). By a considerable margin, Clinton won the total popular vote; her loss was not a national rejection, but came from the constitutional structure, the state-by-state accumulation of electors.

The same disparity came just sixteen years earlier, when Democrat Al Gore also won a national popular majority but was then counted out by the Electoral College (on a bare vote of 271–267), aided by a controversial ruling by the Supreme Court. The combination of two selections of minority Republican presidents in this short period—the first since 1888—raises serious doubts about the democratic fairness of the system.

We can easily imagine other outcomes, if we mathematically (and perhaps magically) construct other outcomes. The simplest reconstruction would be to change the system to direct popular vote—as Clinton supporters would now want. The Democrat would then be the new President.

However, it's not that simple. If there had been a different system in effect, campaign behavior would also be different. Trump has said that he would have devoted more attention to states that he lost decisively, such as California and New York, probably changing his total vote and possibly making him the majority choice. Clinton's vote would also change as she would devote less effort to states she actually lost narrowly, such as Florida and North Carolina. So, who would win? We will never know.

A different magic would add a small number of votes—only 0.12% more—to Clinton's tallies in the three close industrial states. That would give her 47 more electoral votes, and a total win with 279 electoral votes. Or, more generously, imagine a 1% shift of the popular vote from Trump to Clinton. That would almost exactly reverse the election outcome, giving her an electoral vote majority of 307–231 (Silver 2016a).

Of course, these changes cannot be made. Still, they raise questions about the institution of the Electoral College itself. Is it now inherently biased against Democrats and the foundational principle of majority rule? Or, as Trump might have asked, is the system rigged? Perhaps that assertion is true, because the institution gives extra power to small states, since each state's electoral votes are based not only on its population but also include two votes for each state, reflecting each state's equal number of two members in the U.S. Senate. Is it fair that 85,000 voters in Wyoming choose each of three electors, while it takes 252,000 Californians to make the same decision?

Suppose we took away these two "senatorial" electors from each state? Then there would be 100 fewer electoral votes, now a reduced total of 438. That would not change the 2016 result. Trump would now have 246 and Clinton 192, a reduced margin, but still a clear Republican victory. This imagined scenario does not support the argument that small states have an inherent and always unfair advantage in the Electoral College.

One other probe. Are the parties treated equally in terms of winning these electoral votes? Does it take more Democratic popular votes? In Table 3.2, we calculate the number of popular votes that brought one electoral vote to the parties in 2016, in the nation as a whole and in states of varying populations and, consequently, different numbers of current electoral votes. We show the result for four different kinds of states, based on their population size.

**TABLE 3.2** Effects of the Electoral College

| State EV | Clinton | | | Trump | | |
|---|---|---|---|---|---|---|
| | Number of States | Vote per EV | State EV | Number of States | Vote per EV | State EV |
| 3–4 | 13 | 83,366 | 24 | 7 | 77,400 | 19 |
| 5–9 | 17 | 122,376 | 34 | 5 | 125,432 | 81 |
| 10–19 | 15 | 181,809 | 70 | 6 | 143,161 | 118 |
| 20–55 | 6 | 152,156 | 104 | 3 | 211,477 | 87 |
| Average | 51 | 149,622 | 232 | 21 | 153,843 | 305 |

*Notes*: District of Columbia is included in calculations. Maine calculated as with three electoral votes, not including the 2nd congressional district. Nebraska statewide vote only. Calculation of "vote per EV" is a simple division of the candidate's statewide votes by the number of the states' electoral votes.

*Source*: Author's calculations.

Parties do have advantages in some places. Democratic efforts are more "efficient" in the smallest and largest states, Republicans in those of middle-sized populations. Overall, there is no significant variation in party effectiveness or consistent harm to the Democrats. In fact, on average, it takes somewhat fewer ballots for the party to win electoral votes than do Republicans. The problem for the Democrats is that they win fewer states, and that their popular majority in 2016 was "wasted" in overwhelming victories in places such as California; that state alone provided almost twice her national popular majority.

Put another way, the Democratic problem is that the United States is not a single country in presidential elections as it is in the real constitutional world—it is a federal system in which states are given significant roles in the choice of the leader of the nation. It is a diverse nation that defers to cultural differences in states that span a continent from secularist Washington to evangelical Georgia, and a republic that is deliberately hostile to rule by a firewall of only nineteen states on its geographical fringes.

Acknowledging these differences was part of the "federal bargain" that created the Constitution itself, evident as well in the composition of the Congress and the existence of equal state votes in the Senate. It is one of the virtues praised by Alexander Hamilton in *The Federalist*, a safeguard, he wrote, against national "cabal, intrigue, and corruption" that might characterize a single national election (Hamilton 2005). Perhaps the federal system is outdated and America should be a unitary state, with a single leader, male or female, responsible only to a mass majority, perhaps even to the "tyranny of the majority" feared by Alexis de Tocqueville. Until the United States decides to make that extraordinary change in its institutions, the Electoral College does not threaten its democracy.[3]

## Patterns in the Popular Vote

The obscure 538 members of the Electoral College officially chose Donald Trump as the next President, meeting in the separate states in December. But their formal actions were only pre-ordained summaries of the ballots cast by individual voters across the nation. The significance of the election comes from the decisions made in millions of hearts and minds. To probe those decisions, we need to examine the turnout and divisions of groups within the electorate.

### Turnout

The total turnout set a new record for American electoral participation. It surpassed that in 2012 by more than seven million while the percentage of eligible voters who cast ballots, 58.4%, dropped slightly due to population growth (Bialik 2016). Clinton did win a plurality of these votes nationally—48.0% to Trump's 46.1%—but she trailed her Democratic predecessor, Barack Obama.

Turnout, although large and higher, did not benefit Clinton, because many Democratic voting groups showed decreases in their relative shares of the vote. There were small but significant declines apparent in the proportions of ballots returned by partisan identifiers, liberals, African-Americans, lower-income groups, millennial youth, and women. These declines were paralleled by declines in the Democratic vote returned by large industrial cities in critical states, such as Cleveland in Ohio, Milwaukee in Wisconsin, and Scranton in Pennsylvania.

Where participation did rise, changes worked to Trump's benefit: "Republican turnout seems to have surged this year while Democratic turnout stagnated." In party strongholds in six critical states, GOP voting rose 2.9%, while its opponents' ballots declined 1.7% (Leonhardt 2016, SR3). Furthermore, some of these declines may have come from militant efforts by Republicans to remove likely Democrats from the voting rolls (Palast 2016).

The vote for minor candidates more than doubled, to over seven million, less than 6% of the total. Clinton would have won the close states if supporters of the Libertarian and Green parties had switched to her, but there is no clear evidence that they would have supported—or if they would vote at all—in a straight Clinton vs. Trump contest.

Demographic groups voted quite differently from one another, but there were similar changes in all groups compared to the previous election. Almost all showed a decrease in Clinton's share when compared to Obama (Table 3.3 provides detailed data). Four characteristics were particularly important.

**TABLE 3.3** Demography of the Vote in 2016 and 2012

|  | % Vote | % Clinton | % Trump | Shift '12–'16* |
|---|---|---|---|---|
| **Partisanship** | | | | |
| Democratic | 37 | 89 | 9 | −3 |
| Republican | 33 | 7 | 90 | 1 |
| Independent | 31 | 42 | 48 | −3 |
| **Sex** | | | | |
| Men | 48 | 41 | 53 | −4 |
| Women | 52 | 54 | 42 | −1 |
| **Ideology** | | | | |
| Liberal | 26 | 84 | 10 | −2 |
| Moderate | 39 | 52 | 41 | −4 |
| Conservative | 35 | 15 | 81 | −2 |
| **Race** | | | | |
| White | 70 | 37 | 58 | −2 |
| Black | 12 | 88 | 8 | −5 |
| Latino | 11 | 65 | 29 | −6 |
| Asian | 4 | 65 | 29 | −8 |
| **Age** | | | | |
| 18–29 | 19 | 55 | 37 | −5 |
| 30–44 | 25 | 50 | 42 | −2 |
| 45–64 | 40 | 44 | 53 | −3 |
| 65 and older | 15 | 45 | 53 | 1 |
| **Yearly Income** | | | | |
| Under $50,000 | 36 | 52 | 41 | −8 |
| $50–100,000 | 31 | 46 | 50 | 0 |
| Over $100,000 | 33 | 47 | 48 | 3 |
| **Financial Situation—2015–16** | | | | |
| Better Today | 31 | 72 | 24 | −10 |
| About the Same | 41 | 46 | 46 | −12 |
| Worse Today | 27 | 19 | 78 | 1 |
| **Education** | | | | |
| No College | 18 | 45 | 51 | −6 |
| White | 34 | 28 | 67 | −8 |
| Non-White | 16 | 75 | 20 | −7 |
| Some College | 32 | 43 | 52 | −6 |
| College Graduate | 32 | 49 | 51 | 2 |
| White | 37 | 45 | 49 | 3 |
| Non-White | 13 | 71 | 23 | −6 |
| Postgraduate | 18 | 58 | 37 | 3 |
| **Religion** | | | | |
| Protestant | 52 | 39 | 58 | −3 |
| White Evangelical | 26 | 16 | 81 | −5 |
| Catholic | 23 | 45 | 52 | −5 |
| Jewish | 3 | 71 | 24 | 2 |
| Other | 8 | 62 | 29 | −12 |
| None | 15 | 68 | 26 | −5 |

|  | % Vote | % Clinton | % Trump | Shift '12-'16* |
|---|---|---|---|---|
| **Life Status** | | | | |
| Married Women | 30 | 49 | 47 | 3 |
| Unmarried Women | 23 | 62 | 31 | −5 |
| Married Men | 29 | 37 | 58 | −1 |
| Unmarried Men | 19 | 46 | 45 | −10 |
| Gay, Lesbian, Bisexual | 5 | 78 | 14 | 2 |
| Veteran | 13 | 34 | 61 | |
| **Size of Place** | | | | |
| Large city | 34 | 59 | 35 | −3 |
| Suburbs | 49 | 45 | 50 | 6 |
| Rural | 17 | 34 | 62 | −14 |

*Source*: Author's calculations using data from publicly reported national exit polls (e.g., *Washington Post* and *The New York Times*).

## Critical Markers: Partisanship

As has become common, partisan self-identification was the strongest influence. Overwhelmingly, Democrats supported Clinton and Republicans backed Trump. The voters disappointed campaigners' concerns—or hopes—that Sanders devotees or moderate Republicans would stray from their parties. However, there were noticeable defections to the minor candidates, Gary Johnson and Jill Stein, and marginally less Democratic solidarity than in 2012, perhaps affecting the critical states.

The strong partisanship evident in the vote reflected similar strong differences in political ideology between Democratic and Republican identifiers. Nearly four of five Democrats were located on the left of a scale of policies on racial, economic, and cultural issues—and the same attitudes were mirrored by Republicans on the right. On a ten-point scale, the average Democrat scored 3.0 and the average Republican 7.1, but few persons were located in the middle (Abramowitz 2016).

## Critical Markers: Sex

Democrats had founded their campaign on expected major gains among two groups. They hoped that women—now a clear majority of the total electorate—would be especially supportive of Clinton, the first woman nominated for President by a major party, culminating a century of political effort after sexual equality had been written into the Constitution.

There was a "gender gap" in the vote favoring the Democrats, as there had been as early as 1972. Females were more likely to vote for Clinton, surpassing her vote from males by 10–12 percentage points. A good showing, but virtually the same as the gap between Obama and Romney in 2012, and essentially the same edge achieved by other recent Democratic candidates—John Kerry, Al Gore, and Bill Clinton (Fox 2013, ch. 10).

Sisterhood was not powerful in 2016. Its impact was still less when the female vote was examined along with other factors, especially race and social class. Although the gender gap remained among whites, Caucasian women did not show strong affinity for Clinton: only 43% voted for their sexual compatriot (although 12% more than men). She did win a bare majority of women with college degrees (again 12% more than men). There was considerably less gender solidarity among white women of lower education: Clinton gained only a third of their support—and less than a quarter of men of the same level of schooling (Malone 2016).

*Critical Markers: Ethnicity*

The most basic fact about the electorate, often ignored, is that it is still predominantly (70%) white. Other groups have risen in size, and have properly gained more influence. In 2016, racial divisions grew, along with a significant and often disturbing increase in white ethnic identification.

Ethnic minorities have favored Democratic candidates since the development of liberal policy positions in the New Deal and even more strongly since the civil rights movement in the 1960s. With the candidacy of Barack Obama, African-Americans became nearly monolithic in their party loyalty. With Obama's retirement from the White House, black participation and solidarity dropped in 2016.

Yet Democrats were hopeful that ethnic loyalties would still swell their vote. Latinos would soon be the largest non-white group in the electorate, as native-born children of immigrants from Latin America came of voting age and political consciousness. The Republican nomination of Trump would spur Latino involvement, they assumed, because Trump had deliberately defamed the group, from his first campaign day's characterization of Mexican immigrants as illegal, rapists, and criminals to his drumbeat of outlandish plans to build a wall across the border with Mexico, abrogate the North American Trade Agreement, and deport millions of resident aliens from the southern nations.

But the actual impact was less than expected. There certainly were more Latino voters, with some estimates as high as three million new voters from the ethnic group. Uncertain data, however, made it difficult to assess the extent or effect. The National Exit Poll data, included in Table 3.3, showed no increase in the Latino proportion of the electorate and reported an increased share of their vote for Trump, compared to Romney in 2012.

Both conclusions seem debatable. The larger Democratic vote in such states as California, Arizona, and Florida likely came from new Hispanic voters who probably flocked to the polls to oppose a candidate rousing the country against their "threats." Latino researchers make a plausible, but still not definitive, claim that their ethnic group, vastly larger in voting numbers, voted 79% for Clinton (Sanchez 2016; Enten 2016). It is also true, however, that the Latino vote did not bring any new states into the diminished Democratic coalition and could not prevent the loss of states with a large Hispanic population, such as critical Florida.

*Critical Markers: Class*

If Democratic hopes were frustrated, Trump succeeded extraordinarily in his personal strategy to appeal to the white working class, those he would arouse at fervent rallies of "the forgotten" men and women. His was not an appeal simply on race—he barely increased the Republican support among whites generally. But, as Table 3.3 and other data baldly show (Beckman 2016), he won surges of support from whites he targeted: those of lower income, lacking a college degree, evangelical in their religion, frequent church attenders, rural residents, and financially insecure.

Trump's appeal built on longer trends in the demographic bases of the two major parties. The Democrats' previous majorities had been founded on multiple groups including working-class whites benefitting from the economic programs of liberal presidents beginning with Franklin Roosevelt. In more recent periods, the party shifted to an emphasis on group identities and multi-culturalism. These shifts, we will see in the rest of this chapter, had much to do with the party's loss of the presidency.

## The Astonishing Campaign

Most presidential campaigns are both exciting and eventually unsurprising. Political scientists and pundits have developed models of electoral behavior that generally allow early and accurate forecasts of the eventual results (Campbell, October 2016, 649–690). Hundreds of polling organizations follow the voters' shifting responses. Although often flawed in early predictions, polls taken three weeks or less before Election Day almost always have been correct in identifying the presidential winner.

But, in 2016, clarity gave way to confusion in the campaign and in election predictability. The odds always favored Clinton, but her chances varied from close to merely even to nearly 9:1 in her favor (Figure 3.1). A similar pattern could be seen in the average of opinion polls, published daily on a major website, realclearpolitics.com.

Figure 3.1 looks like a balloon that first expands and then deflates. When "air" is blown into the balloon, Clinton opens up a significant lead in the odds and polls. This effect is seen after events favorable to Clinton such as the party conventions and the television debates. Then, the balloon flattens as Trump strengthens from countervailing events such as his aggressive campaigning and controversy over Clinton's use of a private

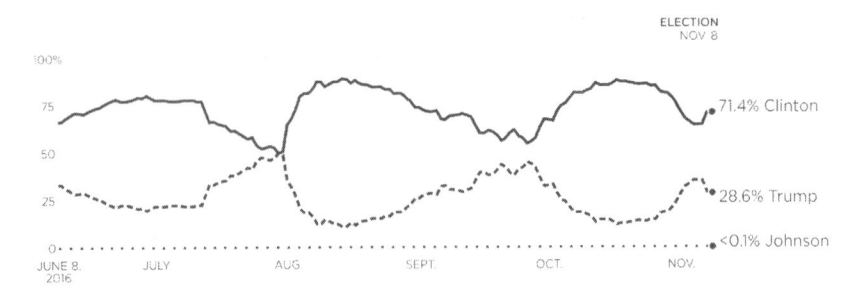

**FIGURE 3.1** Shifting Odds in 2016 Campaign

*Source:* Silver (2016b). Figure constructed by author.

email server. When the election itself nears, the balloon is close to flat again, suggesting the close result that became reality in the final vote.

### Summer Storms and the Party Conventions

Both major candidates had secured their party nominations by the beginning of June, with Clinton holding a strong and growing lead, although a Trump victory still was a significant possibility. As the nation passed Independence Day, however, the odds shifted. The likely cause of the change was an arcane controversy that had dogged Clinton during months of press and Republican investigations.

When serving as Secretary of State, Clinton had bypassed the agency's email network and had established a separate private server. Critics were suspicious, charging that the private system had posed the risk of loss of classified material and they implied, furthermore, that the server had been cleaned of thousands of messages that might reveal her corrupt personal behavior. Adding to her problems, Clinton evaded the issue for months before admitting fault and apologizing.

On July 5, FBI Director James Comey issued the Bureau's official report on the computer operations, which cleared Clinton of any criminal wrongdoing, but left her politically vulnerable. The number of emails containing confidential information was only a trace amount among tens of thousands of messages, and there was no evidence that they had been read by foreign countries. But Comey gave Clinton only the most narrow escape, concluding: "Although there is evidence of potential violations of the statutes regarding the handling of classified information, our judgment is that no reasonable prosecutor would bring such a case." (Federal Bureau of Investigation 2016).

Republicans had hoped that Clinton would be charged and indicted for criminal acts. Seeing Comey as too lenient, they continued to press the issue and pressure him to continue the investigation. Public opinion did move against Clinton, reflecting existing distrust of her honesty as well as anxieties aroused by recent terrorist attacks at home and abroad. As the national conventions opened, the presumptive nominees were nearly an even bet (Clinton 52%, Trump 48%).

Then came the conventions, only one week apart at the end of July, Republicans leading off and then Democrats closing. Actually, Trump dominated both conventions, demanding the admiration of his own party in Cleveland then suffering the disdain of his opponents in Philadelphia. To Trump, the conventioneers were the audience for his personal glorification. The most prominent speakers were his family, his chosen running mate Governor Mike Pence, and himself (at record length). Aside from these dependents, others—who generally avoided mentioning his name—concentrated on attacks against Hillary Clinton, including frenzied calls to "Lock her up."

Trump's last primary opponents went even further, ignoring him completely. Ohio Governor John Kasich refused even to enter the convention arena, while Senator Ted Cruz (TX) ostentatiously refused to endorse his former rival, instead urging viewers to "vote their consciences," an early opening for his anticipated return to the intraparty party contest of 2020.

In his acceptance speech, Trump became more fully self-centered. He mentioned none of his rivals nor any other Republican leader other than the vice-presidential aspirant, Indiana Governor Mike Pence (once). His solipsistic attitude was also evident in his preference for saying "I" (85 times) rather than "we" (62 times). His theme was his personal ability to solve national problems through his own forceful will:

> I'M WITH YOU—THE AMERICAN PEOPLE. I am your voice. . . . I'm With You, and I will fight for you, and I will win for you. We Will Make America Strong Again. We Will Make America Proud Again. We Will Make America Safe Again. And We Will Make America Great Again.
>
> *(Politico staff 2016)*

The Democrats put on a better show, with rousing oratory from the nation's most prominent politicians and entertainers drawn from ethnically diverse groups. Trump was also the focus of the Democrats. Although not cited by name by President Obama or First Lady Michelle Obama, he was a looming presence in theirs and others' speeches. The sharpest attacks came from nominee Hillary Clinton, who assailed her opponent four times for each time she praised President Obama. Secretary Clinton's speech was also a sharp contrast to Trump's egotism, featuring commendations of her primary rival Bernie Sanders, and considerably fewer uses of "I" (62) than of "we" (98).

Clinton's acceptance speech was less stirring than Trump's or those of other Democratic leaders. More like the State of the Union speech of a sitting President, it made promises to the different elements of the party coalition. Preceding her address, the party's multicultural appeal was also shown dramatically by Khizr and Ghazala Khan, Muslim immigrants and the parents of a U.S. Army captain heroically killed in Iraq. "Donald Trump," challenged the father, "Have you ever read the U.S. Constitution?" Offering to lend his own pocket-sized copy, he told Trump, "Look for the words 'liberty' and 'equal protection of law.'" The rhetorical damage grew for a week, while Trump kept the subject in the news, repeatedly denigrating the Gold Star family.

The conventions soon affected the opinion polls, as the odds favoring Clinton rose to an overwhelming advantage, close to 9:1. Seeing the need for drastic change, Trump's advisers and family recast the campaign, bringing in new and more experienced managers, initiating new fundraising among wealthy Republicans and Internet supporters, and disciplining Trump to measured and "presidential" efforts. Clinton sagged, affected physically by a bout of pneumonia and politically by a clumsy effort to conceal her brief illness. The race had tightened again, as attention turned to the expected drama of national televised debates.

### Television Debates and the Final Weeks

Trump now had the opportunity to take command. The race already appeared to be a virtual draw in the polls, Trump had shown his ability to command the debate stage in his routs of sixteen competitors in the Republican primaries. The political seeds sown in the spring might be ready for harvest in the fall. But what followed was a flood of electoral disasters; these events almost drowned Trump and his party until he caught a favoring wave.

In the first presidential debate, held September 26 before a record electronic audience of 84 million, Trump was baited by Hillary Clinton into poses of arrogance, exaggeration, and false claims. He boasted that he avoided personal income taxes "because I'm smart," denied his documented early support of the Iraq war, and focused his personal criticism of Clinton on implicitly sexist claims that she lacked "a presidential look" and "stamina."

For two weeks after the debate, Trump's support fell. He accelerated his own decline by gnawing over Clinton's attack on his alleged sexism. He denied that he had criticized the Venezuelan winner of his own Miss Universe contest for her weight or had denigrated her as "Miss Porkie" and "Miss Housecleaner." He also tarred her as the performer in a "sex tape" that did not exist. On a different front, state tax returns for Trump in 1995, leaked to *The New York Times*, showed that he had claimed a billion-dollar business loss in 1995, potentially freeing him from all tax liabilities for up to two decades.

As the second presidential debate neared, a new sensation came to light, an audio tape of a lewd sexual discussion in 2005, where Trump boasted of his domination of women: "You know I'm automatically attracted to beautiful—I just start kissing them. It's like a magnet. Just kiss. I don't even wait. . . . And when you're a star, they let you do it. . . . Grab them by the p—y. You can do anything" (Fahrenthold 2016). In the following days, ten women publically claimed that Trump had in fact sexually harassed them.

Called to account in the second debate, Trump apologized for his "locker room talk," affirmed his "great respect for women," then pivoted to chastise Bill Clinton for his own sexual behavior, and threatened, if elected, to prosecute Hillary Clinton for her own misdeeds in office. The candidates made their mutual disregard clear for the rest of the ninety minutes, even avoiding a ceremonial handshake and disagreeing on every issue posed, from immigration into the United States to foreign relations outside the nation.

Clinton's lead reached its high point on October 19, the date of the third presidential debate. That confrontation was not unusual for this acrimonious campaign. The candidates largely stayed on policy issues, as Clinton scored a clean sweep of the series. The most serious difference portended a potential governmental crisis after the election. Citing Trump's increasing warnings of election fraud, the moderator asked if he would accept the results, win or lose.

Trump answered that the election was "rigged" because Clinton was "guilty of a very, very serious crime. She should not be allowed to run." For that reason, he casually, even arrogantly, dismissed the question: "I will tell you at the time. I'll keep you in suspense. OK?" Trump's skepticism toward the legitimacy of the electoral process drew a sharp rebuke from Clinton: "That is not the way our democracy works. . . . We've accepted the outcomes when we may not have liked them. And that is what must be expected." ("Transcript of the Third Debate" 2016).

Clinton's lead continued to grow, reaching favorable odds of 7:1. Other indicators were also favorable. Republican candidates for the House and Senate distanced themselves from Trump, as did four of the five previous living party candidates for President. Reporters compiled an extensive list of presumably hostile persons and groups insulted by Trump (Lee and Queally 2016). Large numbers of senior Republicans and former national security experts declared their refusal to vote for him (Graham 2016; Sanger and Haberman 2016). Clinton received endorsements from almost every major newspaper in the country, including many—*USA Today*, *Arizona Republic*, *Dallas Morning News*, *Cincinnati Enquirer* and *Atlantic* magazine—that had almost always supported Republicans in the past (Rutenberg 2016).

Clinton also had the critical advantage of cold cash. Two weeks before the end of the campaign, she had routed Trump in the race for dollars—$1.3 billion to $795 million. In a reversal of party stereotypes, she raised three times as much money from super PACs than her wealthy opponent, who gave only $31 million of his reputedly vast fortune to his own campaign, but Trump got a far larger percentage of his contributions from small donors (27% to Clinton's 16%) ("Election Campaign Finance" 2016). Her funding enabled Clinton to air three times as many television spots as Trump. How could she lose?

Still, Clinton's standing in the polls began dropping in the last two weeks, bringing the race toward a new equilibrium level. Then, another surprise. Just eleven days before the national balloting, FBI Director Comey tersely announced that he was reexamining the email issue because new material might—or might not—be found in a different case, involving alleged sexting by the husband of Clinton's chief aide. Soon, yet another turnaround. Only two days before the election, Comey returned to the stage to announce that he had no new information about Clinton and no reason to reopen the formal investigation.

Another campaign effect might have come from hackings of computers of the Democratic National Committee and the Clinton organization. Damaging material from these groups' files were spread by the renegade website WikiLeaks, and exploited by the Trump campaign. After the election, the hacking itself was attributed to the intelligence services of Russia, acting at the direct behest of the country's president, Vladimir Putin—who both won and reciprocated the open praise of Trump. Only two weeks before the Republican's inauguration, all U.S. intelligence agencies (including Comey's FBI) officially reported, "Russia's goals were to undermine public faith in the U.S. democratic process, denigrate Secretary Clinton, and harm her electability and potential presidency. We further conclude that Putin and the Russian government developed a clear preference for President-elect Trump."[4] Neither the agencies nor independent analysts could demonstrate that the foreign intervention affected the election. But it is conceivable that the Russians supplied the last straw that broke the Democratic donkey's back.

And then the polling booths opened.

## The Qualities of the Campaign

### Debate in a Democracy

As an exercise in citizen democracy, the campaign was an unsightly failure. The electorate was provided inadequate information and shallow choices. Attention was directed primarily toward the candidates' alleged scandals and deficiencies, and far less to the issues of greatest public concern: jobs and the economy. The defects were evident in presentations of both the candidates and the news media.[5]

The candidates ran half a million advertisements, but attacks on their opponents predominated, comprising three-fourths of Clinton's and half of Trump's paid television time. News media did little to correct the imbalance—only 17% of their reports dealt with Trump's economic policies, and even less, 10%, with Clinton's (Vavreck 2016).The imbalance reflected television networks flight from serious news coverage. The past giants of broadcast journalism—ABC, CBS and NBC—devoted a total of thirty-two minutes on their nightly newscasts to policy issues in 2016—compared to one hundred on Clinton's email and 333 on Trump in the Republican nominating contests (Boehlert 2016).

Both major candidates emphasized the asserted defects of their opponent. This was the natural posture for a challenger. The Clinton campaign did not respond with a defense of the incumbent administration, or with a coherent message of a different course. Instead, it made the election a choice of change with Trump or risk with Trump. "It was based on the old rules of the road. If your opponent is the change candidate, turn that change against him. Rather than refreshing change, turn it into dangerous change" (Cillizza 2016). But two negative campaigns did not combine into a positive contribution to the electoral process.

The problems posed by the media and the candidates in 2016 are part of more extensive changes in American politics. Voters are less likely to be true citizens, engaging in meaningful discussion about their common country. Republicans and Democrats are more separated in ideology and literally in space, less likely to live near one another. Shared communications though the print press or television networks have been replaced by partisan websites, interest groups, and even churches. News—or an imitation of news—now comes to the electorate as much through the unauthenticated and fake news of the non-social "social media" of Facebook and Twitter as from professional journalists and experts. Americans talk less about politics and are more hostile toward each other in political discussions—just a quarter of Trump backers and only a fifth of Clinton voters had close friends supporting the other side (Blake 2016). When they did talk, Americans were hostile to their future leader—majorities thought that both Clinton and Trump "represent a threat to the nation's well-being" (Balz and Guskin 2016).

### Trump and Democratic Discussion

The new President has furthered this decay. The essence of citizen democracy is talk, a commitment to discussion, mutual respect among the talkers, an effort to seek truth, and the peaceful resolution of disputes. With his astonishing victory, Trump has marked a political sea change that will surely be imitated by other power seekers. The consequence is likely to be further deterioration in electoral practices.

Trump's candidacy for president was hardly an exercise of reasonable deliberation. It was modeled on his success as an entertainment celebrity, particularly on his role as a chief executive on "The Apprentice." The program won audiences, in part, because Trump's judgment was erratic, his decision-making process was uncertain, his choices hidden until a dramatic conclusion. Conflict between the participants brought excitement and audiences. These same characteristics made him "good copy," the center of attention during the nominating season, resulting in hours of free publicity on the airwaves.

As he rose to the nomination, the real estate developer perfected his techniques. Instead of engaging in polite dialogue, he found ways to dominate his rivals, most obviously by coining insulting labels: "Lyin' Ted" (Cruz), "Little Mario" (Rubio), "Pathological" Ben Carson, "Low energy" Jeb Bush—and eventually "Crooked Hillary" (Clinton).

Trump also violated the canons of political discourse by ignoring facts and inconvenient truths. He first came to political notice by spreading the lie that President Obama was born outside of the United States. More generally, the leading journalistic fact checker, Politifact, found that Clinton told the truth fully or mostly in 76% of her statements, compared to making false or mostly false statements 26% of the time. In contrast, of Trump's statements, 15% were largely or mostly truthful, but 70% were false or mostly false ("Comparing Hillary Clinton, Donald Trump on the Truth-O-Meter" 2016).[6]

The developer also showed an authoritarian bent in his rhetoric, a recurring emphasis on violence—not talk—as the means of resolving disputes. His Middle East policy was to "wipe out ISIS," he termed himself a "law and order" candidate who saw killing as the main feature of minority urban areas, his primary immigration policy was forceful deportation of aliens, and he encouraged forceful retaliation against protestors and journalists at his rallies.

Trump's commitment to the democratic process is uncertain. But he was also clever and innovative. He proved to be a stirring speaker to rapt audiences. He campaigned energetically, turning massive rallies into virtual crusades, inspiring enthusiasm that was unseen or ignored by "experts." He changed campaigning itself from the former emphasis on television and advertising to social media, building a constituency hidden to most observers—while saving campaign funds. He sensed the discontents of the white working class, and successfully transformed his public image from self-indulgent billionaire to a voice for some of the disadvantaged. American politics will not be better for his example, but it will be different.

## The Meaning of the Vote

At last, on November 8, the longest campaign in American history ended. As many as two out of five Americans had already voted on early or absentee ballots. They mailed ballots or went to the polls weary of the cacophony of negative arguments, incessant polls, and fervent commentary, alienated by both major candidates. In the end, they astonished all of the bruited "experts," and simultaneously expressed their collective preference for Hillary Clinton and elected Donald Trump. The voice of the people was loud, but their collective message was garbled. But soon, translators came to parse the speech of the American people.

### *Interpretations of the Vote*

Three principal explanations of the election results have circulated, each citing different causes and examining different time periods.

### *The Fundamentals*

A prominent explanation largely ignores campaign events. Political science predictions take a longer perspective, typically relying on complex statistical models. These forecasts were more accurate than almost all of the polls, including those reported one day before the formal vote (Campbell, November 2016).[7]

The scholarly models essentially agree that elections are decided by conditions in place before the campaign. They use a variety of data, including presidential approval ratings, nomination primaries, different measurements of economic conditions months before Election Day, early polls, and the length of time that the incumbent party has held the White House. In 2016, nine of eleven major studies predicted Clinton's lead in the national popular vote. However, by neglecting the Electoral College and variations among the state votes, they generally failed to predict Trump's victory. One scholar did continue his perfect record of election predictions, using simpler evaluations of the historical setting (Lichtman 2016).

### *Campaign Effects*

Political professionals stress short-term influences. Their focus is particularly on events during the intense period of the campaign itself, the months between the national party conventions and Election Day.

Clinton herself is the most prominent example of this school of thought. In a conference call with major contributors, she blamed her defeat on Comey's late pre-election letters. By again raising the issue of her emails, Clinton said, that issue was revived to her detriment, halting her momentum toward victory. When Comey then closed the investigation only two days before the election, she argued, he inspired Trump voters to surge to the polls.

While we cannot recover the thought processes of the voters, this explanation has major flaws. Empirically, Clinton's lead was already eroding before Comey's intervention, and few poll respondents stated that it had influenced their votes. More fundamentally, it seems improbable that the FBI Director's brief announcements would change preferences shaped over a long campaign. More likely, the effect was not persuasion but rather reinforcement of choices that had been made already, and indeed already cast by many in early voting. It is still more doubtful that the second Comey letter, again dismissing Clinton of criminal liability, would increase Trump's turnout. Why would Clinton's detractors become energized by her vindication?

Some analyses of Clinton's defeat criticized other aspects of her campaign. With the advantage of flawless hindsight, Monday morning quarterbacks now know, for example, that she might have won by devoting more time and advertising in the last weeks to the upper Midwest. But, overall, Clinton ran a good—if inevitably imperfect—campaign. She targeted good combinations of states, raised far more money than her billionaire opponent, dominated television ads, ran a superior national convention, and triumphed in the critical presidential debates. All she lacked was votes.

### A Basket of Deplorables

Quite different is the interpretation by many Clintonites, who were not only disappointed, but depressed virtually to clinical levels by the Republican victory. Clinton had warned in the campaign that as many as half of Trump's acolytes could be put into "the basket of deplorables,"[8] using their votes to express malign hostilities toward women, immigrants, homosexuals, and ethnic minorities. As the returns came in, Democrats reiterated this damning explanation. The editor of the liberal *New Yorker* ably articulated the sentiment:

> The election of Donald Trump to the Presidency is nothing less than a tragedy for the American republic, a tragedy for the Constitution, and a triumph for the forces, at home and abroad, of nativism, authoritarianism, misogyny, and racism. Trump's shocking victory, his ascension to the Presidency, is a sickening event in the history of the United States and liberal democracy. On January 20, 2017, we will bid farewell to the first African-American President—a man of integrity, dignity, and generous spirit—and witness the inauguration of a con who did little to spurn endorsement by forces of xenophobia and white supremacy.
>
> *(Remnick 2016)*

American history certainly provides ample evidence of racism, misogyny, and hostility toward immigrant groups and gays—including slavery and segregation, disenfranchisement of women, the Know-Nothing party, and violence against homosexuals. Even today, hate groups have considerable support. The Trump campaign was not overtly based on such malignant appeals, but it was slow to reject backing from such groups as the Ku Klux Klan, and its rallies did include lewd disparagement of Clinton, encouragement of calls to "Lock her up," and enthusiastic calls to deport Mexican-Americans and restrict Moslems.

Racism and sexism did spur the Trump movement. Whites who denied the existence of racial inequality or who saw women as seeking to control men were considerably more likely to vote for Trump, as shown by Professor Brian Shaffner. But these attitudes were not the only influences. Economic insecurity also played a role: "Ultimately, the competing narratives about why Trump performed so well among whites are not competing at all; they are complementary" (Shaffner 2016).

Despite these expressions of truly un-American attitudes, it is difficult to believe that they were the controlling bases of Trump's victory. Large majorities of the electorate endorsed egalitarian positions, including citizenship for undocumented aliens and equal rights for women, blacks, and homosexuals. In actual voting, Americans have elected increasing numbers of minorities and women, including four new women senators in 2016, chose Barack Obama twice as President, and endorsed marriage equality for gays. Whatever may be hidden in white Americans' hearts, the nation has become more tolerant in its acts.

## *The Voters' Message*

The simplest explanation of the election is that the voters thought it was "time for a change," the typical electoral response after two presidential terms by one party. This sentiment was the most frequent call of the voters, gaining a plurality among choices offered in the national exit poll, with Trump winning six of every seven voters emphasizing this characteristic—the only one on which Trump was rated higher than Clinton, as detailed in Table 3.4.

This Trump vote can be seen as simple "retrospective voting," a common defense by political scientists of the "rationality" of the voters. Busy with their own lives and looking for obvious clues to the complexity of the world, according to this construct, voters can reasonably judge the results of government—keeping the incumbent party in power if they are satisfied, opting for the opposition when unhappy (Fiorina 1981; Popkin 1991). However, retrospective voting is not as simple as it may seem. In a striking and acrid challenge, two scholars warn that the theory "fails to do justice to the very considerable logical and informational difficulties"

**TABLE 3.4** Influences on the 2016 Presidential Vote

| Influences | % of Total | Vote Clinton % | Trump% | Contribution to Vote Clinton% | Trump% |
|---|---|---|---|---|---|
| *Issues* | | | | | |
| Economy | 52 | 52 | 42 | 14.4 | 10.9 |
| Foreign Policy | 13 | 60 | 34 | 4.1 | 2.2 |
| Immigration | 13 | 32 | 64 | 2.2 | 4.2 |
| Terrorism | 18 | 39 | 57 | 3.7 | 5.1 |
| *Traits* | | | | | |
| Bring needed change | 39 | 14 | 83 | 2.8 | 16.2 |
| Right experience | 21 | 90 | 8 | 9.6 | 0.8 |
| Good judgment | 20 | 66 | 26 | 7.2 | 2.6 |
| Cares about People | 15 | 58 | 35 | 4.7 | 2.6 |
| Total Vote % | | | | 48.7 | 44.7 |

*Notes*: Contribution to the vote calculated by multiplying percentage emphasizing the issue or trait (column 2) by percentage voting for the candidate (column 3 or 4). The calculations assume that the impact of the combined issues equaled that of the combined traits. The total effects on Clinton and Trump votes are imprecise. Other significant issues and traits were not included in the poll questions.

*Source*: Author's calculations using data from publicly reported national exit polls (*e.g.*, *Washington Post* and *The New York Times*).

and "may be no more sensible than kicking the dog after a hard day at work" (Achen and Bartels 2016, 92–93). The judgment of the electorate is often inarticulate, limited to the choices presented. As the authoritative V.O. Key put it:

> The voice of the people is but an echo. . . . no more than a selective reflection from among the alternatives and outlooks presented to them. . . . Even the most discriminating popular judgment can reflect only ambiguity, uncertainty, or even foolishness if those are the qualities of the input into the echo chamber. If the people can choose only from among rascals, they are certain to choose a rascal.
>
> *(Key 1966, 6–7)*

In 2016, the electoral message was certainly negative, but also inarticulate. Both candidates were seen unfavorably, as rascals for different reasons. Clinton detailed policy proposals, but her basic defense of the incumbent party was rejected. Trump was even less popular, and provided only vague and often contradictory pledges for the future. Trump's mandate was only for a flag salute, his empty hope to "make America great again."

Yet even that vacuity carried a message, one of anger, for some a desire to return to bygone America, for others to progress to a restored nation. That message was the source of the strong support won by Trump among white men of the working class, as detailed in the demographics of the vote. Inarticulate, it did convey a call first expressed forty years earlier in a classic film, *Network*: "You've got to say my life has value. Stop and yell, 'I'm mad as hell, and I'm not going to take that anymore.'" Neither Trump nor the film's fictional television anchor provided policy content, leaving that task to another day: "I don't know what to do. We'll figure out what to do later." But both the real and the imagined celebrities were effective in their protest.

Trump's appeal was not personal, nor his victory a specific policy mandate. By the middle of October, close to two-thirds of likely voters held unfavorable views of the Republican, thought he lacked the "personality and temperament to serve as president," and believed he "probably has made unwanted sexual advances on women" (Clement and Balz 2016). After the vote, he earned mediocre or failing grades from 70% of the nation for his conduct during the campaign (far worse than Clinton), the only election winner to lack majority approval (Pew Research Center 2016b).

Trump's appeal was a reaction to circumstances, not a personal endorsement, by

> a white working class whose economic interests and experience diverge fundamentally—in terms of culture, class, and history—from those of soccer moms in Bethesda, suburban independents in Fair Lawn, and wired cyberprofessionals in Silicon Valley. . . . The failure of activist government. . . has persuaded forgotten-majority voters that government is more a part of this values-experience disjunction than the solution to it. The direct and long-lasting result is the sour and skeptical attitude toward government that has become so common today.
>
> *(Rogers and Teixeira 2000)*

These voters heard Trump as the voice of their grievances, economic and social. Some regretted the loss of male and white dominance in a nation increasingly diverse and egalitarian. More broadly, their protest reflected economic changes that had brought severe class differences to the United States. The richest tenth of the population had held 35% of the total nation income; its lion's share was now half, a return to inequalities before the New Deal (Piketty 2014, 24, 294–296). Yearly income shows a similar decline. Since 2000, median real income of white males without college degrees declined 16%, more than wiping out gains for the previous quarter of a century (Bernstein 2016). The relative loss of income was paralleled by a loss of future opportunities, as the American dream of social mobility across generations faded. Once, the United States led the world in providing educational opportunities; now it provides less than almost every industrial country. Less than a third of Americans have a higher education level than their parents (Porter 2014). Class anger should be no surprise.

Trump was the willing beneficiary of these grievances. He blamed Obama and Clinton for the economic decline of the working class, directing his attacks to trade agreements and immigration. And his gains were augmented by the inattention of the Democrats. Unintentionally, the party had undermined its electoral base. From the election of Bill Clinton in 1992 to the defeat of Hillary Clinton in 2016, the white share of registered Democrats fell from 76% to 57%, the share of loyalists among persons without college education fell from 55% to 32%, and the share of those with a religious affiliation declined from 90% to 71% (Pew Research Center 2016a).[9]

The change in its base was evidenced by its campaign. The erstwhile "party of the working class" never used that phrase in its 2016 platform, instead focusing on the indeterminate "middle class." It similarly avoided reference to "labor unions," substituting the vaguer phrase "unions." "Whites" were cited only as relatively advantaged in comparison to racial minorities. More attention was given to the LGBT community: a total of twenty-two mentions, including eight for the small proportion of transgendered persons. The Democratic emphasis had shifted from economic class appeals to those based on multi-culturalism and group identity (Democratic Party Platform 2016). The shift was summarized in Clinton's campaign slogan, "Stronger Together." That motto invoked only a worthy inclusive process, not substantive content. Voters taught a hard electoral lesson: "If you are going to mention groups in America, you had better mention all of them. If you don't, those left out will notice and feel excluded" (Lilla 2016).

Each of these interpretations provides insight into the election results. Full interpretation requires years of analysis, but we are unlikely to find a single cause of Trump's unexpected triumph. Eventually, we will probably see the election of 2016 as a perfect political storm.

## Conclusion: The Future of the Republic

In remembering the election of 2016, we may gain more insight from a great analyst of politics, Shakespeare, and his revealing work on political ambition, *Julius Caesar*.

Donald Trump in 2016 resembled Caesar of ancient Rome. Both were indeed ambitious, both saw themselves as unique voices of the masses against a rotted establishment, and both succeeded in politics—Caesar briefly, Trump for few or many years. In their quests for power, they demonstrated similar qualities. Both promised to build walls to protect their land—Caesar against invaders from Gaul, Trump against aliens from Mexico. Both were deaf to warnings of the dangers in their actions and ambitions. Caesar mortally ignored cautions expressed by soothsayers; Trump triumphantly ignored modern warnings from pundits. Both were vain, boastful, and insisted on following their impulsive judgments. Caesar praised himself as steadfast: "I do know but one/That unassailable holds on his rank,/Unshaked by motion: and that I am he" (*Julius Caesar*, III.1.68–70). Trump saw himself as the unique creator of a better America: "I alone can fix it."

Both denigrated established political institutions—Caesar rejecting the advice of the Senate, Trump declaring he would eliminate a failed military and corrupt administrators. Each transformed his country's system of republican government. Caesar's death precipitated civil war and the rapid emergence of an oligarchy ruled by an authoritarian emperor. Trump has brought a transformation of the United States to a new regime based on manipulation of populist outrage.

The tragedy in Julius Caesar is not the death of Caesar. The basic tragedy is the end of the Roman republic itself; "the corruption of the people is the key to the mastery of Rome" (Bloom 2009, 100). Shakespeare condemns the docile citizens of Rome as "You blocks, you stones, and you worse than senseless things," (Julius Caesar, I.1.35) and reinforces his condemnation by dramatizing their rapid changes of opinion in response to Mark Antony's manipulative oratory. Trump would boast that his supporters would remain loyal even if he were to kill someone in public view on Fifth Avenue. This unthinking support is the danger that still exists, a greater and continuing threat to the American republic than the fearful tempest of Trump himself or the possible storms of the Trump presidency.

The election revealed major faults in the republican foundations of the United States. The citizens heard little reasonable debate on the nation's future. The quality of campaigning deteriorated to the level of schoolyard taunts, the choice reduced to "the untrusted against the unstable, the uninspiring against the unfit" (Gerson 2016). The lesson for future candidates will be that appeals to bigotry can work for some voters. The greatest danger to the nation is the scent of fascism in Trump's invocation of violence, his threats to prosecute Clinton and to widen libel laws against a critical press, his readiness to reject an electoral defeat, his personal arrogance.

In this troubled America, we might take solace in Abraham Lincoln's temperate view of the American public: "You can fool all the people some of the time, and some of the people all the time, but you cannot fool all the people all the time."

Maybe. But we might better rely on Benjamin Franklin's admonition to all generations as the Constitutional Convention ended. The Framers created a republic, he boasted, but "only if you can keep it." Will we?

## Notes

\* I dedicate this chapter to the memory of Marlene M. Pomper—wife and friend, editor and guide.
1 In violation of their oaths and political reality, seven faithless electors—two Republicans and five Democrats—cast their formal ballots for other candidates. We report only the record of the voters' true intentions.
2 Others did win election following an incumbent two-term President who himself came to office because of death. These included William Howard Taft after Theodore Roosevelt, Herbert Hoover after Calvin Coolidge, and Harry Truman after Franklin Roosevelt.
3 For further discussion of the Electoral College, see Best (1996).
4 This was reported by the Associated Press (Eric Tucker, Chad Day and Jack Gillum) in "US Report: Putin Ordered Attempt to Help Trump, Hurt Clinton." *The New York Times*. January 6, 2017. P.A1.
5 Compare the campaign of 2016 to an earlier presentation of standards for ideal campaign discussion: Kelley (1960, 12–16).
6 The most egregious "pants on fire" claims were 18% of Trump's and only 2% for Clinton. The remaining statements were rated as neither fully true nor false.
7 Thomas Edsell (2016) suggests that some Trump voters, for reasons of "social undesirability," hid their intended votes when responding to live telephone interviewers.
8 See www.cbsnews.com/news/hillary-clinton-half-donald-trump-supporters-basket-of-deplorables/.
9 In all of these comparisons, change was considerably greater in Democratic demographics than in the nation generally.

## Bibliography

Abramowitz, Alan. 2016. "Donald Trump, Partisan Polarization, and the 2016 Presidential Election." *Sabato's Crystal Ball*, June 30.
Achen, Christopher H. and Larry M. Bartels. 2016. *Democracy for Realists*. Princeton, NJ: Princeton University Press.
Balz, Dan and Emily Guskin. 2016. "In Every State, Pessimism About Trump, Clinton and the Impact of the Election." *washingtonpost.com*, September 7.
Beckman, Milo. 2016. "Religion and Education Explain the White Vote." *fivethirtyeight.com*, September 23.
Bernstein, Jared. 2016. "More on Real Earnings, Real Anger." *washingtonpost.com*, March 11.
Best, Judith A. 1996. *The Choice of the People?* Lanham, MD: Rowman & Littlefield.
Bialik, Carl. 2016. "No, Voter Turnout Wasn't Way Down From 2012." *fivethirtyeight.com*, November 15.
Blake, Aaron. 2016. "47 Percent of Clinton Backers Don't Have Any Close Friends Who Support Donald Trump." *washingtonpost.com*, August 3.
Bloom, Harold. 2009. *The Hero's Journey*. New York: Barnes & Noble.

Boehlert, Eric. 2016. "The Media's Final Email Flop." *mediamatters.org/blog/*, November 7.
Campbell, James E. 2016. "Forecasting the 2016 American National Elections" *PS: Political Science & Politics* 49:4. October. Pp. 649–690. https://doi.org/10.1017/S1049096516001591
———. 2016. "How Accurate Were the Political Science Forecasts of the 2016 Presidential Election?" *centerforpolitics.org/crystalball*, November 17.
Chayefsky, Paddy (screenplay) & Lumet, Sidney (director) (1976). *Network* [Motion Picture]. United States: Metro-Goldwyn-Mayer.
Cillizza, Chris. 2016. "One of Hillary Clinton's Top Aides Nailed Exactly Why She Lost."*washingtonpost.com*, November 14.
Clement, Scott and Dan Balz. 2016. "Washington Post-ABC News Poll." *washingtonpost.com*, October 16.
"Comparing Hillary Clinton, Donald Trump on the Truth-O-Meter." 2016. *politifact.com*, November 29.
"Democratic Party Platform." 2016. *demconvention.com*, July 21.
Edsell, Thomas. 2016. "How Many People Support Trump but Don't Want to Admit It?" *nytimes.com*, May 11.
"Election 2016: Exit Polls." 2016. *The New York Times*, November 9.
"Election Campaign Finance." 2016. *Washington Post*, October 28. www.washingtonpost.com/graphics/politics/2016-election/campaign-finance/
Enten, Harry. 2016. "Trump Probably Did Better With Latino Voters Than Romney Did." *fivethirtyeight.com*, November 18.
"Exit poll results from the National Election Pool." 2016. *washingtonpost*.com, November 29.
Fahrenthold, David. 2016. "Trump Recorded Having Extremely Lewd Conversation About Women in 2005." *Washington Post*, October 8. P. 1.
Federal Bureau of Investigation. 2016. "Statement by FBI Director James B. Comey." *fbi.gov*, July 5.
Fiorina, Morris. 1981. *Retrospective Voting in American National Elections*. New Haven, CT: Yale University Press.
Fox, Richard L. 2013. "The Gender Gap and the Election of 2012." In *Winning the Presidency 2012*, ed. William J. Crotty. Boulder, CO: Paradigm Publishers. Chap. 10.
Gerson, Michael. 2016. "Clinton vs. Trump." *washingtonpost.com*, July 30.
Graham, David. 2016. "Which Republicans Oppose Donald Trump? A Cheat Sheet." *theatlantic.com*, November 6.
Hamilton, Alexander. 2005. *The Federalist*, No. 68, in *The Federalist*, J.R. Pole. Cambridge, MA: Hackett Publishing Co.
Kelley, Stanley, Jr. 1960. *Political Campaigning: Problems in Creating an Informed Electorate*. Washington, DC: Brookings.
Key, V.O. Jr. 1966. *The Responsible Electorate*. Cambridge, MA: Harvard University Press.
Lee, Jasmine C. and Kevin Queally. 2016. "The 282 People, Places and Things Donald Trump Has Insulted on Twitter: A Complete List." *nytimes.com/politics*, October 23.
Leip, Dave. 2016. "Atlas of U.S. Presidential Elections," www.uselectionatlas.org/RESULTS/index.html; and "2016 General Election Turnout Rates," United States Election Project, www.electproject.org/2016g.

Leonhardt, David. 2016. "The Democrats' Real Turnout Problem." *New York Times*, November 20. P. SR3.
Lichtman, Allan J. 2016. Interviewed by Peter Stevenson, "The Fix." *washingtonpost.com*, November 9.
Lilla, Mark. 2016. "The End of Identity Liberalism." *New York Times*, November 20. P. SR1.
Malone, Clare. 2016. "Clinton Couldn't Win Over White Women." *fivethirtyeight.com*, November 9.
Palast, Greg. 2016. "The Election Was Stolen—Here's How." *gregpalast.com*, November 12.
Pew Research Center. 2016a. "The Parties on the Eve of the 2016 Election: Two Coalitions, Moving Further Apart." *people-press.org*, September 13.
———. 2016b. "Low Marks for Major Players in 2016 Election—Including the Winner." *people-press.org*, November 21.
Piketty, Thomas. 2014. *Capital in the 21st Century*. Cambridge, MA: Harvard University Press.
Politico staff. 2016. "Full Text: Donald Trump 2016 RNC Draft Speech Transcript." July 21. www.politico.com/story/2016/07/full-transcript-donald-trump-nomination-acceptance-speech-at-rnc-225974.
Popkin, Samuel L. 1991. *The Reasoning Voter*. Chicago: University of Chicago Press.
Porter, Eduardo. 2014. "A Simple Equation: More Education = More Income." *nytimes.com*, September 10.
Remnick, David. 2016. "An American Tragedy." *newyorker.com*, November 9.
Rogers, Joel and Ruy Teixeira. 2000. "America's Forgotten Majority." *theatlantic.com*, June.
Rutenberg, Jim. 2016. "The Editorialists Have Spoken. Will Voters Listen?" *nytimes.com*, October 5.
Sanchez, Gabriel. 2016. "Don't Believe Those Exit Polls Saying 25 Percent of Latinos Voted for Trump." *vox.com*, November 10.
Sanger, David E. and Maggie Haberman. 2016. "50 G.O.P. Officials Warn Donald Trump Would Put Nation's Security 'at Risk'." *nytimes.com*, August 8.
Shaffner, Brian. 2016. "White Support for Donald Trump Was Driven by Economic Anxiety, But Also by Racism and Sexism." *vox.com*, November 16.
Shakespeare, William. *Julius Caesar*.
Silver, Nate. 2016a. "What a Difference 2 Percentage Points Makes." *fivethirtyeight.com*, November 10.
Silver, Nate. 2016b. "Who will win the presidency?" *fivethirtyeight.com*, November 8.
"Transcript of the Third Debate." 2016. *New York Times*. October 20. www.nytimes.com/2016/10/20/us/politics/third-debate-transcript.html?_r=1
Vavreck, Lynn. 2016. "Candidates Fed a Focus on Character Over Policy." *The New York Times*, November 25. P. A20.

# 4

# EXPLAINING THE VOTE

*Charles L. Prysby*

*Finality is not the language of politics.*

— Benjamin Disraeli

It was probably the strangest presidential election in modern history. Both candidates were judged unfavorably by the electorate. Both candidates attacked each other's character in a relentlessly negative campaign. One candidate called his opponent a crooked liar and said that he would put her in jail if he were elected; the other candidate painted her opponent as a racist misogynist who boasted about assaulting women. The eventual winner was a wealthy businessman and celebrity who had never held any elected office; the loser had a lengthy political resume. Donald Trump prevailed even though many Republican leaders opposed him during the presidential primaries and were only lukewarm in their support after he won the nomination. Even more surprising, Trump triumphed in spite of a campaign in which he was widely criticized for making many insulting and outrageous comments, and Hillary Clinton lost despite clearly winning each of the three debates. Throughout the campaign, almost all of the pundits and political scientists predicted a Clinton victory, even right up to just before Election Day. Explaining the vote in this presidential election would seem to be a difficult task.

To best understand how and why people decided to vote for Clinton or Trump, we can begin by considering the major factors that influence the presidential vote decision. A very basic model of voting behavior views the vote as affected by both stable, or long-term, political orientations and election-specific, or short-term, attitudes (Lewis-Beck, Jacoby, Norpoth and Weisberg 2008, 22–28; Miller and Shanks 1996, 189–211). Party identification and ideology are the important stable orientations, stable in the sense that few voters change their party identification or ideology much from one year to the next. These two orientations, which are more strongly related to each other now than in the past, influence how voters perceive and interpret the political world, thereby influencing the vote (Campbell, Converse, Miller and Stokes 1960, 120–145; Green, Palmquist and Schickler 2002, 204–229). While party identification and ideology exercise great influence on the vote, in every election some Democrats and Republicans defect and vote for the candidate of the other party, due to the influence of election-specific attitudes on the vote. Moreover, independent voters are heavily influenced by these attitudes, which explains why their vote often shifts substantially from one presidential election to the next. Three major short-term attitudes shape voting behavior: (a) evaluations of government performance, particularly regarding the incumbent President; (b) attitudes on public policy issues; and (c) assessments of the personal characteristics of the candidates. These are attitudes that frequently differ greatly from one presidential election to the next and can shift significantly during the presidential election year. One useful way to understand the outcome of the 2016 presidential election is to analyze these orientations and determining whether either candidate had an advantage on any of these factors in 2016.

This analysis attempts to explain the popular vote, which Clinton won by a narrow margin: she received 48.1 percent of the total vote, Trump won 46.0 percent, and various minor party candidates together captured nearly 6 percent (*New York Times* 2016). Despite losing the popular vote by over 2.8 million votes, Trump easily won the Electoral College vote, with a total of 306 votes to Clinton's 232. The disparity between the popular and Electoral College vote was much greater in 2016 than it was in 2000, the other presidential election in recent history when the popular vote winner failed to win the Electoral College vote. In 2000, George W. Bush very narrowly lost the popular vote, 48.9 percent to 49.2 for Al Gore, and he won just 270 Electoral College votes—the bare minimum needed for a victory, and that was only after he prevailed in a hotly disputed recount in Florida. While an analysis of the Electoral College and its impact of presidential elections is an interesting topic, it is beyond the scope of this chapter. Explaining the popular vote in 2016 will be a sufficiently challenging topic for this study.

## Party Identification and Ideology

Party identification strongly influences voting behavior. This is especially true in the current era of highly partisan polarization. Ideology and party identification are more strongly aligned now than they were in the past.

Fewer liberal Republicans and conservative Democrats remain, and both sets of partisans are more ideologically consistent, making both parties more ideologically cohesive and more ideologically distinct from each other (Abramowitz 2010; Levendusky 2009). The result is greater party loyalty in voting, as both sets of partisans have increasingly negative views of the other party. Although about one-third of the voters label themselves as independents, most also indicate that they lean toward one of the two major parties, and these leaners are similar to weak partisans in both attitudes and voting behavior. True independents are more moderate and more persuadable, but they account for only about 10 percent of those who vote.

Clinton had a small advantage on party identification in 2016: 33 percent of registered voters identified themselves as Democrats and 29 percent called themselves Republicans, with the remainder mostly identifying as independents, but with a few saying other or none (Pew Research Center 2016a). Most of the independents leaned toward one party or the other, but even including independent leaners in with partisans still results in a 4-point advantage for Democrats, 48 percent to 44 percent. This was less than the 9-point advantage that Obama held in 2012. Of course, an advantage among registered voters does not necessarily translate into the same advantage among those who vote. In 2004, for example, Democrats held a 4-point advantage on party identification among all registered voters, but the exit polls that fall indicated that they had no advantage among those who voted in November (Prysby 2013, 117). A number of public opinion polls in 2016 showed that Trump supporters were more enthusiastic about their candidate than were Clinton supporters, and this led to speculation that Republicans would turn out to vote at a greater rate than Democrats (Washington Post 2016). However, the 2016 exit polls indicate that Democrats held the same 4-point advantage among those who voted as they held among all registered voters. Of course, it is possible that Democrats who liked Trump were more likely to vote than were other Democrats, but we cannot determine if this was the case with the data currently available.

The exit polls show that voting was very much along party lines: 88 percent of Republicans voted for Trump and 89 percent of Democrats for Clinton; independents went for Trump by 46 percent to 42 percent (National Election Pool 2016). The defection rates for Democrats and Republicans were slightly higher than they were in 2012, which is not surprising considering the unfavorable evaluations of both presidential candidates in 2016. The relatively high level of loyalty among Republicans was somewhat surprising because there were reasons to expect substantially more defections. For one thing, a number of prominent Republican officeholders did not support Trump. For example, GOP Senators Mark Kirk (IL), Kelly Ayotte (NH), Rob Portman (OH), and Lisa Murkowski (AK) all did not endorse their party's presidential candidate, and other Republicans were lukewarm in their support (Yourish, Pearce and Lee 2016). Also, many of the controversial statements made by Trump throughout the year seemed to bother even Republican voters. But in the end, Trump was able to win the vote of most Republicans, doing only slightly worse among Republicans than Mitt Romney did in 2012. His ability to hold nearly 90 percent of the Republican vote, which was critical to his victory, largely reflects the strength of party ties in an era of intense partisan polarization. Whatever reservations Republican voters may have had about their party's candidate, most viewed the Democratic candidate as worse. They saw Clinton as ideologically unacceptable and personally abhorrent. Democratic voters displayed a very similar pattern of attitudes toward Trump, which led to their strong vote for Clinton. Also essential to Trump's victory was his success among independent voters. This must be attributed primarily to short-term forces, not to party loyalty, so we now turn to these factors.

## Evaluations of Presidential Performance

Evaluations of presidential performance involve judgments of how well the President has achieved widely shared policy goals, such as peace and prosperity (Miller and Shanks 1996, 370–388). These evaluations should be distinguished from orientations on issues of public policy, which are questions of what the government should or should not do. How well the public evaluates the performance of the incumbent President strongly influences the election outcome. This is particularly true when the incumbent President is running for reelection, but even when this is not the case, the candidate of the President's party has a better chance of winning election when the incumbent President has a favorable approval rating. Two examples of recent Republican presidential candidates illustrate this effect: George H. W. Bush was elected in 1988 with the help of President Ronald Reagan's favorable rating at the end of his two terms in office, and John McCain failed to win election in 2008 partly because of President George W. Bush's unfavorable approval rating at the time.

In 2016, President Barack Obama had a positive and improving approval rating. Gallup poll results show his approval rating in the first quarter of 2016 to be about 50 percent, and that improved to 53 percent in late September and to 55 percent in late October before returning to 53 percent just prior to election day (Gallup 2016). No doubt the steadily improving economy played a role in these numbers. The recovery from the Great Recession of 2008–2009 began in 2010, and the economy continued to improve steadily, even if sometimes slowly, throughout the remainder of Obama's presidency. Unemployment fell from its high of around 10 percent to below 5 percent by the fall of 2016 (Sides, Tesler and Vavreck

2016). Jobs continued to be added during Obama's second term, and real income—which was slow to rise early in the recovery—began to increase at a greater rate. More importantly, people perceived an improving economy: consumer sentiment returned to its pre-recession levels (Sides, Tesler and Vavreck 2016).

Although Obama's favorable approval rating provided some advantage to Clinton, it may not have been the substantial advantage that she hoped for. Despite the 53 percent approval of Obama's performance as President, there was substantial overall dissatisfaction with the federal government: nearly one-half of the voters stated that they were dissatisfied with the federal government and about another one-quarter said that they were angry (National Election Pool 2016). Voters may not have blamed Obama for much of what was wrong with the government, but they still seemed to have wanted change in Washington, not a continuation of the existing situation. Clinton was not seen by many voters as a candidate who would provide that change. Trump, because he was an outsider who campaigned against the actions of both Democrats and Republicans in Washington, was viewed by many as someone who could. The exit poll data indicate that about 40 percent of the voters said that the ability to bring about change was the candidate quality that matter the most to them; of that group, over 80 percent voted for Trump (National Election Pool 2016).

It also is the case that it is difficult for one party to hold the White House for more than two consecutive terms. In the past 70 years, that feat has been accomplished just once, when Republican George H. W. Bush won in 1988 after serving as Reagan's Vice President for two terms, and Bush lasted just one term in office. One analysis of presidential elections indicates that a party can expect to receive about 4 percent less of the popular vote after two terms in the White House than it would receive after one term with the same state of the economy and level of presidential approval (Abramowitz 2016). Voters seem inclined to give an incumbent President a second term but reluctant to grant a party a third consecutive term in the White House.

## Orientations on Issues of Public Policy

Public policy issues did not dominate the campaign in 2016, even though the candidates differed greatly on most issues. For example, Trump promised to repeal Obamacare, while Clinton said that she would keep and improve it. Clinton's immigration proposal would have allowed most of those living in the U.S. illegally to stay, while Trump promised to deport large numbers of immigrants. Trump proposed large tax cuts that would disproportionately benefit upper income individuals; Clinton argued that the rich should pay more in taxes. Clinton wanted to continue the

Obama administration's environmental policies, but Trump claimed that climate change was just a Chinese hoax. Trump promised to drastically change existing trade deals; Clinton argued that more moderate changes were better. Clinton wanted stronger gun control legislation; Trump was against this. Clinton favored abortion rights; Trump opposed them. Thus, although Trump may not have been a traditional Republican conservative, he and Clinton disagreed on a wide range of issues (Clinton 2016; Trump 2016). Furthermore, supporters of both candidates frequently stated that they were attracted to their candidate because of some of these issues. Trump supporters often cited immigration and trade policies as reasons for their candidate preference, for example. Clinton supporters often emphasized their support of such things as abortion rights, a more liberal immigration policy, protecting Obamacare, and a more progressive tax policy.

While questions of the character of the candidates may have dominated the election campaign, policy issues surely had an effect on the vote. The question then is whether one candidate had an overall advantage on issues of public policy. That is a difficult question to answer. We cannot simply look at whether a majority of voters held Trump's position or Clinton's position. For one thing, different issues will be important to different voters. Thus, a voter who disagrees with a candidate on many issues may nevertheless decide to vote for that candidate because of the candidate's position on a few issues that are of great importance to that voter. One can imagine some voters supporting Trump largely because of his proposal to tear up existing trade deals and bring manufacturing jobs back to economically distressed areas. Similarly, some voters might have decided to support Clinton because of her liberal positions on social issues even though they might have disagreed with her on economic and other issues. Public opinion polls rarely measure intensity of opinion very well, so we can only speculate about this factor.

Another determinant of how issue orientations affect a voter is how the voter perceives the candidates on the issues, and considerable research indicates that voters often fail to see differences that exist or even incorrectly perceive where candidates stand on certain issues, which adds to the difficulty of determining whether one candidate had an advantage on policy issues in the eyes of the voters. In some cases public opinion polls ask respondents which candidate they prefer on an issue, rather than asking about where the respondent stands on the issue, and questions of this nature have the advantage of incorporating the voter's perception of where the candidate stands, whether that perception is right or wrong.

For those reasons, the available polling data do not provide a definitive picture of how voters evaluated the candidates on issues of public policy, but they do not suggest that Trump had any substantial advantage on this dimension. For example, the national exit poll asked voters whether the new President should continue Obama's policies, pursue more liberal ones, or pursue more conservative ones. About 48 percent wanted more conservative policies, while 45 percent preferred a continuation of Obama's policies or more liberal ones (National Election Pool 2016). If we assume that voters would have perceived Trump as the one who would have moved the current policies in a more conservative direction and Clinton as the one who would have done the opposite, then Trump had only a very slight advantage. A Gallup poll conducted in late October asked registered voters whether they agreed with each of the candidates on the issues that mattered the most to them; 45 percent said that they agreed with Clinton and 46 percent with Trump, which also shows the two candidates fairly even on issues in the eyes of the voters (Newport 2016). Other polling data show similar results regarding very general questions about which candidate was seen as better overall on the issues. This fairly even evaluations of the two candidates reflects the influence of party identification: Democrats were very likely to see Clinton as superior on issues, just as Republicans were prone to see Trump the same way.

While the above data suggest that the voters were evenly divided on which candidate was preferable on policy issues, questions about specific issues show an overall advantage for Clinton. Table 4.1 presents results from three pre-election polls, all of which asked voters which candidate they preferred on a number of specific issues. This wording has the advantage of taking into account how the voters perceived the candidates on the issues, but it can have the disadvantage of measuring the voter's perception of how capable a candidate is of handling a problem rather than how much the voter agrees with the candidate's policy position, especially when the poll asks about such general issues as handling of the economy or national security. Nevertheless, these polls provide another picture of whether one candidate had a significant advantage regarding public policy issues.

The first poll reported in Table 4.1, the Gallup poll conducted in mid-September, asked registered voters which candidate they preferred on a number of issues and found that Clinton led on slightly more issues and had an average advantage of 19 points on the issues she was favored on, compared to only a 7-point advantage for Trump on the issues he was favored on. Clinton's biggest advantages were on social issues (abortion, gay marriage), the treatment of minority groups, environmental issues, and education; in each case, her lead was over 25 points. Trump did best on several economic issues, including dealing with the federal budget deficit, regulating Wall Street, taxes, creating jobs, and dealing with the size and efficiency of the federal government, but his advantage on each of these issues was less than 10 points. The AP-GfK poll showed Clinton at least slightly better than Trump on each of the nine issues asked of respondents, and the Pew Research Center poll taken in late October also showed

**TABLE 4.1** Voter Evaluations of the Presidential Candidates on Public Policy Issues

| | Clinton | Trump |
|---|---|---|
| *Gallup Poll* (registered voters, Sept. 14–18) | | |
| Economy | 47 | 50 |
| Employment and jobs | 47 | 52 |
| Regulation of Wall Street and banks | 43 | 52 |
| Trade policy | 51 | 47 |
| Distribution of income and wealth | 50 | 44 |
| Taxes | 45 | 51 |
| Federal budget deficit | 44 | 53 |
| Size and efficiency of the federal government | 44 | 52 |
| Climate change | 62 | 29 |
| Health care and the Affordable Care Act | 56 | 41 |
| Education | 61 | 36 |
| Immigration | 55 | 42 |
| Treatment of minority groups | 65 | 30 |
| Social issues such as gay marriage and abortion | 63 | 33 |
| Gun policy | 45 | 52 |
| Terrorism and national security | 48 | 47 |
| *AP-GfK Poll* (likely voters, Oct. 20–24) | | |
| Economy | 42 | 36 |
| International trade | 42 | 34 |
| Creating jobs | 39 | 35 |
| Health care | 46 | 29 |
| Immigration | 43 | 35 |
| Race relations | 51 | 17 |
| Gun laws | 39 | 35 |
| National security | 42 | 33 |
| The threat from the Islamic State group | 38 | 34 |
| *Pew Research Poll* (registered voters, Oct. 20–25) | | |
| Economy | 46 | 47 |
| Trade policy | 49 | 46 |
| Health care | 55 | 40 |
| Immigration | 55 | 42 |
| Race relations | 62 | 30 |
| Crime | 43 | 48 |
| Gun policy | 48 | 47 |
| Terrorism | 49 | 47 |

*Note:* Entries are the percent of respondents who thought that the candidate would do a better job of handling the specified issue.

*Sources:* Author's composition from assessing data in Auter 2016; GfK Public Affairs 2016; Pew Research Center 2016b. "As Election Nears, Voters Divided Over Democracy and 'Respect'" (2016).

Clinton doing better than Trump overall: significantly more voters thought that Clinton would do better on dealing with health care, immigration, and race relations; the two candidates were rated about equally in dealing with the economy, trade policy, gun policy, and terrorism; and Trump was preferred when it came to dealing with crime.

Taken as a whole, the responses to questions about specific issues suggest a small advantage for Clinton, but this conclusion should be tempered by the qualifications mentioned previously. It could be, for example, that the voters who favored Trump on some of the issues felt extremely strongly about those policies, while the voters who favored Clinton on many issues were much less intense in their concern about those issues. There is some evidence that this may be the case. For example, the national exit poll asked voters which issue was the most important one facing the nation, and examining the vote by the responses to this question shows some interesting patterns. Only 13 percent identified immigration as the most important issue, but those who did voted 2:1 for Trump (National Election Pool 2016). The public opinion data cited in this section indicate that overall opinion on this issue was not in line with Trump's positions; in fact, the Pew data indicate that a majority of people favored Clinton on this issue. This suggests that the minority of voters who saw this as the key issue in the election were ones who favored Trump, and they probably were more strongly influenced by this issue than were the larger group of voters who favored Clinton on the issue but did not rate it as so important. Of course, this is just one issue. We would need more complete data on issue intensity to conclude that Trump benefitted overall from strong feelings on key issues among those who agreed with him on those issues. However, the fact that the very general questions about which candidate the voter preferred overall on issues show Trump even with Clinton indicates that this is a plausible interpretation.

## Assessments of Candidate Character Traits

Voters also consider the personal characteristics of the candidates. Research indicates that the most important character traits to most voters are leadership ability, competence, integrity, and empathy (Holian and Prysby 2015, 22–44). Leadership involves the candidate's ability to be decisive, lead, be in command, inspire, and accomplish goals. Competence refers to the candidate's experience, knowledge, intelligence, and dependability. Integrity denotes honesty, trustworthiness, sincerity, and morality. Empathy deals with whether the candidate is perceived to be compassionate and concerned about people, especially most people or "ordinary" people. It tends to be connected more to public policy preferences than do the other traits; candidates who rate high on empathy are ones who are seen as favoring policies that would help most people or the average person. Media pundits frequently argue that voters are drawn to warm and friendly candidates, and this might be considered to be a fifth trait dimension, but the research indicates that most voters are not particularly concerned with this trait (Holian and Prysby 2015, 29–43). Voters focus more on traits that are relevant to being a good President, such as being a strong leader or being trustworthy, and less on whether the candidate would be a good dinner companion.

Character traits received extensive attention in the 2016 presidential election. Even in the three presidential debates, many of the questions dealt more with the character of the candidates than with their proposed policies. Media coverage of Clinton and Trump focused heavily on their personal attributes, especially their personal shortcomings. Both candidates attacked each other's character throughout the campaign, and the voters assessed both candidates rather unfavorably in personal terms. Nevertheless, the data indicate that Clinton did better than Trump overall on the four character traits that have been important in past presidential elections. Table 4.2 presents data on voter assessments of these character traits from three pre-election polls plus the national exit poll, and these data show an overall advantage for Clinton.

Clinton's strongest trait, in the eyes of the voters, was competence. This is hardly surprising, since Clinton had served as Secretary of State and as a U.S. Senator, not to mention having been a very political First Lady for eight years, and she seemed well versed in public policy. In contrast, Trump had no political experience and often seemed ill informed about government policy during the campaign. In the national exit poll, 52 percent of the voters said that Clinton was qualified to be President, whereas only 38 percent said that about Trump. The pre-election polls reported in Table 4.2 show a similar pattern for this question. Indeed, the Pew Research and the AP-GfK polls both found a 30-point advantage for Clinton on this question, substantially greater than the advantage that she had in the exit poll.

Clinton's weakest area was integrity. Only around one-third of the electorate viewed her as honest and trustworthy. However, integrity was hardly a Trump strength. In the national exit poll, Trump was seen as slightly less honest and trustworthy than was Clinton. In the three pre-election polls reported in Table 4.2, Trump had a small advantage on honesty in two of them and a slight disadvantage in the third. Clinton's low marks on integrity can be attributed to several factors, including questions about her use of a private e-mail server while she was Secretary of State, concerns about the very large speaking fees that she received after resigning as Secretary of State, possible conflicts of interest between the Clinton Foundation and her public service, along with several issues that involve Bill Clinton when he was President in the 1990s. The sources of concern about Trump's integrity are less clearly identified, but they probably include questions about his business practices, particularly his use of bankruptcy laws to avoid paying his creditors, concerns about how little he may have paid in taxes, and feelings that he was insincere in many of his campaign promises.

**TABLE 4.2** Voter Assessments of the Presidential Candidates on Character Traits

| | Clinton | Trump |
|---|---|---|
| *Pew Research Poll* (registered voters, Oct. 20–25) | | |
| Strong leader | 52 | 46 |
| Inspiring | 42 | 35 |
| Not reckless | 55 | 29 |
| Well qualified to be president | 62 | 32 |
| Good judgment | 43 | 34 |
| Honest | 33 | 37 |
| Moral | 43 | 32 |
| *AP-GfK Poll* (likely voters, Oct. 20–24) | | |
| Decisive | 55 | 50 |
| Qualified | 58 | 28 |
| Honest | 32 | 30 |
| Not corrupt | 50 | 54 |
| Compassionate | 43 | 24 |
| *New York Times/CBS News Poll* (likely voters, Oct. 28-Nov. 1) | | |
| Would bring about real change | 36 | 50 |
| Would unite the country | 40 | 34 |
| Right temperament for being president | 58 | 33 |
| Qualified to be president | 56 | 43 |
| Honest and trustworthy | 34 | 40 |
| Understands needs and problems of people like yourself | 49 | 40 |
| *National Exit Poll* (actual voters, Nov. 8) | | |
| Right temperament to be president | 55 | 35 |
| Qualified to be president | 52 | 38 |
| Honest and trustworthy | 36 | 33 |

*Note*: Entries are the percent of respondents who had a favorable assessment of the candidate on the specified trait.

*Sources*: Author's composition from assessing data in Cohn 2016; GfK Public Affairs 2016; National Exit Pool 2016; Pew Research Center 2016b.

Also, there were allegations about his treatment of women, highlighted by a video recording that had him boasting about groping women, which was released late in the campaign and was the subject of questioning in the second debate. All of this raised serious questions about his morality in the minds of many voters, and the Pew Research poll data show his weakness in this aspect of integrity.

The two most important character traits to voters usually are leadership and empathy. Leadership is a character trait that Republican presidential candidates often do better on, but the available public opinion data do not show such an advantage for Trump. The Pew Research poll found that Clinton was viewed slightly better on being a strong leader and being inspiring, and the AP-GfK poll found that likely voters were somewhat more likely to see Clinton as decisive, all of which are aspects of leadership. Voters were particularly concerned about whether Trump had the right temperament for being President, as the data in Table 4.1 show; in fact, the Pew Research poll found that only 29 percent of the voters thought that Trump would not be reckless, compared to 55 percent for Clinton. However, the New York Times/CBS News poll found that Trump was viewed as significantly more likely to bring about change, and being able to accomplish things is one dimension of leadership. In sum, it seems that Clinton had an advantage on several aspects of leadership, but there were some aspects in which Trump may have been seen as better.

Empathy is a character trait that Democrats usually do better on than do Republicans. Every Democratic presidential candidate from 1980 on, when the American National Election Studies first began to include questions about character traits in their election year surveys, has been seen as the more empathetic candidate (Holian and Prysby 2015, 52–84). This is because Democrats traditionally have pushed for policies that provide benefits to ordinary citizens, such as Social Security, Medicare, a higher minimum wage, and, most recently, Obamacare. The same Democratic advantage on empathy is present in the 2016 data as well. On the question of being compassionate, Clinton had a sizable advantage in the AP-GfK poll, and the New York Times/CBS News poll found that more voters thought that she understood the needs and problems of people like themselves. Earlier pre-election polls, not reported in Table 4.1, also showed that Clinton was seen as more empathetic: an early October CNN poll found that Clinton had a 13-point advantage on the question of being in touch with the problems facing the middle class, and a Washington Post/ABC News poll in September had her with a 12-point advantage on understanding the problems of the people (Washington Post 2016). While Clinton appears to have the expected Democratic advantage on empathy, Trump may have been able to reduce the size of his disadvantage to something less than what a typical Republican would have. Perhaps his emphasis on bringing jobs back to economically distressed areas convinced a number of voters that he was concerned about their well-being.

## Conclusion: Adding It All Up

The data examined in this chapter indicate a clear advantage for Clinton. She had a 4-point advantage on party identification. President Obama's approval rating improved during the year to about 53 percent by the time of the election, and there was positive economic news that fall. On issues of public policy, Trump was at best even with Clinton and perhaps a little behind. Finally, Clinton held a clear advantage on candidate character traits, which dominated the campaign news and which many pundits thought would be critical to the decisions of the voters. Compared to Trump, Clinton was seen as considerably more experienced and knowledgeable, as more empathetic, as somewhat better on leadership, and about even on integrity. All of the above would seem to add up to a clear victory for Clinton. She did win the most votes, of course, but her 2-point popular vote victory is lower than what the data suggest should have been the outcome, and a stronger popular vote for Clinton quite likely would have produced an Electoral College victory.

A few reasons can be suggested for why Trump received more popular votes than the underlying attitudes examined here would predict. First, Trump won almost 90 percent of the vote of Republicans, which was just as good as Clinton did among Democrats. That probably reflects the strong combined influence of party identification and ideology in the current era of high partisan polarization. Whatever misgivings some Republicans may have had about Trump, they undoubtedly believed that he was more likely to pursue a conservative agenda than was Clinton, and since Republicans are largely conservatives, this was surely an important consideration. Media accounts after the election often focused on how Trump voters were different from those who supported Romney and other Republicans, but it is worth remembering than most of those who voted for Trump were Republicans who would have voted for almost any Republican candidate, especially against a Democrat like Clinton.

Republican votes were not enough for victory. Trump also needed a strong vote from independents and other persuadable voters. Among this set of voters, Trump did appeal to many who would not have voted for any Republican candidate, and he won enough of these voters in some key Midwestern states to give him the victory. One possible reason for Trump's ability to do this is that many voters found him very appealing because he was an outsider who railed against the system. A combination of strong distrust of the federal government combined with intense dissatisfaction with Washington politics may have made a candidate like Trump more successful in 2016 than would have been the case in previous presidential elections. While voters generally gave better marks to Clinton on character traits, they did see Trump as much more likely to bring about real change in Washington. Exactly what change voters were thinking of when they said that is unclear, but they may have felt that the intense partisan bickering, continued partisan gridlock, and increasingly hostile partisan tone made the federal government unable to deal with problems that they were concerned about. For many independent voters, a vote for Trump may have been a repudiation of the leadership of both parties and even of the system as a whole.

Added to or overlapping with the above reason is another likely contributing factor: the economic dissatisfaction that was expressed by many voters in the election, especially whites who were less educated. Although the economy continued to improve during Obama's second term, it was a modest rate of improvement that did not overcome problems that had been developing over a longer period of time. The decline in well-paying blue-collar jobs and the growing income inequality in the country left many Americans feeling that they did not have a bright economic future and that their children would not be as well off as they had been. Trump's focus on trade policies as a fundamental source of these economic problems appeared to resonate in many areas of the country where manufacturing jobs had been lost. The fact that a similar argument was made on the Democratic side by Bernie Sanders in his campaign for the nomination, and that it was applauded by many Democratic voters, surely made Trump's argument more credible in the general election.

Finally, one set of responses from the national exit poll seems insightful. Asked whether they had a favorable or unfavorable opinion of each candidate, 44 percent indicated they had a favorable opinion of Clinton, compared to 38 percent for Trump. Thus, Clinton had a 6-point advantage on this question, which presumably measures the voter's attitudes toward both the character traits and the policy positions of the candidate, yet she had only a 2-point advantage in the popular vote. When we examine how people voted by how they responded to this question, we find an interesting pattern. Nearly all of the 41 percent who saw only Clinton as favorable voted for her, and the same was true of the 36 percent who felt that way toward Trump. However, the 18 percent who saw both candidates as unfavorable were not divided evenly; had they been, Clinton would have done better in the popular vote. Instead, they broke heavily for Trump, 49 percent to 29 percent, with the remainder voting for another candidate. We can only speculate about why they did that, but it seems plausible that many of these voters were ones who deeply dissatisfied with whole system, and when faced with two candidates that they did not like, they were willing to vote for the one who promised to drastically change things.

The 2016 presidential election was one in which the factors that affect voters did not play out in quite the same way that they have played out in previous elections. In 2012, for example, the factors examined in this study accurately pointed to an Obama victory (Prysby 2013). This year, they indicated a bigger popular vote for Clinton than she received. Strong desires for change in the political system appeared to have carried Trump to victory in spite of his disadvantages on a number of factors. Interestingly, those winds of change were not blowing so hard in 2012 even though many of the underlying sources, such as partisan polarization or economic problems, were present then. This study has gone as far as it can with the data available at this point in time, but when other data—such as the American National Election Studies survey—become available, we should be able to better explain the interesting dynamics of voting behavior in 2016 and determine if the speculations put forth at the end of this study are an accurate explanation of the outcome of the election.

## Bibliography

Abramowitz, Alan I. 2010. *The Disappearing Center*. New Haven, CT: Yale University Press.
———. 2016. "Will Time for Change Mean Time for Trump?" *PS: Political Science & Politics* 49. October. Pp. 659–660.
Auter, Zack. 2016. "Voters Prefer Trump on Economy, Clinton on Most Other Issues." Gallup, Sept. 26. http://www.gallup.com/poll/195809/voters-prefer-trump-economy-clinton-issues.aspx?version=print.
Campbell, Angus, Philip E. Converse, Warren E. Miller and Donald E. Stokes. 1960. *The American Voter*. New York: John Wiley & Sons.
Clinton, Hillary. 2016. "Hillary Clinton on the Issues." Hillary for America. Web site of the Clinton Presidential Campaign. www.hillaryclinton.com/issues.
Cohn, Nate. 2016. "Polling Still Shows Hillary Clinton with a Lead, but not a Safe One." New York Times, Nov. 4. http://www.nytimes.com/2016/11/05/upshot/polling-still-shows-hillary-clinton-with-a-lead-but-not-a-safe-one.html.
Gallup. 2016. "Presidential Job Approval Center." www.gallup.com/poll/124922/Presidential-Job-Approval-Center.aspx.
GfK Public Affairs. 2016. The AP-GfK Poll, October. http://ap-gfkpoll.com/poll-archives.
Green, Donald, Bradley Palmquist and Eric Schickler. 2002. *Partisan Hearts and Minds*. New Haven, CT: Yale University Press.
Holian, David B. and Charles L. Prysby. 2015. *Candidate Character Traits in Presidential Elections*. New York: Routledge.
Levendusky, Matthew. 2009. *The Partisan Sort*. Chicago: University of Chicago Press.
Lewis-Beck, Michael S., William G. Jacoby, Helmut Norpoth and Herbert F. Weisberg. 2008. *The American Voter Revisited*. Ann Arbor, MI: University of Michigan Press.
Miller, Warren E. and J. Merrill Shanks. 1996. *The New American Voter*. Cambridge, MA: Harvard University Press.
National Election Pool. 2016. National Exit Poll. Conducted by Edison Research. www.cnn-con/elections/results/exit-polls.
Newport, Frank. 2016. "Clinton Holds Clear Edge on Having Presidential Qualities." *Gallup*. www.gallup.com/poll/196952/clinton-holds-clear-edge-having-presidential-qualities.aspx.
New York Times. 2016. Election 2016: Presidential Election Results. www.nytimes.com/elections/results/president.
Pew Research Center. 2016a. "2016 Party Identification Detailed Tables." Pew Research Center. http://www.people-press.org/2016/09/13/2016-party-identification-detailed-tables.

Pew Research Center. 2016b. "As Election Nears, Voters Divided Over Democracy and 'Respect'." October 27. http://www.people-press-org/2016/10/27/as-election-nears-voters-divided-over-democracy-and-respect/.

Prysby, Charles. 2013. "Explaining the Presidential Vote." In *Winning the Presidency 2012*, ed. William J. Crotty. Boulder, CO: Paradigm Publishers.

Sides, John, Michael Tesler and Lynn Vavreck. 2016. "The Electoral Landscape of 2016." *Annals* 667. September. Pp. 50–71.

Trump, Donald. 2016. "Policies." Make America Great Again. Web site of the Trump Presidential Campaign. www.donaldjtrump.com/policies.

*Washington Post.* 2016. Washington Post-ABC News National Poll, conducted September 5–8. www.washingtonpost.com/wp-stat/polls/postpollarchive.html.

Yourish, Karen, Adam Pearce and Jasmine Lee. 2016. "Where Republicans in Competitive Races Stand on Trump." *New York Times*, October 11.

# 5

# THE RACES FOR CONGRESS IN 2016

## A Tale of Two Elections

*Paul S. Herrnson and Raymond J. La Raja**

> *The more things change, the more they stay the same.*
> — Jean-Baptiste Alphonse Karr

The conventional wisdom at the onset of the 2016 election season was that it would be a year when the Democrats won seats in Congress and former Secretary of State Hillary Clinton would run a formidable presidential campaign against Jeb Bush, Marco Rubio or some other mainstream Republican. However, Bernie Sanders's aggressive challenge to Clinton for the Democratic presidential nomination and Donald Trump's unstoppable drive in the Republican contest and outlandish general election campaign put to rest these expectations. The early narratives for 2016 were that voters would choose between continuity and change and there were strong odds a woman would finally break the nation's highest political glass ceiling. The storyline featured Clinton at the top of the Democratic ticket against one of a number prominent Republican politicians. As the presidential campaign unfolded, the narrative broadened to include the "year of the outsider" to accommodate Trump's unlikely emergence as the frontrunner in the Republican primaries and the GOP nominee.

Politicians and political consultants in congressional elections struggled to adapt to the new scenario. In addition to questions about how many seats the Democrats could be expected to pick up in the House and the possibility of their winning control of the Senate, a host of new possibilities came into focus. Would Clinton's early challenges in the primaries reverberate down the ballot, undercutting the aspirations of other female candidates and their supporters? Would Trump's sudden rise to prominence have an alternative effect, fueling the candidacies and campaigns of political outsiders and their anti-Washington allies? Would the pro-Democratic national tide anticipated prior to Trump's and Clinton's nominations come to fruition, or would Clinton's projected coattails diminish as a result of the populist frenzy that bore similarities to the Tea party movement that captured the national stage in 2009?

In the course of addressing these questions, this chapter places the 2016 congressional elections in a broad context by describing the issues and concerns voters considered paramount and the effects of the presidential campaign on the national political conversation. It then turns to the impact of this context on the candidacy decisions of those who ran for the House and Senate and the responses of the Washington elites and other donors who participated in campaign financing. Next are a discussion of the strategies the candidates used to appeal to voters and an analysis of the primary and general election outcomes. Relying on evidence from the congressional races, we conclude that 2016 was a tale of two elections, particularly with respect to women and outsider candidates. While partisan loyalties drove much of the election results in both the presidential and congressional races, the relatively weak connection between the candidacies and campaigns have implications for the relationship between members of the Trump administration and Congress, political reform, and other aspects of policymaking.

## Two Types of Elections

There are two overarching types of congressional elections. The first, sometimes referred to as a "status quo," or "localized" election, is characterized by contests that focus primarily on the abilities, experiences, and public service records of the candidates and on issues of major concern to local voters. Because of the many advantages they enjoy over challengers, an overwhelming number of incumbents who seek reelection in status quo election cycles win.

The second type of election cycle, often referred to as a "nationalized" or "tidal wave" election, is one in which national political, economic, or social forces create an environment that strongly favors one party—usually the party out of power—and results in a sea change in the partisan composition of Congress and other elective institutions. An election that is nationalized in one party's favor leads to greater enthusiasm and participation by that party's contributors, activists, and electoral base, thereby increasing the support that party and its candidates are able to attract. It also increases the level of support congressional and other candidates receive from the independent or swing voters whose backing is often the key to victory in marginal districts.

The ability to campaign on the same, or very similar, issues greatly benefits candidates who belong to the favored party in a nationalized election. When local and national issues dovetail, candidates whose communications are consistent with those of their party and its interest group and media allies find it easier to break through the cacophony of voices heard in competitive elections. This is especially beneficial to congressional challengers, who are at a disadvantage in getting their message heard by voters. Nationalized elections result in virtually all of the favored party's incumbents successfully defending their seats, an unusually large number of its challengers getting elected, and the success of most of its open-seat candidates.

## Run Up to the Election

Conflicting dynamics made it more difficult than usual to assess what kind of election this would be. On the one hand, ongoing concerns associated with the economy, immigration, fear of terrorism and other seemingly intractable issues resulted in voter frustration with national politicians. Much of this hostility was directed toward Congress, which plausibly makes voters want to "throw the bums out." This scenario might have led to heavy losses for the Republican majority. Given the large number of Senate seats being defended by Republicans in states with close presidential contests in 2012, it seemed entirely plausible. In the House, Democrats faced longer odds to take a majority, needing to win 30 seats. Most prognosticators believed it would take a tidal wave to bring in that many Democratic House members, especially given the lopsided partisanship in many districts (Harwood 2016).

On the other hand, the President was a Democrat, which makes it less likely the voters will blame just one party. Obama's popularity was contingent on partisan identity of voters: Republican partisans and independents who lean toward the GOP disliked him, while Democrats and independents predisposed toward their party were highly supportive. Neither party's congressional candidates could rely on the divided popularity of the President to help them in closely contested districts where the partisan balance among voters was close. The environment provided few opportunities for these candidates to claim credit or assign blame for the federal government's performance or the state of the nation.

More critically for congressional candidates in close elections was how they positioned themselves vis-à-vis the presidential candidates. Trump was clearly a provocative candidate. Several of his stances on trade, immigration, and social security were the antitheses of positions long held by the mainstream of the Republican party. He also ignited controversies with his statements about preventing Muslims from entering the country, calling Mexican immigrants rapists, and belittling the parents of a fallen war hero. Most dramatically, he was caught on a 2005 videotape bragging about groping women. Such behavior is typically outside the norms for major party nominees and created a dilemma for GOP congressional candidates on whether to endorse or run away from him. Many Republicans in close races did not want to anger staunch GOP voters by shunning Trump, but also wanted to hold vital swing voters who disapproved of Trump's behavior. Most danced around the subject by trying to obscure how much or how little they supported him.

Most—but not all—Democratic candidates allied themselves closely with Clinton. They were hopeful that Trump's candidacy would be a catastrophe for the GOP that would keep Republican voters from the polls and win over independents for Clinton. A large Clinton victory offered the prospect of a nationalized election with candidates riding into office on Clinton's coattails. There was considerable mention in the mainstream media about a landslide election in the Electoral College in favor of the Democrats. As late as mid-October, there were even hopes that a 10-percentage point Clinton victory—which was not out of the question at the time—would enable the Democrats to win back control of the House (Harwood 2016).

## The Strategic Context

Candidates, consultants, party officials and interest group strategists assess the political environment, including the circumstances in each district and the national dynamics. At the local level, important considerations include the intentions of the incumbent and other potential candidates, and the partisan history of the seat. Relevant national-level factors include whether it is a presidential or midterm election year, the state of the economy, the President's popularity, international affairs, and the public's current attitudes toward the federal government.

In the United States, candidates assume most of responsibility for running their campaigns. While party labels matter, candidates cannot rely entirely on the party or its top standard-bearers to help them win. Political parties and interest groups play important roles in elections, but they have traditionally remained in the background, providing funds, strategic advice, issue and opposition research, targeting data, voter mobilizing drives, and assistance with fundraising and navigating the world inhabited by campaign consultants. Increasingly, parties and groups have spent huge sums on "independent ads" to help favored candidates, and in some of the most competitive races these organizations outspend the candidate committees. Nonetheless, the norm remains that candidates are the focal point of campaigns and they are expected to sustain and manage a personal campaign committee to get elected. This arrangement puts a lot of pressure on getting resources and coming up with a strategic message.

Another key aspect of congressional elections is the significant advantages that accrue to incumbents. Officeholders are very hard to unseat. First, they typically possess a favorable share of partisan voters in their districts, making it difficult for challengers from another party to unseat them. Second, being a member provides perks of office that allow them to bring resources to the district and advertise through mailings to constituents. Third, and related, members frequently showcase themselves throughout the year by appearing at local events and getting good attention from local media, which is typically very friendly to them. Fourth, as powerful officeholders it is easier for them to raise money from Washington PACs. All of these advantages create the expectation that they are formidable to beat, which makes it less likely that strong challengers will emerge to challenge them (Jacobson and Kernell 1981; Stone, Maisel and Maestas 2004). For this reason more than 90 percent of House incumbents and 80 percent or more of Senate running for reelection typically win. In 2016, this figure for the House was 97 percent, which was slightly higher than in 2014 when it was 95 percent. In the Senate, 90 percent of incumbents were reelected in 2016 compared to 82 percent in 2014 (Center for Responsive Politics 2016c).

Potential candidates also assess public opinion. They know that citizen attitudes about the direction of country and economy all play a role in shaping voter decisions at the ballot box. To the degree that people are dissatisfied they are likely to blame the incumbent party, particularly the party of the President. The public was very discontented with the way things were going in the nation. According to Gallup, just 29 percent of Americans said they were satisfied in September 2016.[1] Public dissatisfaction has been in decline since 2002 and reached as low as 10 percent during the years 2009–2010 after the Great Recession. Since then, it stabilized at a higher level through the Obama years, although it remains relative low compared to the late 1980s and late 1990s (both periods when the economy was doing well). Going into the 2016 election, public opinion was difficult to read for prospective candidates. Satisfaction in the direction of the country was relatively low, but the economy had been improving steadily. These two factors seemed at odds in contemplating which party would be favored.

Related but somewhat distinct, is public opinion about the President. High approval tends to benefit congressional candidates of the President's party and low ratings typically have the opposite effect. Obama's approval had been rising toward the close of his presidency. He remained very popular among members of his own party and moderately popular among independents, but intensely unpopular among Republicans. On balance, this should have been a slight benefit to Democratic candidates, or at least provided some neutral turf upon which to wage an election. On the other hand, an election in which voters appear to want change could spell problems for the incumbent party in the White House—especially for a candidate, like Clinton, who was trying to win a third consecutive term for the Democrats. She framed her governing agenda as a continuation of the Obama presidency. Based on exit polls of voters, it appears that Clinton was not able to generate the same enthusiasm for her campaign as the previous Obama campaigns. The resulting depressed turnout of the Democratic coalition precluded a "wave election" even though she won the popular vote.

Finally, there is the potential impact of the presidential campaign. Clinton had the challenge of winning a third consecutive term for the Democrats, a situation in which opposition party and independent voters are usually more enthusiastic for their candidate than those in support of the incumbent party. The first sign of dampened excitement for Clinton was her struggle to gain the votes of younger generation of voters compared to her chief rival in the Democratic nomination, Bernie Sanders, the independent socialist Senator from Vermont. However, larger concerns loomed within the Republican party. Trump's popularity among the primary electorate relative to more mainstream Republicans was fostered by a deep unhappiness with the status quo and political elites similar to that which gave rise to the Tea party. The success of his populist message suggested that outsiders in congressional campaigns might do well. Traditional Republican elites, however, had concerns about his fitness for office, given his lack of political experience and his controversial remarks about immigrants, Muslims, and women. Indeed, many fellow Republicans running for Congress feared a backlash against their candidacies. This threat seemed so real that many tried to distance themselves from him during the campaign or at least keep him at arm's length.

In sum, the strategic context for the 2016 congressional elections was composed of a mix of variables that made many outcomes uncertain. Despite the structural advantages for incumbents, the presidential primaries suggested a groundswell of support for outsiders like the GOP nominee Trump and Democratic primary contender Bernie Sanders. These dynamics indicated a strong dissatisfaction with the status quo, which could generate energy against incumbents. The situation was particularly fraught for the GOP because many of their voters appeared energized for change after two terms with President Obama, but the nomination of Trump potentially undercut this advantage because he seemed so unpredictable.

## Candidate Emergence

Experienced politicians focus on the immediate circumstances in their districts when contemplating a candidacy. Quality challengers also give some consideration to the national mood, particularly if they believe that dissatisfaction with the status quo or the government's performance will be an advantage for their party. Such sentiments give challengers who have previously held office and unelected politicians—those who previously ran for Congress, served as a party official, held an appointed position in government, or had some other significant political experience a better chance to win. They may even create opportunities for some political amateurs (candidates with limited political experience) to win.

As is the case in most presidential election cycles, the race for the White House had the potential to drown out the political discussion in individual congressional elections. Trump ran on the theme that it was "time for change," while Clinton's message emphasized "staying the course." Reputable prediction models—focusing on the state of the economy, presidential popularity and the number of years an incumbent party held the White House—gave a slight advantage of winning to the Republicans (Abramowitz 2016). But Trump was not a typical candidate, which created greater uncertainty with these models. He had no elective office experience and ran a brash and controversial campaign that highlighted strongly populist themes. Given the mood that propelled Trump through the nominations one might think being an outsider also would helpful to congressional candidates.

At the same time, female potential candidates may have also been inspired to jump in the race because it was clear for a long time that Clinton would be running. Women previously had run for a major-party nomination. What made 2016 different than 2008, when Clinton was defeated by Obama—and 1972 when New York Democratic Congresswoman Shirley Chisholm became the first African-American woman to run for the Democratic nomination, and 1964 when Senator Margaret Chase Smith of Maine sought to lead the Republicans—was that it was common knowledge among most political insiders, journalists, and Americans who follow politics that Clinton and her allies had all but cleared the field of her strongest known opponents. Many political insiders believed this could be the year for Clinton to shatter the political glass ceiling, and her candidacy could inspire the candidacies and victories of other women.

Nevertheless, data recording the background characteristics of congressional candidates demonstrate that the 2016 election was fairly typical in terms of the numbers of outsiders who ran for the House and Senate and the outcomes of their elections. The story begins before the congressional primaries, when incumbents decided whether to run for reelection or leave office. Fifty-one members retired or ran for another office, and four resigned The next stage involved nonincumbents' declarations of candidacy for a party nomination. There was little to no departure from previous primary elections. As Figure 5.1 shows, there was a slight surge in the number of outsider or "amateur" candidates, meaning those who lacked

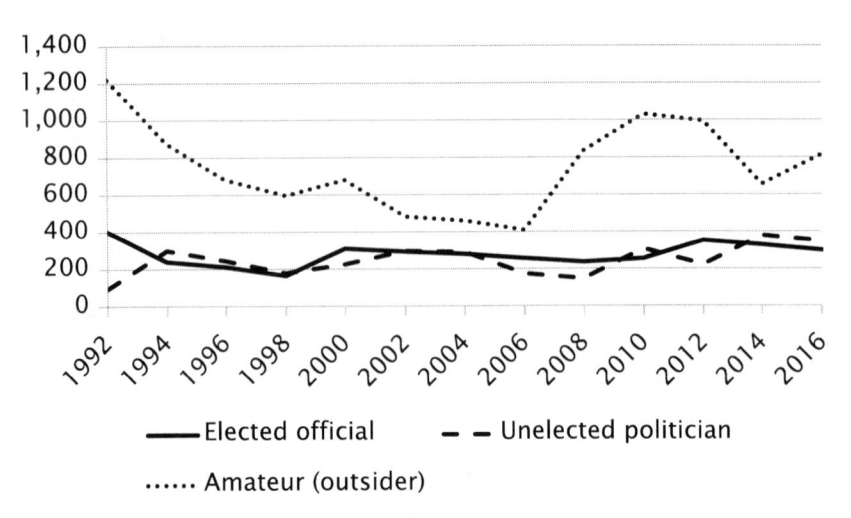

**FIGURE 5.1** House Candidates: Outsiders

*Source:* Data compiled by the author from candidates' web sites, other public sources, and Herrnson (2016).

significant political experience. The 814 outsiders who ran in 2016 reflects an increase over 2014 of 655, but many fewer amateurs ran in 2016 than in the 2008, 2010, and 2012 elections—which were associated with the rise of the Tea party—or the surges of 1992 and 1994, which preceded and led to the Republican takeover of Congress. None of this was out of the ordinary. At the same time the number of unelected politicians—i.e. those with some form of political experience—declined very slightly from 379 in 2014 to 348 in 2016, which was not much different from previous years.

Figure 5.2 shows a continuation of the trend of modest growth in the number of women House candidates. A total of 315 women ran in 2016, compared to 250 in 2014. However, the pool of female candidates was nothing out of the ordinary, especially when compared to that of their male counterparts, who in 2016 outnumbered the women by 5:1, which is a similar ratio as 2014.

What can we make of the figures for outsider House candidates? As is usually the case, most potential and actual candidates decided whether to run after contemplating whether local voters might embrace the causes they sought to champion, giving some thought to the likely competition, and pondering the effects of the race on their families (Canon 1993). Their decision-making may not have been as systematic or strategic as that of politicians with significant elected or unelected political experience, but it had in common with them a strong local focus (Maisel and Stone 1997). The national conditions leading to Trump's ascendance in the Republican

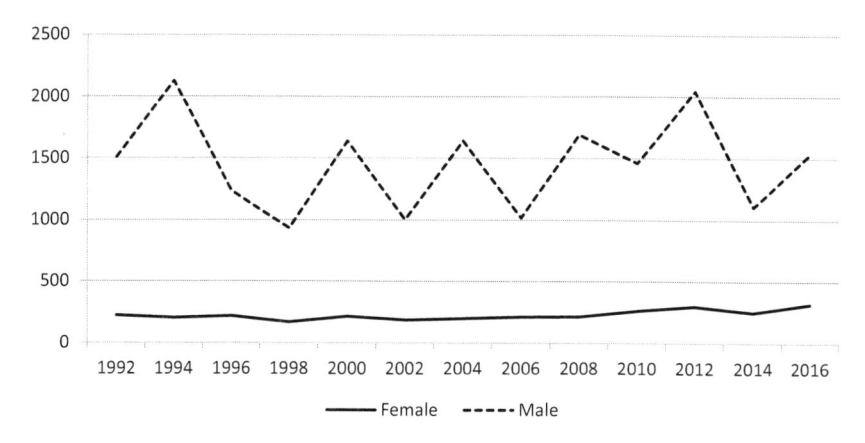

**FIGURE 5.2** House Candidates: Women

*Source:* Data compiled by the author from Center for American Women and Politics (2016); candidates' web sites; and other public sources.

presidential primaries appear to have done little to boost the number of outsider candidates. Trump's candidacy itself also does not appear to have inspired more outsiders to run than usual.

Similarly, women who had some interest in running for the House appear to have been reading different tea leaves than Clinton. Her decision, like that she made in 2008, was influenced by national factors and the product of many years of planning. Would-be female House candidates responded to opportunities that would be recognizable in conversations at local coffee houses rather than conference rooms in the nation's capital. Many undoubtedly found Clinton's 2008 and 2016 presidential candidacies inspirational, but then they weighted factors closer to home when considering their own possible bids for office rather than follow the lead of a political icon.

## The Campaign for Resources

Candidates for most offices must organize their own campaigns to have any chance of victory. The first campaign—the campaign for votes—is a very public campaign designed to win votes. The second campaign—the campaign for money and the other the resources needed to wage run a competitive campaign for votes—occurs early, and largely behind the scenes. Most congressional incumbents begin raising funds shortly after the previous election. Their objective is each to amass a war chest large enough to ward off or defeat a challenger. They devote long hours to fundraising, unless it becomes obvious they will face a strong challenger in neither the primary nor the general election. At that point, many scale back their fundraising efforts. Some continue to raise funds that they redistribute to congressional colleagues locked in close races or party committees that also participate in the redistribution of wealth (Herrnson 2016).

Most congressional challengers and open-seat candidates begin fundraising later than incumbents, in large part, because they first need to choose whether or not to run for office and, as previously noted, more time and effort usually goes into assessing that option than an incumbent's decision to run for reelection. Raising significant dollars early in the campaign season is important to a nonincumbent's election prospects. A good start demonstrating political viability enables candidates to begin to hire campaign staff, reach out to potential supporters, attract media coverage, and raise their political profile among potential supporters. This process repeats itself, wherein early success in the money race leads to hiring more campaign staff and consultants, more media coverage and recognition as a strong candidate, and the ability to collect more money. With rare exceptions, a successful campaign for resources is an essential component to a successful campaign for votes (Herrnson 2016).

Importantly, the campaign for resources extends beyond campaign contributions. It also is intended to attract endorsements and the independent efforts of party committees and interest groups. Much of it is now spent independently both by party committees, and allied groups. Decisions by the federal courts in 2010 paved the way for more outside spending in congressional elections.[2] Candidates, of course, would prefer to control as much money within their own committees, rather than rely on outside spending, with which they cannot legally coordinate. In 2016, the Wesleyan Media Project estimated that $276.6 million was spent in House elections and $593.3 million in Senate elections on broadcast television, national network and national cable (Wesleyan Media Project 2016). A significant portion of these ads were sponsored by independent groups affiliated with the congressional parties, or interest groups such as the Chamber of Commerce or Freedom Partners Action Fund, which is an ideological arm of the industrialists Charles and David Koch.

Because of these outside groups, political spending in House races has elevated since 2008 (pre-Citizens United[3]). As Figure 5.3 shows, congressional spending has been close to the $4 billion mark since 2010 according to the Center for Responsive Politics. In 2016, campaign spending appears to be at a record level, outpacing 2014 by almost 9 percent (controlling for inflation).

Campaign money—especially independent spending—is concentrated in the tightest races. Indeed, in such races outside spending often exceeds the amount that candidates spend. Table 5.1 shows, for example that in the top 10 spending races for the U.S. House, outside groups outstrips the amounts spent by candidates in eight of those races. In Nevada's District 3, independent groups spent $15.8 million—against the sum of $3.6 million

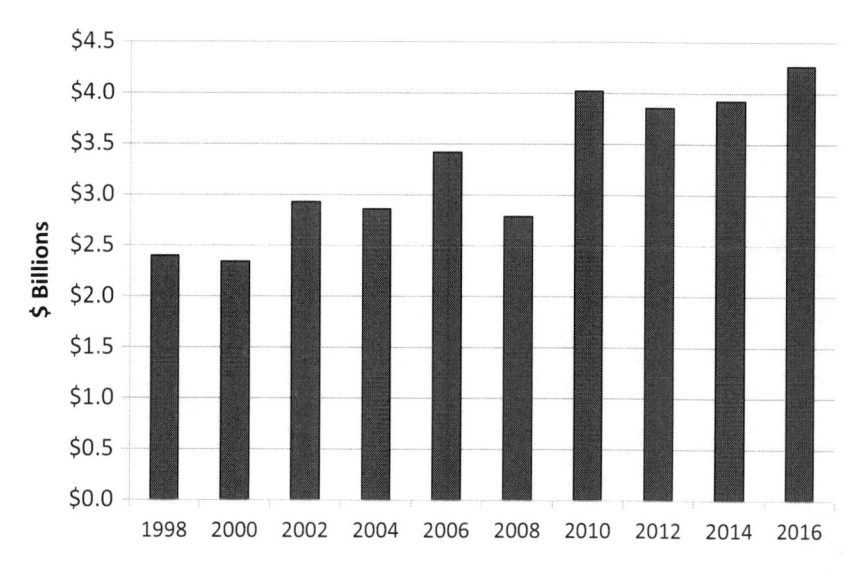

**FIGURE 5.3** Spending in Congressional Races
*Source:* Center for Responsive Politics (2016a).
*Note:* All dollar amounts adjusted for inflation.

for both candidates—which reflects 80 percent of spending in the contest. On the Senate side, the contest in Pennsylvania outpaced spending in all races with a whopping $162.2 million, of which $121 million was independent spending. While party committees played a large role here so did partisan interest groups such as Freedom Partners Action Fund ($7.2 billion) and the U.S. Chamber of Commerce ($6.1 million), both in support of the Republican incumbent Patrick Toomey in his race against Democratic challenger Katie McGinty.

Returning to the question of whether 2016 was the year of the outsider or the year of the woman, pre-election fundraising patterns suggests it was not.[4] Regarding outsiders running for the House, the level of money raised by amateurs appeared no better in 2016 relative to that raised by elected officials or unelected politicians in prior years. Figure 5.4 shows average fundraising through September for amateurs was $282,000, which is 22 percent of elected officials' fundraising. This proportion is no different than it was in the 2014 midterms. Unelected politicians fared slightly worse in fundraising 2016 compared to 2014, while elected politicians did somewhat better.

The fundraising totals comparing men and women tell a similar story of stability. The average fundraising amounts for general election House candidates demonstrates that differences between men and women are not very large. Figure 5.5, which shows data through September 2016, suggests that female candidates continued to raise fewer dollars than men, but

**TABLE 5.1** Top Congressional Races for Spending

*House*

| Rank | Race | Candidate | Indep Spending | Total | % Indep |
|---|---|---|---|---|---|
| 1 | Virginia District 10 | $8,078,629 | $14,618,676 | $22,697,305 | 64% |
| 2 | Minnesota District 08 | $6,394,555 | $15,778,187 | $22,172,742 | 71% |
| 3 | Florida District 18 | $13,592,735 | $7,226,778 | $20,819,513 | 35% |
| 4 | Pennsylvania District 08 | $4,697,925 | $15,614,715 | $20,312,640 | 77% |
| 5 | Colorado District 06 | $6,585,964 | $12,965,671 | $19,551,635 | 66% |
| 6 | Nevada District 03 | $3,634,991 | $15,813,800 | $19,448,791 | 81% |
| 7 | Illinois District 10 | $10,507,915 | $8,352,229 | $18,860,144 | 44% |
| 8 | Florida District 26 | $5,213,478 | $13,191,556 | $18,405,034 | 72% |
| 9 | New York District 19 | $7,790,699 | $9,468,016 | $17,258,715 | 55% |
| 10 | Maine District 02 | $6,783,510 | $10,068,301 | $16,851,811 | 60% |

*Senate*

| Rank | Race | Candidate | Indep Spending | Total | % Indep |
|---|---|---|---|---|---|
| 1 | Pennsylvania Senate | $40,516,131 | $121,690,105 | $162,206,236 | 75% |
| 2 | New Hampshire Senate | $30,063,341 | $88,906,240 | $118,969,581 | 75% |
| 3 | Nevada Senate | $21,201,476 | $90,643,954 | $111,845,430 | 81% |
| 4 | Ohio Senate | $31,741,599 | $52,281,410 | $84,023,009 | 62% |
| 5 | Florida Senate | $30,003,871 | $49,174,435 | $79,178,306 | 62% |
| 6 | North Carolina Senate | $19,206,056 | $59,943,874 | $79,149,930 | 76% |
| 7 | Missouri Senate | $21,853,818 | $45,095,769 | $66,949,587 | 67% |
| 8 | Indiana Senate | $19,981,337 | $45,234,817 | $65,216,154 | 69% |
| 9 | Wisconsin Senate | $35,144,671 | $28,284,459 | $63,429,130 | 45% |
| 10 | Illinois Senate | $25,405,056 | $4,940,998 | $30,346,054 | 16% |

*Source*: Center for Responsive Politics (2016b).

## Figure 5.4

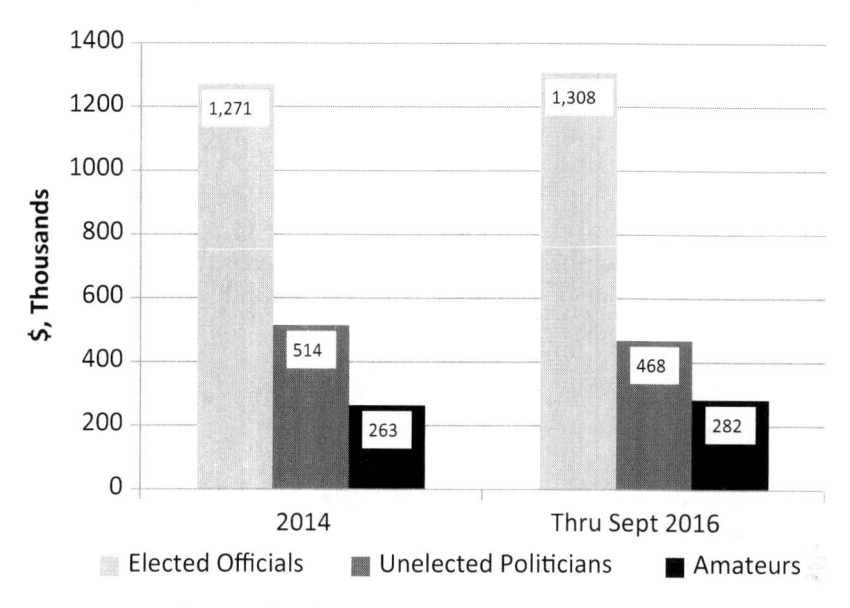

| | 2014 | Thru Sept 2016 |
|---|---|---|
| Elected Officials | 1,271 | 1,308 |
| Unelected Politicians | 514 | 468 |
| Amateurs | 263 | 282 |

(\$, Thousands)

**FIGURE 5.4** Fundraising for the House: Insiders vs. Outsiders, 2014 & 2016

Source: Compiled by the author from Federal Election Commission, candidates' web sites, other public sources, and Herrnson (2016).

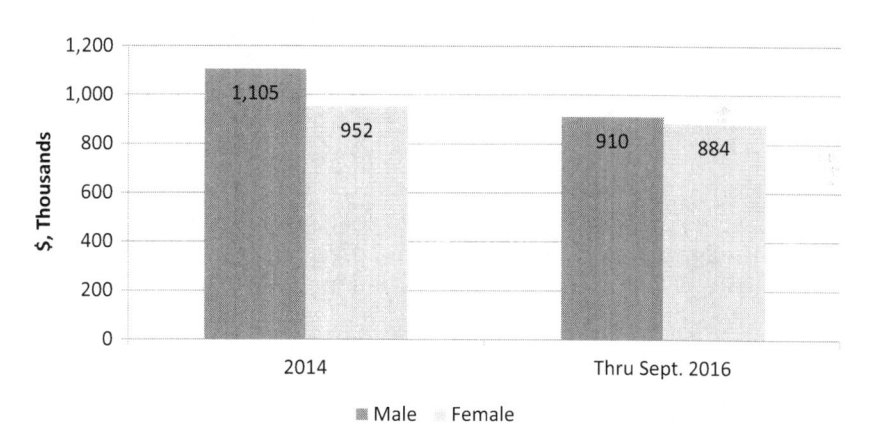

## Figure 5.5

| | 2014 | Thru Sept. 2016 |
|---|---|---|
| Male | 1,105 | 910 |
| Female | 952 | 884 |

(\$, Thousands)

**FIGURE 5.5** Fundraising for the House: Men vs. Women, 2104 & 2016

Source: Compiled by the author from Federal Election Commission, candidates' web sites, other public sources, and Herrnson (2016).

not by much. In the top Senate races, women fared well in head-to-head matchups with male candidates, such as in Nevada where Catherine Cortes Masto outraised Republican Joe Heck $16 million to $11 million. Similarly, the Democratic challenger in Illinois, Tammy Duckworth, outraised Republican incumbent Mark Kirk $15 million to $12 million.

## The Campaign for Votes

Despite the national context that affected the presidential and some congressional campaigns, the outcome of the 2016 congressional elections points clearly to a status quo election in which incumbents in both parties held their seats and neither party swept the open seat races. Democrats advanced just two seats in Senate and six in the House, leaving the Republicans with marginally smaller majorities in both chambers. In picking Trump for President, voters gave one party control over the elected branches of the national government, an advantage that President Obama enjoyed at the start of his first term. The Trump victory was a significant surprise, and because the election was so close, neither party benefitted from coattails. Both presidential candidates were viewed unfavorably by an unusually high number of voters, and the winner could not claim a popular mandate. Instead, most voters doubled down on partisan loyalties, which meant few incumbents faced serious challenges.

Steadfast partisan voting appears to be the new norm. Such loyalties, combined with growing ideological and demographic differences between the parties' electorates explain why votes for the presidency are so congruent with those for Congress, regardless of who is the presidential nominee. Despite the challenge Trump presented to Republican policy orthodoxy, as well as the sound and fury of his campaign, at the end of the day his campaign was not overly influential in determining the outcomes of many congressional elections. To be sure, Trump's appeal to rural and white working-class voters may have boosted votes for congressional Republicans in districts where these demographics were salient. This may have helped in toss-up districts such as New York's 22nd or Maine's 2nd district because these were disproportionally working class and rural compared to most congressional districts. And Trump's appeal to a faction of voters may have helped Republicans in key Senate races in the Rust Belt. At the same time, the Clinton campaign appeared to perform strongly in districts and states with greater than average share of college educated voters (Cohn 2016), but these were already Democratic strongholds.

Given the unpopularity of both presidential nominees, many candidates attempted to run on persona and local issues and away from the party's presidential candidates. This is a typical strategy for many congressional incumbents, who do not want their campaigns to be distorted by what is going on at the top of the ticket. House members and senators routinely communicate to constituents prior to the election using both congressionally funded mail, email, websites and social media, and campaign-funded communications. Republican incumbents in marginal seats—and many other GOP candidates in tight races who were concerned about Trump's unpredictability—took extra steps to distance their campaigns from those at the top of the ticket, in several instances refusing to support the GOP presidential nominee, such as Republican incumbent Mia Love in Utah's 4th district. To be sure, presidential candidates intruded on local races when their remarks or actions set the news agenda. In such instances, the candidates were forced by their opponents to respond to controversial remarks by the presidential candidates, (e.g. Trump's tweets, statements at rallies and videos), or events (Clinton's emails from a private server at the State Department, the announcements of the FBI investigation, and the DNC emails unloaded in final months by WikiLeaks).

Trump, in particular, was an extraordinarily complex presidential contestant for candidates of his own party. The GOP's most prominent elected official, Speaker of the House Paul Ryan (R-WI), had difficulty giving his full support to Trump. When the *Washington Post* unearthed a 2005 video of Trump boasting about his groping of women, Ryan and leading Republicans began to walk back their endorsements of him and several insisted that he drop out of the race. Immediately after the video release, Ryan requested that Trump not appear with him at a campaign event in Wisconsin. The Speaker looked as if he was writing off the Trump candidacy when he suggested in a GOP conference call to members that they should choose their own path to victory and, according to one participant, he said "do what's best for you in your district" (Barabak and Mascaro 2016). This was a signal to Republican candidates to localize the race as much as possible and distance themselves from the top of the ticket.

## House Races

Since the typical congressional election has an incumbent who is not threatened seriously, most campaign messages remained positive relative to the presidential campaign. Incumbents have cultivated a positive image and relationship with constituents, and do not want to see that fray with a negative campaign. For this reason they frequently ignore opponents and rarely resort to sharp attacks on challengers unless the race gets very close. In contrast, challenges and open seat campaigns need to be more aggressive in getting out their messages. In the open seat race for New York's 22nd district, for example, Republican Claudia Tenney, tried to show toughness to take on Washington problems by appearing in commercials on a motorcycle with a black leather jacket, holding a gun at a shooting range, and appearing with veterans and her son who is a Marine. She won against a Democratic candidate, but this race was not about gender or outsider status, so much as a strategy for motivating a base of conservative voters and demonstrating courage with independent voters to "take on Washington."

The success rates for women and outsiders were not impressive. Figure 5.6 shows the percentage of women and men who prevailed in 2014 compared to 2016. The percentage of women candidates in 2016 who won a nomination was 17 percent; the general election was 20 percent;

**118** Chapter 5

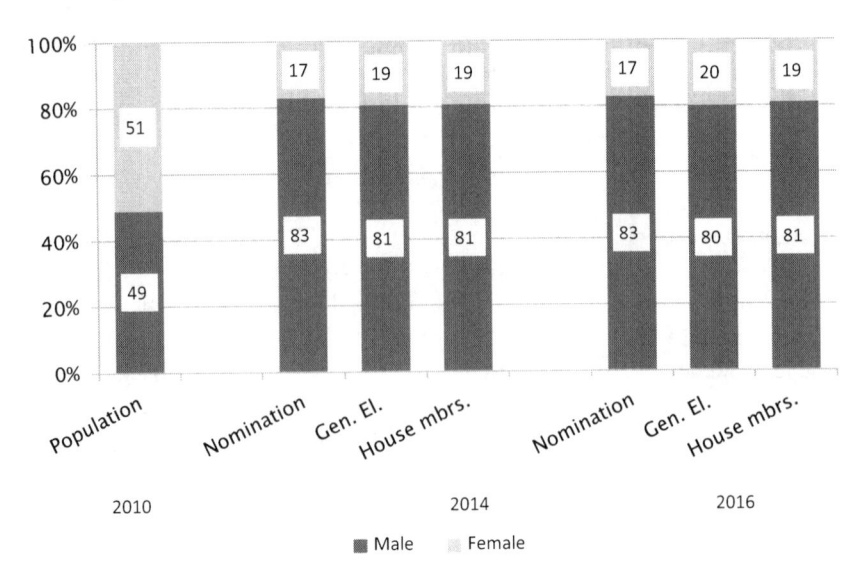

[Bar chart showing male/female percentages across Population (2010: 49 male, 51 female), and for 2014 and 2016: Nomination, Gen. El., House mbrs. — 2014: 83/17, 81/19, 81/19; 2016: 83/17, 80/20, 81/19]

**FIGURE 5.6** House Elections: Women

*Source:* Compiled by the author from Herrnson (2016), candidates' web sites, and other public sources.

and being a House member was 19 percent. These figures are virtually identical to those in 2014. Figure 5.7 adds to the story. It shows the rates at which different types of candidates prevailed relative to the number of candidates of that type. So, for example, among all women candidates, just 26 percent gained a position in the House. This success rate was slightly greater than for male candidates at 23 percent. Outsider candidates had very low success rates with just 2 percent of them winning a seat, compared with 19 percent of unelected officials and 58 percent of elected officials.

Maine's 2nd District illustrates some of challenges to making this a year of the woman. This district pitted a rematch of one-term Republican incumbent Bruce Poliquin against Democratic challenger Emily Cain. This is among the most rural districts in the nation and is peppered with old mill towns. Both candidates tried to make the race local and avoid being affected by national issues and the unpredictability of the presidential campaign. To some extent the strategy worked for the Democratic candidate who picked up more rural voters than Clinton. Both candidates emphasized anti-trade positions and support for gun rights. The Republican candidate refused to say whether he would vote for Trump, but he appeared to benefit from the same national forces propelling Trump.[5] Despite the contest being considered a true toss-up (the district went slightly for Obama over Romney in 2012, 44 percent to 42 percent), the Republican won with almost a 10 percent margin. The race was inundated with independent

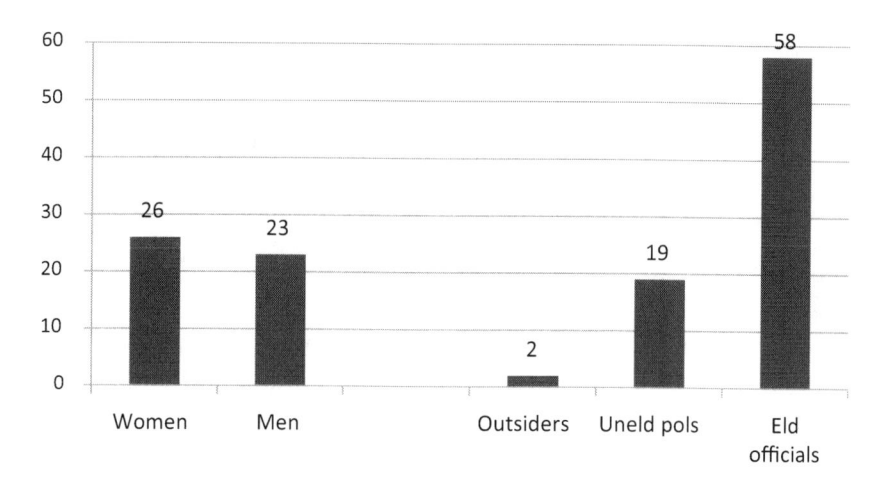

```
60                                                                    58
50
40
30    26
            23
20                                              19
10
                              2
 0
    Women   Men          Outsiders  Uneld pols   Eld
                                                officials
```

**FIGURE 5.7** House Success Rates

*Source:* Compiled by the author from candidates' web sites and other public sources.

spending from party committees and allied interest groups such as the National Rifle Association in support of the Republican candidate and a super PAC compromised of liberal groups supporting the Democrat.

In the adjacent state of New Hampshire, the outcome was different even though the district was also rural/suburban and overwhelmingly white. This time a woman won, but it was mostly because the incumbent Republican faced a scandal. The seat was held by Republican Frank Guinta, facing a fourth race against Carol Shea-Porter. Democrats thought she was not moderate enough for this district to win and hold it, and her record suggests as much. She lost the seat against Guinta in 2010, regained it in 2012, lost it in 2014, and regained it in 2016. In other words, she only held the seat during presidential years when the electorate is typically more favorable to Democrats. Importantly, Guinta was a weakened candidate because he was involved in campaign finance scandals that caused even members of his own party to repudiate him. The fact that the independent candidate won almost 10 percent of vote shows that there was significant dissatisfaction with both major party candidates.

Amateur candidates appeared in some key races even though it was not necessarily their amateur status that won the day. Moreover, even in these races Trump was not much of an issue, despite the fact that the Democrats tried to make it one. In an open-seat contest in Florida's 18th district, for example, the amateur Democratic candidate Randy Perkins was a wealthy businessman facing an amateur Republican and U.S. Army veteran Brian Mast. Perkins tried to link the Republican candidate to Trump, most pointedly after Trump's video emerged. The charges did not seem to stick and Mast continued to stand by Trump. While this race featured discussion of national issues, the candidates tried to focus on local issues, too, including projects regarding Indian River Lagoon and the Everglades, and which candidate would be better in securing jobs for the district (Editorial Board, Treasure Coast Newspapers 2016). At the end of the day, however, the vote shares correlated highly with the vote shares received by the presidential candidates in these districts.

This race seems emblematic of an increasing trend in congressional elections. Regardless of the candidates and local issues, the rates of party voting are extremely high for presidential contest and congressional seats (Jacobson 2015). In 2012, district level vote shares for President and House candidates correlated at greater than 0.95[6], with only 6 percent of districts having split verdicts. Similar dynamics appear to have been operating in the 2016 election. People who supported the President's performance were highly likely to vote for Clinton and Democratic congressional candidates. Those who did not were going to vote for the Republican candidates, regardless of who was the GOP nominee. In House elections especially, party line voting strongly favors Republicans because they have structural advantages in the distribution of partisans across congressional districts (Jacobson 2015).[7] This is one reason why it is so difficult for Democrats to pick up seats in the House, particularly in a status quo election.

In pre-Labor Day predictions, Cook Reports listed 56 races as potentially competitive. Among these, there were just five seats that were occupied by a Republican in districts that were likely or leaning for a Democratic pick-up. The Democrats swept these (FL-10, 13, VA-4, NV-4 and NH-1). However, they had the potential to pick up many more in 16 toss-up seats occupied by Republicans. Democrats won just four of these seats and gave up a seat they controlled in Nebraska's 2nd district. Democrats also lost two seats they previously controlled in districts that were leaning or likely Republican (Cook Political Report 2016). All told, they picked up just six House seats for the 115th Congress, resulting in a 241–194 majority for the Republican party.

### Senate Races

The balancing act for candidates dealing with Trump at the top of the ticket was especially challenging in Senate races where the presidential campaign loomed larger. In the competitive contests, most Republicans did a dance that criticized Trump and tempered their support for him, without entirely throwing him overboard. For the most part, candidates did not campaign as if this was a "change election" in the same manner as Trump. According to the Wesleyan Media Project, Senate ads mentioned the word "change" just 4 percent of time, and that was in support of Senate

Democrats trying to take back the Senate majority. Most ads on the GOP side tried to paint the Democratic candidates as too liberal, tying them to President Obama—who Republican voters tend to see as extremely liberal. Democratic challengers, in contrast, used ads that claimed, rather conventionally, that Republicans officeholders were beholden to "special interests" and helping the wealthy.

Even if congressional elections were not about change, this does not mean voters tolerated candidates who they viewed as Washington "insiders." Three Senate races stand out in particular: Wisconsin, Indiana, and Missouri. These seats in the Midwest were all controlled by Republicans and retained by them. Somewhat paradoxically, the Democratic challengers were all tagged as Washington insiders. This was particularly true in Indiana, where Evan Bayh, a Democratic veteran of state politics, was beaten badly by Representative Todd Young because the Republicans were able to portray Bayh as a creature of Washington whose connections to Indiana had eroded. A similar fate was in store for former Democratic Senator Russ Feingold, who was trying to win back his seat against incumbent Ron Johnson in Wisconsin. Johnson effectively portrayed Feingold as a career politician. Both Democratic candidates lost by much wider margins than anyone ever expected. It cannot be overlooked that the Republican candidates in these states were beneficiaries of a surge in rural and white working-class voters who came to the polls in support of Trump and voted for the Republican Senate candidate. In Missouri, however, Democrat challenger Jason Kander almost pulled off a major upset against Republican incumbent Roy Blunt. Kander was able to portray Blunt as an out-of-touch Washington crony. Kander's surprisingly strong showing was boosted by his military background and by an unusual ad in which he put tougher an assault rifle blindfolded. Blunt tried to tie the Democrat closely to Obama, who is very unpopular in Missouri, and in the end this may have saved him. Trump won the state by huge margin of 18 percentage points, while Blunt won by just 3.2 percentage points.

A second feature of these Senate campaigns is that women did fairly well in some close contests, but only boosted their numbers in the Senate by one seat. In states that are firmly or trending Democrat, women won in Illinois, Nevada, and New Hampshire, while suffering a surprising loss in Pennsylvania. At the same time, women were not yet able to break through against incumbents in the red states of Arizona and North Carolina, which are undergoing rapid demographic changes that increasingly favor Democrats.

In the Nevada open seat being vacated by Senate Minority Leader Harry Reid, Catherine Cortez Masto, a Democrat became the first Latina senator, defeating GOP Representative Joe Heck. A war veteran, Heck tried to campaign as moderate in a state with rapidly increasing numbers of Latino and Democratic voters affiliated with union workers from the casinos and hotels. At first, Heck was critical of Trump during the primaries, and then tried to support him tepidly. His back-and-forth appeared to alienate his Republican base. At the same time, Masto was helped by a significant voter mobilization effort by the Clinton campaign.

In Illinois, another blue-leaning state, the Democratic challenger Tammy Duckworth beat Senate Republican incumbent, Mark Kirk. Kirk tried to completely disassociate himself from Trump, at one point tweeting that "DJT is a malignant clown—unprepared and unfit to be president of the United States" (DeBonis and Phillip 2016). Kirk was a moderate Republican (he supports gay rights) and tried to localize the election but he angered a faction of his base by refusing to support Trump (Davey 2016). Duckworth was a member of the U.S. House and her military background likely helped her beyond her Democratic base. She lost her legs in the Iraq War after the helicopter she co-piloted was shot down. In the end, she won by an unusually large margin against the incumbent, 54 percent to 40 percent.

A female Senate candidate lost in Pennsylvania, a state that many believed had become firmly Democrat. Once Trump won the nomination, Republicans were especially fearful that the incumbent Patrick Toomey would lose to challenger Katie McGinty because he would not retain educated voters in the Philadelphia and Pittsburgh suburbs. It was the most expensive race in the country, as the parties and interest groups spent extravagantly on independent ads. McGinty tried to frame herself as pro-business Democrat, even though she had strong pro-environment credentials. She also allied herself closely with Clinton. Toomey, on the other hand, never endorsed Trump and avoided questions about whether he would vote for him. In the end, Trump may have helped him by boosting turnout in the Republican base and winning a significant share of working-class white voters who went to the polls.

The closest Senate contest pitted two experienced women against each other. In New Hampshire, the popular Senator Kelly Ayotte (R-NH) had to do the "Trump dance" of how closely she wanted to tie herself to him. She was flummoxed in the campaign by conflicting statements she made about him, in one instance saying she "absolutely" saw him as a role model, and later saying she would not vote for him. She was being challenged by Governor Maggie Hassan, a Democrat who was also popular in the Granite State. Hassan allied herself with Clinton but tried to woo independents by saying she supported better screening of Syrian refugees before they could come to New Hampshire. Both candidates tried to talk in bipartisan terms about opioid epidemic and other local issues. In the end, Hassan won this race by a hairbreadth of 0.1 percent.

In red states with shifting demographics, women made valiant bids to unseat incumbents but fell short. In Arizona, for example, Republican Senator McCain initially faced a surprising tough reelection campaign against Representative Ann Kirkpatrick. Despite being denigrated by Trump for not being a war hero because he was captured, McCain said he would support the Republican nominee out of party loyalty. He then rescinded this support after the video release of Trump in 2005 because of his "demeaning comments about women and boasts about sexual assaults" ("Did Democrats Regain Control of the Senate? No. Here Are 10 Races We Watched" 2016). Kirkpatrick, like other Senate Democrats, allied herself closely with Clinton. The McCain campaign attacked her relentlessly for her support of President Obama's Affordable Care Act. McCain ended up winning the race by a comfortable margin, 53.4 percent to 41.1 percent.

The race was closer in North Carolina (51.1 percent to 43.2 percent), where Democratic challenger and state legislator Deborah Ross tried to portray the incumbent Republican Richard Burr as a Washington insider. In return Burr, casted his opponent as being too liberal by reminding voters about her work for the American Civil Liberties Union, while emphasizing his support for gun rights and his key position on the Senate Intelligence Committee where he could challenge an Obama foreign policy that his base saw as weak.

## Conclusion: A Tale of Two Elections

The dynamics of the 2016 presidential primaries appeared to presage upheaval across the electoral field. And yet this was not the case for congressional elections. We did not observe a surge in support for outsider or amateur candidates, even if many voters disliked insiders. While the voters in presidential contests elected the most iconic outsider in the history of U.S. presidential elections since Andrew Jackson, the congressional races went forward with barely a trace of throwing out incumbents and conventional candidates.

Regarding the potential for the "year of the woman" with Hillary Clinton at the top of the ticket, we did not see an increase in women in downballot races despite key wins in Senate races. Three new Senators are women. One defended an open seat vacated by Harry Reid in Nevada, Catherine Cortez Masto (D). The other two beat incumbents. In Illinois, Tammy Duckworth (D) defeated Senator Mark Kirk (R) and in New Hampshire, Maggie Hassan (D) defeated another woman, Senator Kelly Ayotte (R). At the same time, however, two women Senators, Barbara Mikulski (D-MD), and Barbara Boxer (D-CA) retired. Mikulski was replaced by Representative Chris Van Hollen, and Boxer was replaced by

California Attorney General Kamala Harris—who beat out U.S. Representative Loretta Sanchez. Thus, there was only a net increase of one woman to the Senate from 20 to 21 in the 115th Congress (16 Democrats and five Republicans). Meanwhile, in the House the number of women declined by one from 84 to 83, which reflects just 19 percent of the chamber.[8]

The conclusion we draw is that this was a status quo election for Congress, regardless of the fireworks in the presidential race.[9] It was indeed a tale of two elections. What we see going forward based on outcome of congressional election is a continuation of the intense policy and electoral battles fought at the margins. These close margins make it less likely that parties in Congress will compromise, each seeing keeping distinctive positions in a strategic gambit to pursue majorities in the next election (Lee 2016). As the minority party, Democrats are likely to be more unified during the 115th Congress, while Republicans will continue to face factionalism between members of the anti-government Freedom Caucus and the more mainstream conservatives.

The most significant change is that the government is now unified under one party. The last time this happened was 2008 with Obama's first election. As a result, Democrats were able to push through the Affordable Care Act. However, that highly partisan effort created an electoral backlash that might give Republicans pause. In the subsequent 2010 midterm, Democrats lost their majority in the House and almost in the Senate. The energized Republicans were able to push back hard on much of Obama's policy agenda for the rest of his presidency. In races further down the ballot, the Democrats lost more than 800 state legislative elections and control over many state governments. Not only did this affect their capacity to control the redistricting process in 2010, these purges have hurt the party long-term with a smaller crop of legislators moving through state legislative chambers in preparation for leadership in higher office. In the 2018 elections, Republicans could face similar situation if they overreach in pushing policies during the first term that do not reflect a broader consensus in the nation.

Given the differences between Trump and mainstream Republicans, we can expect periodic conflict between the President and members of his own party in Congress. While Republicans are united on policies such as reducing taxes and eliminating government regulations, it is not clear they have a consensus plan to repeal and replace Obamacare. Moreover, large differences exist over immigration and trade, where the new President's position is more restrictive than others in his party. In foreign policy, he will likely face significant resistance from Senators in both parties where a bipartisan consensus exists on a liberal world order shaped by the United

States willingness to shoulder security burdens, such as NATO and other treaties in support of a Pax Americana. Trump wants other countries to their pay their "fair share" while Congress is more likely to preserve a status quo that gives the United States a dominant global presence and maintains international stability.

The stakes of this election were particularly high for shaping the direction of the federal courts. The unexpected death of Supreme Court Justice Antonin Scalia in February 2016 gives the President an immediate opportunity to shape the direction of the Court. Senate Majority Leader Mitch McConnell was able to put off the confirmation of Obama's selection for the Court in declaring that the vacancy should be filled by the next President. In the end, McConnell's strategy worked. Democrats did not take back the Senate and the new President is a Republican, which, as expected, led to a more conservative appointment to the Supreme Court and could lead to additional conservative appointments if other justices leave the bench in the next few years.

With the stakes so high, both parties are preparing immediately for the 2018 elections. The President's party typically loses seats after his first two years in office, a product of public disappointment after much optimism. Trump did not have coattails to help Republicans win in Democratic-leaning or toss-up competitive seats. For this reason, the number of newly elected House members who might be vulnerable will not be large. In the Senate, it seems unlikely that Democrats will win a majority because they are mostly defending 23 seats compared to just eight for the Republicans. At the same time, many of the seats Democrats must defend are in states that Donald Trump won.[10] A disastrous presidency, of course, could change all these predictions and sweep in the Democrats. With so many unpredictable features regarding the new administration, including Trump's ability to govern, it is hard to tell what the impact on the next Congress will be.

In the end, this was a tale of two elections. If the presidential election was a surprise win by a rabble-rousing outsider, the congressional elections were a relatively sedate rendering of the status quo to choose the 115th Congress.

## Notes

\* The authors would like to thank University of Connecticut undergraduate research assistant, Jared Quigley, and UConn Political Science Honors Bennett RA program for its support.
1 See Gallup 2016, September 7–11, available at www.gallup.com/poll/1669/general-mood-country.aspx

2 See especially *SpeechNOW.org v. Federal Election Commission*, 599 F.3d 686 (D.C. Cir. 2010); *Citizens United v. Federal Election Commission*, 558 U.S.310 (2010).
3 The Supreme Court's 2010 ruling in *Citizens United v. Federal Election Commission*, which declared corporations, trade associations, labor unions, and other incorporated groups were free to use general treasury funds to make independent expenditures in elections, led to a substantial increase in outside spending in House races.
4 This analysis includes data through September 2016 rather than the full election cycle reporting, which ended December 31, 2016.
5 There were other close races where a surge in white working-class voters almost unseated Democratic incumbents including Rep. Tim Walz (D, MN-1), Rep. Collin Peterson (D, MN-7), and Rep. Matt Cartwright (D, PA-17). See *Sabato's Crystal Ball* (2016).
6 Correlated simply means that two variables change together. In this case, the vote share received by the party's congressional candidate fluctuated almost perfectly (a score of 1 would be perfect correlation) with the vote shares for the party's presidential nominee.
7 Romney, for example, ran head of Obama in 226 districts compared to 209 despite Obama's Electoral College and popular vote win.
8 The number of minorities increased slightly and mostly represented by Democratic lawmakers (49 African-Americans, 38 Hispanics and 15 Asian-Americans) (Marcos 2016).
9 It appeared to be a status quo election in state legislative elections, as well. Republicans continued their dominance, picking up 138 seats in the Rust Belt—probably with the help of Trump—while Democrats picked up 95 seats, many in Southwestern states with an increasingly Latino electorate (Sabato 2014; Narea and Shephard 2016).
10 This includes Florida, Indiana, Missouri, Montana, North Dakota, Ohio, Pennsylvania, West Virginia, and Wisconsin.

## Bibliography

Abramowitz, Alan. 2016. "Forecasting the 2016 Presidential Election: Will Time for Change Mean Time for Trump?" *Sabato's Crystal Ball*, August 11. www.centerforpolitics.org/crystalball/articles/forecasting-the-2016-presidential-election-will-time-for-change-mean-time-for-trump/ (accessed December 19, 2016).

Barabak, Mark Z. and Lisa Mascaro. 2016. "Republican Split Deepens as House Speaker Ryan Abandons Trump, Says Every Candidate for Themselves." *Los Angeles Times*, October 10. www.latimes.com/politics/la-na-pol-trump-republicans-20161010-snap-story.html

Canon, David T. 1993. "Sacrificial Lambs or Strategic Politicians? Political Amateurs in U.S. House Elections." *American Journal of Political Science* 37:4. Pp. 1119–1141.

Center for American Women and Politics, Rutgers University. 2016. "Women Candidates in 1992–2016," www.cawp.rutgers.edu/sites/default/files/resources/canprimcong_histsum.pdf

Center for Responsive Politics. 2016a. "Cost of Elections." https://www.opensecrets.org/overview/cost.php

Center for Responsive Politics. 2016b. "Most Expensive Races." https://www.opensecrets.org/overview/topraces.php?cycle=2016&display=currcandsout

Center for Responsive Politics. 2016c. "Reelection Rates Over the Years." www.opensecrets.org/overview/reelect.php

Cohn, Nate. 2016. "The Upshot: The New Blue and Red: An Educational Split Is Replacing the Culture War." *New York Times*, October 19. www.nytimes.com/2016/10/20/upshot/the-new-blue-and-red-educational-split-is-replacing-the-culture-war.html?action=click&contentCollection=The%20Upshot&module=RelatedCoverage&region=Marginalia&pgtype=article

Cook Political Report. 2016. "2016 House Results by Race Rating." November 8. http://cookpolitical.com/house/charts/race-ratings

Davey, Monica. 2016. "Tammy Duckworth Unseats Mark Kirk in Illinois Senate Race." *New York Times*, November 8. www.nytimes.com/2016/11/09/us/politics/illinois-senate-tammy-duckworth.html?_r=0=

DeBonis, Mike and Abby Phillip. 2016. "Ryan Calls Off Plans to Campaign With Trump; GOP-ers Rush to Distance Themselves." *Washington Post*, October 7. www.washingtonpost.com/news/powerpost/wp/2016/10/07/ryan-mcconnell-silent-on-lewd-trump-video/?utm_term=.b66979f74286

"Did Democrats Regain Control of the Senate? No. Here Are 10 Races We Watched." 2016. *New York Times*, November 8. www.nytimes.com/2016/11/08/us/politics/senate-races.html?action=click&contentCollection=Politics&module=RelatedCoverage&region=EndOfArticle&pgtype=article

Editorial Board, Treasure Coast Newspapers. 2016. "Editorial Endorsement: U.S. House, District 118." *TC Palm*, October 23. www.tcpalm.com/story/opinion/editorials/2016/10/23/editorial-endorsement-us-house-district-18/92423412/

Harwood, John. 2016. "To Flip the House, How Big Would a Clinton Victory Margin Need to Be?" *New York Times*, October 24. www.nytimes.com/2016/10/25/upshot/to-flip-the-house-how-big-would-a-clinton-victory-margin-need-to-be.html

Herrnson, Paul S. 2016. *Congressional Elections: Campaigning at Home and in Washington*, 7th ed. Washington: CQ Press.

Jacobson, Gary C. 2015. "Barack Obama and the Nationalization of Electoral Politics." *Electoral Studies* 40: 471–481.

Jacobson, Gary C. and Samuel Kernell. 1981. *Strategy and Choice in Congressional Elections*. New Haven, CT: Yale University Press.

Lee, Frances E. 2016. *Insecure Majorities*. Chicago: University of Chicago Press.

Maisel, L. Sandy and Walter J. Stone. 1997. "Determinants of Candidate Emergence in U. S. House Elections: An Exploratory Study." *Legislative Studies Quarterly* 22:1. Pp. 79–96.

Marcos, Cristina. 2016. "115th Congress Will Be the Most Diverse in History." *The Hill*, November 16. http://thehill.com/homenews/house/306480-115th-congress-will-be-most-racially-diverse-in-history

Narea, Nicole and Alex Shephard. 2016. "The Democrats' Biggest Disaster." *New Republic*, November 22. https://newrepublic.com/article/138897/democrats-biggest-disaster

Sabato, Larry J. 2014. "Why Parties Should Hope They Lose the White House." *Politico*, December 1. www.politico.com/magazine/story/2014/12/presidents-bad-for-their-parties-113241

Stone, Walter J., L. Sandy Maisel and Cherie D. Maestas. 2004. "Quality Counts: Extending the Strategic Politician Model of Incumbent Deterrence." *American Journal of Political Science* 48:3. Pp. 479–495.

Wesleyan Media Project. 2016. "Clinton Crushes Trump 3:1 in Air War; Nearly $600 Million in Ads for Senate Races." Table 7. http://mediaproject.wesleyan.edu/releases/nov-2016/#table7

# 6

# WOMEN AND THE 2016 PRESIDENTIAL ELECTION

## Unrealistic Expectations of Cohesiveness

*Susan A. MacManus\**

> *There are plenty of subplots in the unfolding [2016] presidential election, but the gender fight is among the most interesting of them—and one that will be critical to the outcome.*
> — Charlie Cook, *National Journal*, June 27, 2015
> (1.5 years before the election)

> *Start with the first female nominee of a major party in the 240-year history of the United States: Democrat Hillary Clinton now leads in a campaign that could smash what she famously dubbed "the highest, hardest glass ceiling." [. . .] Whatever happens on Election Day, this year has been a gender earthquake.*
> — Susan Page, *USA Today*, November 1, 2016
> (one week before the election)

> *For all of the talk that Trump's comments about women—and the allegations of sexual assault made against him by a dozen women—would mean historic turnout among female voters (and a historic margin of defeat for Trump), it simply never materialized.*
> — Chris Cillizza, *The Washington Post*, November 10, 2016
> (two days after the election)

Women have been the majority of voters in every election since 1964. In the 2016 election, they were everywhere in every phase of the election—from campaign strategists and managers; TV anchors and reporters; debate moderators; and surrogates on the campaign trail, including daughters

Chelsea Clinton and Ivanka Trump, to presidential candidates—Hillary Clinton (Democratic party), Carly Fiorina (Republican party), and Jill Stein (Green party). From start to finish, however, the dominant story was the candidacy of Hillary Clinton—anticipated since 2008 when she lost the Democratic nomination fight to Barack Obama.

---

**Ten Firsts in Election 2016**

1. First time a woman was nominated for President by a major party (Hillary Clinton—Democratic party).
2. First election with women as serious candidates from both major parties (Clinton, Carly Fiorina-Republican party).
3. First time a winning presidential campaign was run by a female campaign manager (Kellyanne Conway—Donald Trump).
4. First Asian-American presidential debate moderator, and youngest debate moderator since 1988 (Elaine Quijano, CBS News).
5. First time a Democratic candidate carried white college-educated women.
6. First election since 1996 a Democrat won married women.
7. First time with a sharp generational difference among women (millennial females vs. older females).
8. First time both candidates (male, female) were regarded unfavorably by the electorate heading into the election.
9. First campaign a candidate (Clinton) was under active FBI investigation during the campaign.
10. First campaign in which a man's hairstyle was a bigger media focus than a woman's.

---

Many had projected that Clinton's potential to break the glass ceiling would generate record levels of participation and cohesiveness among female voters—much as Obama's candidacy had torn down the racial barrier by mobilizing minorities and young voters. Republican Donald Trump's crude and lewd statements about a wide range of women seemed to reinforce that projection. But it was an unrealistic expectation from the start:

> The dream that women would vote for a woman overlooked the seductive pulls and interactions among party, class and racial identity that have long divided women as much as their gender was assumed to unite them.
>
> *(Chira 2016)*

By Election Day, Clinton could not replicate Obama's share of the women's vote. He won 56 percent of the female vote in 2008 and 55 percent in 2012. Clinton received 54 percent in 2016—the decline in large part due to a dip in turnout and support from Democratic leaning millennial women who either did not vote or chose a minor party candidate like Green party candidate Jill Stein or Gary Johnson of the Libertarian party.

## Historical Pattern of Overestimating Female Solidarity

The tendency to overestimate the cohesiveness of the female vote is nothing new. In fact, it dates back to the suffragists. By one account,

> [I]n 1911, the National Association Opposed to Women's Suffrage had 350,000 female members in 25 states and defeated close to 40 local and state referendums aimed at getting women the vote (and that was back when the population of the U.S. was about a third of what it is now).
>
> *(Tyre 2016)*

In 1920, after ratification of the 19th Amendment giving women the right to vote, a *New York Times* editorial praised the women who had issued their first formal demand for the right to vote at the Seneca Falls Convention (1848). At the same time, it projected that women would not all vote alike: "It is doubtless true that women will divide much as men have done among several parties. There will be no solid 'woman vote'" (MacManus 2014).

Today, campaign strategists warn against one-size-fits-all prescriptions for how to win the women's vote, particularly in presidential elections with marked demographic, socioeconomic, and *partisan* differences across the states. After all, the Electoral College, not the popular vote, chooses the winner.

In 2016, as in virtually every presidential election, states differed in the vote share they gave to each presidential candidate. For example, in the most partisan competitive states—Florida and Ohio—the women's vote was more evenly split between Clinton and Trump than in other less competitive states (Table 6.1). Women in Rust Belt states with more Democratic leaning electorates (Michigan, Pennsylvania, and Wisconsin) delivered slight majorities to Clinton. In sharp contrast, in two *strongly* Democratic states—California and New York—*two-thirds* of the female vote went to the Democratic candidate. Likewise, women in Kentucky and Missouri, two of the strongest Republican leaning states, delivered majorities to Trump.

**TABLE 6.1** National Election Results Mask Vastly Different Female Voting Patterns in States

| Partisan Lean | State | Women Share of Electorate | Women's Vote for Clinton (D) | Women's Vote for Trump (R) |
|---|---|---|---|---|
| | | % | % | % |
| National | | 53 | 54 | 41 |
| Swing | Florida | 53 | 50 | 46 |
| | Michigan | 52 | 53 | 42 |
| | Ohio | 53 | 49 | 46 |
| | Pennsylvania | 53 | 55 | 42 |
| | Wisconsin | 51 | 53 | 43 |
| Strongly Democratic | California | 51 | 66 | 30 |
| | New York | 56 | 66 | 31 |
| Strongly Republican | Kentucky | 51 | 40 | 54 |
| | Missouri | 53 | 43 | 53 |

*Note:* Total for other candidates/refused responses not included.

*Source:* Author compiled data from national exit polls as reported by CNN at www.cnn.com/election/results/exit-polls.

Party affiliation matters greatly. As political scientist Jennifer Lawless has noted: "Whether there's a D or an R in front of your name is way more a cue to the voters than the presence or absence of the Y chromosome" (Chira 2016). But schisms among women occurred even within the ranks of the same party—perhaps none more obvious than the generational divide of millennials vs. older women—within the Democratic Party.

At a post-election forum at Harvard University, Clinton's campaign manager acknowledged the lower-than-expected millennials' turnout rate and vote share for Clinton was a major reason she lost the race. Signs of her trouble connecting with millennials within the Democratic Party had surfaced in her first run for the presidency. A cumulative analysis of state exit poll results in 2008 found that Obama got 58 percent of the millennial vote, Clinton 38 percent. In the 2016 primary, Bernie Sanders received 71 percent of their vote compared to Clinton's 28 percent. In fact, Sanders beat her among millennials in all the 27 Democratic primary and caucus states with exit polls, except Mississippi and Alabama (Brownstein 2016).

### Women's Vote Rationales Were Worlds Apart

To better understand the differences of opinion among women about Clinton's historical candidacy, it is important to lay out the divergent perspectives (within and between women from different backgrounds) that surfaced during the campaign with regard to key questions.

### *Vote for Clinton Just to Make History?*

From the start, the Clinton campaign strongly promoted the historical nature of her candidacy—promising to break down the gender barrier or smash the glass ceiling, thereby paving the way for all the women behind her. In her acceptance speech at the Democratic National Convention in Philadelphia, she highlighted what she saw as the significance of her candidacy:

> Tonight, we've reached a milestone in our nation's march toward a more perfect union: the first time that a major party has nominated a woman for President.
>
> Standing here as my mother's daughter and my daughter's mother, I'm so happy this day has come. I'm happy for grandmothers and little girls and everyone in between.
>
> Happy for boys and men, too—because when any barrier falls in America for anyone, it clears the way for everyone. When there are no ceilings, the sky's the limit. So let's keep going, until every one of the 161 million women and girls across America has the opportunity she deserves.
>
> *("Transcript" 2016)*

In fundraising letters appealing to women donors, she noted:

> Women are the cornerstone of this campaign. I'm proud that 60 percent of our donors are women, and even prouder that we're building a country where we can finally say to all our daughters, "Yes, you can be anything you want when you grow up, even President of the United States."
>
> *(Williams 2016b)*

And when Trump accused her of playing the "woman's card," she proclaimed at her rallies: "If I'm playing the woman card, then *deal me in*!" (Wilhelm 2016).

For many older female voters, history was a powerful motivator. "I just want to see a woman president before I die" and "I've been waiting for this my whole life" were common sentiments (Ballhaus 2016). Many were equally driven by what her win would mean to future generations. First Lady Michelle Obama told convention delegates: "Because of Hillary Clinton, my daughters and all our sons and daughters now take for granted that a woman can be President of the United States." In the eyes of a 68-year-old Hispanic female member of the New York delegation, "the possibility of electing the first female president—it's extraordinary. For my granddaughters—and when my great-granddaughters are born—they'll have the ability to aspire to something like that. In other Latin American countries, it has been done" (Tumulty and Phillip 2016).

Many older women admired Clinton's boldness in running for the nation's top political office: "Here's the thing about women. We don't wake up in the morning thinking we're going to be the next President of the United States. . . which is why I'm supporting Hillary" (Wagner 2015).

But the making-history argument for supporting Clinton did not have the same pull among a number of millennial feminists, primarily because their life experiences—shaped by the intersection of "their gender *and* their race *and* their class" (Filipovic 2016b)—are broader and more complex than Clinton's, and not absent of strong female mentors:

> Many have grown up outperforming boys in the classroom and seeing women as their professors and doctors (not to mention senators and governors). [Clinton's] own wealth and race also undermine her appeal: Just as Americans are increasingly nonwhite, so too are feminists; just as being gay, lesbian, bisexual or transgender is increasingly normalized, so too are LGBT folks more visible and vocal in feminist activism. For young women, feminism today must take into account all of these constituencies and elevate the voices of the most marginalized.
>
> *(Filipovic 2016b)*

In addition, the making-history reason differed sharply by generation. A 22-year-old female student at the University of South Dakota articulated it well. For her mother, the prospect of having a woman President was the deciding factor in her vote for Clinton. But for the student, there was no urgency: "I would love to have a woman president, but I'd like the right woman president. I want this to be based on the ideas and what they're going to do for our country" (Gaudiano and Przybyla 2016).

### *Should Gender Be the Only Voting Cue?*

Much of the Clinton campaign messaging to female voters ("I'm With Her") reflected the "not-at-all subtle message [of] Hey ladies, vote for Hillary" (Murphy 2015). This assumption did not sit well with a number of female millennials who were more issue-oriented. One such voter, who announced she was voting for Bernie Sanders in the primary, reacted negatively to feminists who had verbally attacked her for the decision (Chapin 2016):

"Some women I encounter act as if I've betrayed some kind of secret society. I reject this brand of feminism. I'm not only voting for my gender. *I'm voting for other issues*" (emphasis added). In her case, she liked Sanders' issue stances on free college tuition, a $15 minimum wage, and cleaning up Wall Street corruption better than Clinton's platform. She added that historical firsts like Clinton's did not move her, and pointed to the failure of the Obama presidency to improve black people's lives as an example.

Young feminist supporters of Bernie Sanders irked older icons of the women's movement. Longtime feminists like Gloria Steinem and Madeleine Albright saw Clinton's election as a special moment—a capstone to the movement. Their message to young women averse to Clinton's candidacy was "Shame on you." Albright was even more direct: "There's a special place in hell for women who don't help each other." Steinem suggested younger women were just out to meet young men: "When you're young, you're thinking, 'Where are the boys? The boys are with Bernie'" (Rappeport 2016). The pushback was intense. Social media blazed with comments that to these older feminists, Clinton might well represent the final and best chance to send one of their own to the White House, but to younger ones, gender was not the *single* factor on which they wanted to base their vote.

The idea of gender as the reason to vote for Clinton did not resonate among young conservative women, either. A young female graduate student at a conservative college describes why:

> Women, [the liberal left] suggest, are like bees: simple, homogeneous creatures, who all have the same interests and concerns. Consequently, all women should vote for Hillary Clinton, a woman who will represent these interests and concerns. *When a woman breaks away from the hive, [liberals say] it is because she does not recognize her true interests and has betrayed not only the sisterhood, but herself* (emphasis added). In reality, of course, women have different interests and concerns. Therefore, it is not unreasonable that they would vote accordingly. . . . Most women are not so simply deceived by such opportunistic slogans for female empowerment. . . . Liberal assumptions underestimate women.
>
> *(Bornhorst 2016)*

### *Can a Woman Vote for Lewd and Demeaning Man?*

Female Clinton supporters were the most troubled by women who voted for Trump in spite of his detestable sexist comments: "It's rather jarring to be part of a generation of female Americans who fought for women's rights, and then to watch as your fellow female Americans vote the ultimate male chauvinist into the White House" (Tyre 2016).

Many Republican women were also critical of Trump's degrading statements. But to some, especially religious conservatives, Trump's crude and crass statements did not rise to the level of Clinton's corruption or override his commitment to change the direction of the country. As one woman put it: "I think women see the big picture—women are smart. The fact that [Trump] said something crude is not going to change my mind about the good he can do for our country" (Stolberg 2016). For others, how Trump treated women did not weigh as heavily on them as "how they had been treated by the establishment elite of which Hillary was absolutely part of" (Zablit 2016).

### *Was Sexism a Factor in Vote Decisions?*

For many older Democratic women, the answer was a resounding "Yes." A *Time* magazine piece reflected this viewpoint: the "stench of sexism engulfed Clinton's quixotic bid for the presidency, magnifying her flaws and minimizing her considerable strengths" (Alter 2016). Some minority feminists lashed out at white female Trump supporters for themselves being sexist: "Most white women don't want to be part of an intersectional feminist sisterhood. Most white women just want to be one of the guys" (Zablit 2016).

A columnist for *National Review*, a conservative magazine, expressed the opposing view:

> When it comes to Clinton's numerous flaws and resounding electoral failure, the culprit sure doesn't seem to be sexism. . . . Sexism certainly exists, but to blame it for Clinton's loss—the failed candidacy of an ossified political fixture with enough toxic baggage to crush 17 glass ceilings—is absurd. In the Rorschach test of life, some people will always see sexism lurking around every corner, hysterically labeling each slight as a sign of eternal misogyny. It must be an exhausting way to live.
>
> *(Wilhelm 2016)*

### *Double Standard for Female Candidates?*

Beginning with Clinton's primary contest against Bernie Sanders, some analysts wrote that Clinton was suffering from headwinds not as perceptible as outright sexism, but instead something "more pervasive and far subtler—unconscious, even"—socially ingrained gender stereotypes (Milbank 2016). They pointed out a variety of double standards to which she was subjected: criticism for yelling during speeches, although it was a favorite tactic of her rival Bernie Sanders; an inability to make "lofty promises" for fear of being dismissed as unrealistic, while Sanders proposed policies—and gained followers—for policies widely considered as non-starters in Washington; and how to be "tough and warm at the same time," although men such as Ronald Reagan and George W. Bush, who called for "compassionate conservativism," had no such issues (Milbank 2016).

Women candidates have long suffered disproportionate attention to their age, looks, hairstyle, clothing, accessories, and even the pitch of their voices. Women running for office today, including Clinton, are keenly aware of the age-old style-versus-substance problem they face—the media's focus on women is style, but on men, it's substance (MacManus 2017).

To head off that type of media coverage, when Clinton entered the race, she made light of her age: "I will be the youngest woman president in the history of the United States and the first grandmother as well" (qtd. in MacManus 2017). She even joked about her bottle-blonde hair: "They are not going to see me turn white in the White House," as most presidents have, because "I've been coloring my hair for years." It did not insulate her from stylistic "indignities and prejudices" (Filipovic 2016b)—she is too loud; her voice is shrill; she sounds combative; she needs to smile more; her pantsuits look like jumpsuits (the only stylistic criticism she did not endure was about her hair; Trump took that honor).

What disturbed so many of Clinton's female supporters was the longstanding challenge women candidates face of trying to come across as decisive and impassioned without being shrill. The director of the Center for American Women and Politics at Rutgers University pointed to bias among commentators on cable news shows and Twitter: "The campaign is filled on both sides with men doing a lot of yelling, and that doesn't seem to get called out in the same way" (Page 2016b) as when Clinton speaks. Democratic Congresswoman Barbara Boxer concurred: "A man is assertive where a woman is aggressive. A man has spirit where a woman is loud" (qtd. in Page 2016b). At a Democratic women's political forum, Clinton herself acknowledged the disparity: "When women talk, some people think we're shouting" (qtd. in Williams 2016b).

Then there is the double standard of power. Studies show that "when men seek power, they're perceived as more competent, while when women seek power, they face 'contempt, anger, and/or disgust'" (Bazelon 2016). Obviously, nothing reflects power more than being President of the United States.

Clinton also had to endure what some regarded as a double standard in opinions about her character. Research has shown that "when it comes to honesty and trustworthiness, Americans automatically give an edge to women." But other studies have found that "women pay a higher price than men when they aren't seen as honest, and have a harder time regaining trust if they lose it" (Page 2016b). While pre-election polls repeatedly showed that both Clinton and Trump were viewed unfavorably by a majority of voters, Clinton's female supporters, including some in the media, were firmly convinced the press highlighted her negatives more than Trump's shortcomings. A Harvard study confirmed their suspicions (Sutton 2016). As Rebecca Traister pointed out in *New York Magazine*, "When she campaigns, 'the coverage curdles and becomes cold'" (qtd. in Bazelon 2016).

Near the end of the campaign, President Obama, one of Clinton's most powerful surrogates on the campaign trail, affirmed the existence of a double standard: "There's a reason we haven't had a woman president. Hillary Clinton is consistently treated differently than just about any other candidate I see out there" (qtd. in Wilhelm 2016). Former President Bill Clinton laid the blame for double standards mostly on men: "I know there's a bunch of guys that are upset about having a woman president. They just don't want to 'fess up to it'" (qtd. in Wilhelm 2016). However, a CBS poll taken in June 2016 reported a high percentage of Americans supportive of the idea of a woman President—and no gender gap in that opinion:

> Four out of five voters say the U.S. is ready to elect a woman for president, a doubling of the percentage that said so twenty years ago. Eighty-two percent of men, and 76 percent of women, agree, as do majorities of Republicans, Democrats and independents. Seventy-two percent of voters say they hope to see a woman president in their lifetime, up from 63 percent eight years ago. Seventy-six percent of women, and two thirds of men, hope to see this happen.
> (Dutton, De Pinto, Backus and Salvanto 2016)

But some women (Clinton supporters) accused other *women* (Trump supporters) of being sexist as well—traitors to their gender who sold out the sisterhood with their "internalized misogyny" (Carpenter 2016). A conservative female CNN political commentator took great offense: "Don't say Clinton was disadvantaged because she was a woman because as a Clinton she had every advantage possible. She had money, the staff, the ads, and institutional support needed for a successful run" (Carpenter 2016). Another expressed it differently: "When women want the 'wrong' things, feminists tend to write it off to entrenched sexism and internalized misogyny. But it's 2016, not 1960. Why not credit women with free will and respect their choices?" (Sommers 2016).

### Media Double Standards for Women?

To some conservative women, the more serious double standard is how the media casts female Trump supporters compared to female Clinton supporters on issues ranging from marriage and children to abortion. In the words of a pro-life, family feminist who voted for Trump, "abortion on demand has hurt women, not helped them, and Hillary would have made it worse." (Browder 2016). She and other women holding such a view complain they are marginalized and scorned by the "elite media."

Similarly, poor, less-than-college-educated, working-class white women believe that the media disparaged their life circumstances and castigated them for their support of Trump—as ignorant, not to mention deplorable, racist, sexist, homophobic, xenophobic, and Islamophobic (Taranto 2016). Many of these women "[resented] the fact that everything they believe in is mocked by the media elite, Hollywood" (Chira 2016).

## *What Personal Attributes of a Candidate Matter Most?*

Among older Democrats, Clinton got high marks for her experience, both in the public sector—as First Lady, U.S. Senator from New York, and Secretary of State—and in the nonprofit sector—for her work for children and women's rights (Children's Defense Fund). To a retired black female federal employee,

> The fact that her life mission and work was about family and children, that resonated with me and with other black women. She's been about public service all her life. [But, most of all] my vote for her was based on her qualifications. She was the most qualified person for the job.
>
> *(Williams 2016a)*

Others respected Clinton's passion and performance under fire. In the words of a Clinton volunteer in Iowa in the early days of the campaign: "Women gravitate toward her. No matter what the situation, she is so level-headed, she is so calm, she meets it with such absolute fierceness" (Ballhaus 2016).

Experience and qualifications were not the stumbling blocks. Polls consistently showed that voters thought Hillary was extremely well-qualified for the job. It was her likability that posed more of a problem for her than for Trump, confirming that women who are more authoritative are less liked and perceived to be out for themselves (Filipovic 2016a). Studies have found that voters are less willing to vote for a qualified female candidate that they don't like:

> For women candidates, likability is linked to electability, and that's not the case for men. . . . When women are pushed off or fall off their honesty-and-ethical pedestal [her emails via the private server in her home], it is very, very hard for them to climb back up, and that isn't

the case for men. . . . Male candidates face lower expectations that they will be honest, and voters are quicker to forgive them when they aren't.

*(Page 2016b)*

The likeability problem extended to millennial women as reflected in various polls that found big majorities viewing her as "untrustworthy, calculating, and unprincipled. . . . saying what is politically convenient" (Brownstein 2016). This was terribly disconcerting to older feminists. *New York Times* columnist Maureen Dowd wrote of the irony of Clinton's address to women at her alma mater Wellesley College:

> Hillary Clinton first grabbed the national spotlight 47 years ago as an idealistic young feminist, chiding the paternalistic establishment in her Wellesley commencement speech. So *it's passing strange to watch her here, getting rebuffed by young women who believe that she lacks idealism, that she overplays her feminist hand and that she is the paternalistic establishment* (emphasis added). . . . She's not likable enough for the young women who were supposed to carry her forward as a Joan of Arc.
>
> *(Dowd 2016)*

The younger feminists were put off by her coziness with Wall Street firms like Goldman Sachs, yielding highly lucrative speaking fees and large campaign contributions, her sharp dismissal of women alleging rape by her husband when he was governor of Arkansas, her slowness to embrace gay marriage, and a host of other sins (for example, see Atkins 2016). Many also saw her use of young female celebrities like Lena Dunham and Katy Perry as insulting. Said one (Carpenter 2016):

> A free Katy Perry concert wouldn't even come close to buying off my vote. I may, for once in my life, agree with Lena Dunham about the aspects of anti-woman behavior that are prevalent in America, *but it simply wasn't the top voting issue.*
>
> *(emphasis added)*

## Clinton: Continuation of Obama's Policies or Change Agent?

Clinton consciously tied her campaign to Obama's presidency, hoping to replicate (even expand) his winning coalition of millennials, minorities, and single women. In accepting the nomination at the Democratic National Convention, she told delegates, "America is stronger because of President Obama's leadership, and I am better because of his friendship" (qtd. in Cillizza 2016a). In one mailer, she even wrote: "One vote—your vote—can determine how history remembers Barack's Presidency" (Glueck and Cheney 2016).

In turn, President Obama was one of Clinton's most popular surrogates on the campaign trail. He understood she was the vessel by which his policy legacies would be transported. He told the African American community that he "[would] consider it a personal insult, an insult to my legacy" if they failed to vote for Clinton (Bandler 2016) (as it turned out, the highest support for Clinton came from black women).

Clinton herself put forward what some have called "the most feminist agenda of any nominee in history" (Filipovic 2016b), calling for keeping abortion safe and legal; more government-supported child care; universal pre-kindergarten for every 4-year-old; increased salaries for child care workers, and child care scholarships for student-parents; expanded funding for on-campus child care centers; a cap on middle- and low-income families' child care spending; equal pay for equal work; funding for Planned Parenthood; and appointment of U.S. Supreme Court justices who would not overturn *Roe vs. Wade*.

But to some younger women, Clinton had been a public figure their entire lives and represented the political establishment. Said one: "Even though having a woman in the White House would be new and different, it's hard to feel like Hillary Clinton is new and different" (Gaudiano and Przybyla 2016).

Some Republican women saw her as "the [self-] anointed inheritor of President Obama's third term who would continue unpopular programs like Obamacare with its huge and rising deductibles, refuse to label anything a terrorist attack, and increase taxes, spending, and regulation" (Carpenter 2016). Others said they were going to vote against her, not because she is a woman, but because she is an establishment figure—and they wanted change: "HRC could never be anything but a consummate Washington insider at a time when many, many voters, women as well as men, wanted change" (Tyre 2016).

## *What is a "Woman's Issue" and What is a "Woman"?*

Clinton's female supporters put high priorities on reproductive rights, universal child care, equal pay, pro-choice policies (best protected by U.S. Supreme Court justices she would nominate), and more inclusive definitions of gender.

To conservative women, her views on some of these issues (abortion, gender definitions) were not in sync with theirs: "Readily available contraception may be a fact of life, but women, both churched and unchurched, remain deeply divided about abortion." And they felt that "cultural mores were changing too fast" when those "in the trans-movement insisted that being a woman was no longer a matter of biology and a lifetime of accrued experience but one of preference" (Tyre 2016). A 29-year-old, pro-life mother of four had issues with a number of Clinton policies (maternity, health care, child care) that she saw restricting her freedom of choice. She viewed Clinton as an ambitious politician "out of touch with most American women's family values" in spite of her attempts to "play up her maternal and feminine soft side" (Chapin 2016).

However, none of these issues drove working-class white women to reject Clinton in favor of Trump more than the economy, as noted by Fox Business Network morning host Maria Bartiromo:

> The elites, the establishment, the media, they had no idea what the people wanted and had no idea where the people were in terms of economic issues, in particular jobs. . . . It was very much about the working man and woman. . . . There's a big portion of the population out there who was saying, 'You know that I'm the forgotten. . . . I'm the one who has not seen their wages move in 20 years.'
>
> *(qtd. in Shelbourne 2016)*

### Voting Patterns (from National Exit Poll)

Nationally a majority of women (54 percent) voted for Clinton, but 46 percent did not (41 percent voted for Trump and 5 percent chose a third party or write-in candidate). The hopes and dreams of many women were dashed when Trump was declared the winner by the Electoral College. The outcome was totally unexpected and came as a shock. Most pre-election polls had projected she would get a much higher percentage, especially in light of the multitude of crude and crass statements her opponent had uttered throughout the long, grueling campaign. As it turned out, expectations of a highly cohesive women's vote that dominated news coverage of the race from the beginning were unrealistic. The results affirmed what has been true throughout history—women are not highly cohesive in their voting patterns. Gender is often less a voting cue than party, ideology, race, education, economic circumstance, and age.

### *Sharp Generational Divide*

In the 2016 presidential election, generational differences were sharper than in the past, even within the same party, prompting some to describe the race as millennials vs. baby boomers. It was the first election in which millennials, now America's largest generation and its most racially diverse, most highly educated, and most debt-ridden, exerted their political clout. Millennials ended up helping elect Trump—not because they voted for him (although 39 percent did) but because 8 percent of the 18–34-year-olds voted for minor party candidates Jill Stein (Green Party) or Gary Johnson (Libertarian Party) or independents, or did not vote at all. At a post-election forum at Harvard University, Clinton's own campaign manager, Robby Mook, attributed her loss to the millennials:

> Where the campaign needed to win upward of 60 percent of young voters, it was able to garner something in the high 50s at the end of the day. That's why we lost. Younger voters, perhaps assuming that Clinton was going to win, migrated to third-party candidates in the final days of the race.
>
> *(qtd. in Black 2016)*

### *Gender and Race/Ethnicity*

Clinton's campaign had some bright spots. Overall, 13 percent more females than males voted for Clinton (Figure 6.1). Among both white and black women, 12 percent more voted for Clinton than did their male counterparts. Among Latinos, 6 percent more Latinas (women) voted for her than Latinos (men).

Black women, who made up 7 percent of all voters, were by far the most cohesive voting bloc for Clinton, with 94 percent voting for her. More than two-thirds (69 percent) of Latinas also cast their ballots for Clinton; Latinas were 6 percent of the electorate. In sharp contrast, white women were 37 percent of all voters, and a majority (52 percent) voted for Trump.

### *Education and White Female Voters*

Educational differences were sharp among white women voters. White female college graduates made up a larger share of all voters than their non-college-educated counterparts (20 percent vs. 17 percent, respectively). But that does not tell the real story. Clinton won a majority (51 percent) of white college-educated women, becoming the first Democrat to do so. But Trump garnered 61 percent of the votes cast by non-college-educated white females.

### *Party Affiliation*

Both candidates held on to their respective partisans of both genders fairly well, although Clinton lost fewer Democratic women's (7 percent) than

□ Clinton (D)  □ Other  ■ Trump (R)

**GENDER**
| Group | Clinton | Other | Trump |
|---|---|---|---|
| Male (47%) | 41 | 7 | 52 |
| Female (53%) | 54 | 5 | 41 |

**GENDER AND RACE/ETHNICITY**
| Group | Clinton | Other | Trump |
|---|---|---|---|
| White men (34%) | 31 | 7 | 62 |
| White women (37%) | 43 | 5 | 52 |
| Black men (5%) | 82 | 5 | 13 |
| Black women (7%) | 94 | 2 | 4 |
| Hispanic men (5%) | 63 | 5 | 32 |
| Hispanic women (6%) | 69 | 6 | 25 |
| Others (6%) | 61 | 8 | 31 |

**GENDER AND EDUCATION**
| Group | Clinton | Other | Trump |
|---|---|---|---|
| White college-grad women (20%) | 51 | 5 | 44 |
| White non-college women (17%) | 34 | 5 | 61 |
| White college-grad men (17%) | 39 | 8 | 53 |
| White non-college men (16%) | 23 | 6 | 71 |
| Non-whites (29%) | 74 | 5 | 21 |

**GENDER BY PARTY AFFILIATION**
| Group | Clinton | Other | Trump |
|---|---|---|---|
| Democratic men (14%) | 87 | 4 | 9 |
| Democratic women (23%) | 91 | 2 | 7 |
| Republican men (17%) | 7 | 4 | 89 |
| Republican women (16%) | 9 | 3 | 88 |
| Independent men (17%) | 38 | 12 | 50 |
| Independent women (14%) | 47 | 11 | 42 |

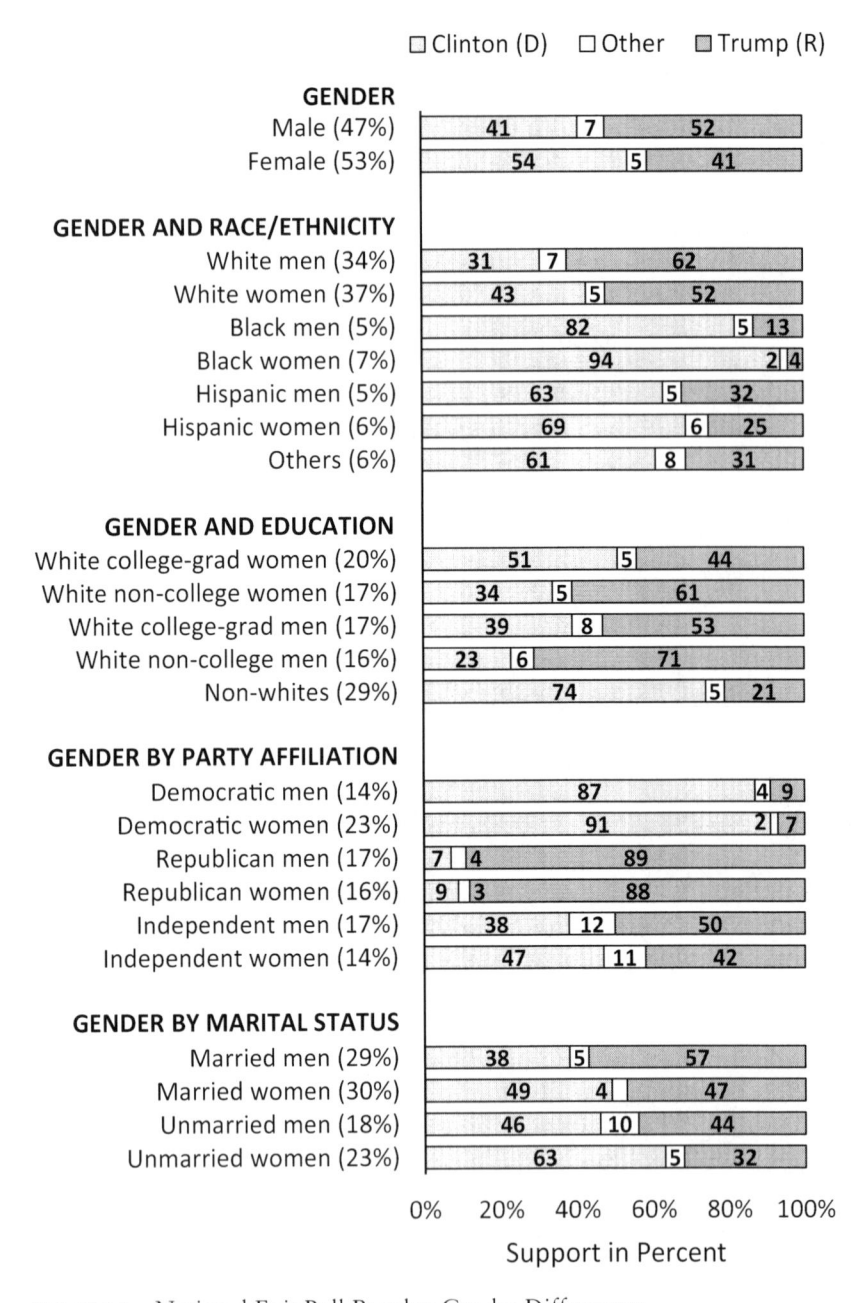

**GENDER BY MARITAL STATUS**
| Group | Clinton | Other | Trump |
|---|---|---|---|
| Married men (29%) | 38 | 5 | 57 |
| Married women (30%) | 49 | 4 | 47 |
| Unmarried men (18%) | 46 | 10 | 44 |
| Unmarried women (23%) | 63 | 5 | 32 |

Support in Percent

FIGURE 6.1  National Exit Poll Results: Gender Differences

*Note:* "Hispanic men" and "Hispanic women" refer to the original exit poll categories of "Latino men" and "Latino women," respectively.

*Source:* Compiled by the author from national exit polls as reported by CNN at www.cnn.com/election/results/exit-polls.

men's (9 percent) votes to Trump. But Trump lost more Republican women's votes (9 percent) than men's (7 percent) to Clinton (the Clinton campaign had heavily targeted Republican suburban women, who historically have been swing voters).

The pattern was quite different among independents who made up 31 percent of all voters. Among women independents, 47 percent voted for Clinton, 42 percent for Trump, and 11 percent for a third party or independent candidate. Support for Clinton among independent men was a low 38 percent. Much of the third party support came from younger voters.

## *Marital Status*

Married women made up a larger share of the voters in 2016 than unmarried women (30 percent vs. 23 percent). Unmarried females were a key part of Obama's winning coalition in both 2008 and 2012 and were heavily targeted by the Clinton campaign in 2016. Unmarried women did support her at a higher level than married women (63 percent vs. 49 percent). However, Clinton got a plurality (49 percent) of the married women's vote. It was the first time a Democrat had gotten more of that vote than the Republican candidate since her husband's win in 1996.

## Conclusion: A Final Look at Women in 2016

The glass ceiling, which some described as more like "reinforced concrete" (Demick 2016), held, leaving a number of women "worried that they'll die before a woman is ever elected president" (Collins 2016). Others like Caitlin Frazier, senior editor for social media at *The Atlantic*, are more optimistic:

> As a presidential candidate, Clinton was vanquished. But as a feminist icon, she's certain to live on. Her supporters have already begun to use her as a convenient shorthand to represent the challenges of their own lives, seeing their struggles in hers. To them, she's the women who withstand the painful misogyny of American society. She's telling your daughter to raise her hand in class, even if the boys make fun of her. She's pantsuits and she's the more than 3 million members of the Facebook group Pantsuit Nation. She's every qualified woman who had an unqualified man beat her out for a job. She's the 'I Voted' stickers on Susan B. Anthony's grave. She's the cracks in the glass ceiling that didn't break. She's what could have been. She's the promise of what someday will be.
>
> *(Frazier 2016)*

In her concession speech, Clinton herself ended on an optimistic note: "I know we have still not shattered that highest and hardest glass ceiling, but some day someone will and hopefully sooner than we might think right now" ("Hillary Clinton's Concession Speech" 2016).

A big lesson learned anew from this election is that women in America are diverse politically, economically, and culturally. Projections of high levels of electoral cohesiveness among them can create unrealistic expectations. There is no singular "woman's vote," but there are "women's votes."

## Note

\* I would like to acknowledge my appreciation for the assistance of my Research Associate and University of South Florida graduate, Anthony A. Cilluffo, in the preparation of this chapter.

## Bibliography

Alter, Charlotte. 2016. "Hillary Clinton Collides Again With Highest Glass Ceiling," *Time*, November 9. http://time.com/4564142/hillary-clinton-gender/ (accessed December 14, 2016).

Atkins, David. 2016. "Why Millennials Don't Like Clinton—And What She Can Do About It." *American Prospect*, September 23. http://prospect.org/article/why-millennials-don%E2%80%99t-clinton%E2%80%94and-what-she-can-do-about-it (accessed December 14, 2016).

Ballhaus, Rebecca. 2016. "Women Join Up to Boost Clinton." *Wall Street Journal*, January 18. www.wsj.com/articles/women-join-up-to-boost-clinton-1453164571 (accessed December 12, 2016).

Bandler, Aaron. 2016. "Obama: You'll Be Insulting Me If You Don't Vote for Hillary." *Daily Wire*, September 19. www.dailywire.com/news/9258/obama-youll-be-insulting-me-if-you-dont-vote-aaron-bandler (accessed December 12, 2016).

Bazelon, Emily. 2016. "What Women Owe Hillary Clinton." *New York Times Magazine*, July 29. www.nytimes.com/2016/07/29/magazine/what-women-owe-hillary-clinton.html (accessed December 12, 2016).

Black, Aaron. 2016. "Yes, You Can Blame Millennials for Hillary Clinton's Loss." *Washington Post*, December 2. www.washingtonpost.com/news/the-fix/wp/2016/12/02/yes-you-can-blame-millennials-for-hillary-clintons-loss/ (accessed December 12, 2016).

Bornhorst, Alyssa. 2016. "Why Identity Politics Didn't Energize Women for Hillary." *The Federalist*, November 22. http://thefederalist.com/2016/11/22/identity-politics-didnt-energize-women-hillary/ (accessed December 12, 2016).

Browder, Sue Ellen. 2016. "I'm a Card-Carrying Feminist Who Voted for Donald Trump." *The Federalist*, November 22. http://thefederalist.com/2016/11/22/im-a-card-carrying-feminist-who-definitely-voted-for-donald-trump/ (accessed December 12, 2016).

Brownstein, Ronald. 2016. "Millennial Voters May Cost Hillary Clinton the Election." *The Atlantic*, September 19. www.theatlantic.com/politics/archive/2016/09/hillary-clinton-millennials-philadelphia/500540/ (accessed December 12, 2016).

Carpenter, Amanda. 2016. "What to Blame Women for Trump's Win? Start with Hillary Clinton." *Washington Post*, November 21. www.washingtonpost.com/news/powerpost/wp/2016/11/21/if-anyone-wants-to-blame-women-for-trumps-win-they-ought-to-start-with-hillary-clinton/ (accessed December 12, 2016).

Chapin, Angelina. 2016. "'I'm Not With Her': Why Women are Wary of Hillary Clinton." *The Guardian*, May 23. www.theguardian.com/us-news/2016/may/23/women-female-voters-us-election-hillary-clinton (accessed December 12, 2016).

Chira, Susan. 2016. "The Myth of Female Solidarity." *New York Times*, November 12. www.nytimes.com/2016/11/13/opinion/the-myth-of-female-solidarity.html (accessed December 12, 2016).

Cillizza, Chris. 2016a. "Democrats, You Had the Worst Year in Washington." *The Washington Post*, December 9. www.washingtonpost.com/classic-apps/democrats-you-had-the-worst-year-in-washington/2016/12/09/db96b054-be41-11e6-94ac-3d324840106c_story.html?utm_term=.875b132003c7 (accessed December 12, 2016).

———. 2016b. "The 13 Most Amazing Findings in the 2016 Exit Poll." *Washington Post*, November 10. www.washingtonpost.com/news/the-fix/wp/2016/11/10/the-13-most-amazing-things-in-the-2016-exit-poll/ (accessed December 12, 2016).

Collins, Gail. 2016. "The Glass Ceiling Holds." *New York Times*, November 11. www.nytimes.com/2016/11/13/opinion/sunday/the-glass-ceiling-holds.html (accessed December 12, 2016).

Cook, Charlie. 2015. "The Gender Subplot." *National Journal*, June 26. www.nationaljournal.com/s/25109 (accessed December 14, 2016).

Demick, Barbara. 2016. "Many Women Thought Clinton Would Shatter the Glass Ceiling, Not Run Into a Concrete Wall." *Los Angeles Times*, November 10. www.latimes.com/politics/la-na-pol-trump-women-20161109-story.html (accessed December 12, 2016).

Dowd, Maureen. 2016. "Hillary Battles Bernie Sanders, Chick Magnet." *New York Times*, February 7. www.nytimes.com/2016/02/07/opinion/sunday/hillary-battles-bernie-sanders-chick-magnet.html (accessed December 12, 2016).

Dutton, Sarah, Jennifer De Pinto, Fred Backus and Anthony Salvanto. 2016. "Clinton Maintains Lead After Claiming Nomination—CBS News Poll," *CBS News*, June 15. www.cbsnews.com/news/clinton-maintains-lead-after-claiming-nomination-cbs-news-poll/ (accessed December 14, 2016).

Filipovic, Jill. 2016a. "Go Ahead, Play the Woman Card." *New York Times*, May 2. www.nytimes.com/2016/05/02/opinion/campaign-stops/go-ahead-play-the-woman-card.html (accessed December 12, 2016).

———. 2016b. "What's With Hillary's Woman Problem?" *Politico Magazine*, September/October. www.politico.com/magazine/story/2016/09/hillary-clinton-feminism-white-house-2016-women-214217 (accessed December 12, 2016).

Frazier, Caitlin. 2016. "The Iconic Hillary Clinton." *The Atlantic*, November 13. www.theatlantic.com/politics/archive/2016/11/hillary-clinton-icon/507503/ (accessed December 12, 2016).

Gaudiano, Nicole and Heidi Przybyla. 2016. "Sanders a Hit With Millennial Women." *USA Today*, January 15. www.usatoday.com/story/news/politics/elections/2016/01/14/bernie-sanders-hillary-clinton-women-millennials/78810110/ (accessed December 12, 2016).

Glueck, Katie and Kyle Cheney. 2016. "Early Voting Shows Upsurge of Women." *Politico*, October 21. www.politico.com/story/2016/10/early-voting-women-battleground-states-230176 (accessed December 12, 2016).

"Hillary Clinton's Concession Speech." 2016. CNN, November 9. www.cnn.com/2016/11/09/politics/hillary-clinton-concession-speech/ (accessed December 12, 2016).

MacManus, Susan A. 2014. "Voter Participation and Turnout: The Political Generational Divide Among Women Voters." In *Gender and Elections: Shaping the Future of American Politics*, ed. Susan J. Carroll and Richard L. Fox. New York: Cambridge University Press.

———. 2017. "Women and Campaigns—Generational-Based Microtargeting and Tackling Stereotypes." In *Campaigns on the Cutting Edge*, 3rd ed., ed. Richard J. Semiatin. Los Angeles, CA: CQ Press.

Milbank, Dana. 2016. "The Sexist Double Standards Hurting Hillary Clinton." *Washington Post*, February 12. www.washingtonpost.com/opinions/the-sexist-double-standards-hurting-hillary-clinton/2016/02/12/fb551e38-d195-11e5-abc9-ea152f0b9561_story.html (accessed December 12, 2016).

Murphy, Patricia. 2015. "Why Are Women Ditching Hillary?" *The Daily Beast*, September 13. www.thedailybeast.com/articles/2015/09/13/why-are-women-ditching-hillary.html (accessed December 12, 2016).

Page, Susan. 2016a. "How Women Have Defined the 2016 Election." *USA Today*, November 1. www.usatoday.com/story/news/politics/elections/2016/11/01/how-women-have-defined-the-2016-election-hillary-clinton/93049292/ (accessed December 14, 2016).

———. 2016b. "Why Are You Yelling? The Questions Female Candidates Still Face." *USA Today*, June 6. www.usatoday.com/story/news/politics/elections/2016/06/05/hillary-clinton-female-candidates-political-landscape-democrat-president/85343998/ (accessed December 14, 2016).

Rappeport, Alan. 2016. "Gloria Steinem and Madeleine Albright Rebuke Young Women Backing Bernie Sanders." *New York Times*, February 7. www.nytimes.com/2016/02/08/us/politics/gloria-steinem-madeleine-albright-hillary-clinton-bernie-sanders.html (accessed December 12, 2016).

Shelbourne, Mallory. 2016. "Bartiromo Knocks View of 'Elites' During Campaign." *The Hill*, December 11. http://thehill.com/homenews/campaign/309831-bartiromo-media-had-no-idea-what-economic-issues-mattered-to-americans (accessed December 12, 2016).

Sommers, Christina Hoff. 2016. "Commentary: How to Make Feminism Great Again." *Washington Post*, December 8. www.chicagotribune.com/news/opinion/commentary/ct-feminism-patriarchy-working-class-women-20161208-story.html (accessed December 12, 2016).

Sutton, Kelsey. 2016. "Harvard Study: General Election Media Coverage 'Overwhelmingly Negative' in Tone." *Politico*, December 7. www.politico.com/blogs/on-media/2016/12/report-general-election-coverage-overwhelmingly-negative-in-tone-232307 (accessed December 12, 2016).

Stolberg, Sheryl Gay. 2016. "The Women Who Helped Trump to Victory." *New York Times*, November 12. www.nytimes.com/2016/11/11/us/politics/the-women-who-helped-donald-trump-to-victory.html (accessed December 12, 2016).

Taranto, James. 2016. "Doubling Down on 'Deplorable.'" *Wall Street Journal*, December 9. www.wsj.com/articles/doubling-down-on-deplorable-1481303167 (accessed December 12, 2016).

"Transcript: Hillary Clinton's Speech at the Democratic Convention." 2016. *New York Times*, July 28. www.nytimes.com/2016/07/29/us/politics/hillary-clinton-dnc-transcript.html (accessed December 12, 2016).

Tumulty, Karen and Abby Phillip. "As Clinton Makes History, Some Already Take It for Granted." *Washington Post*, July 26. www.washingtonpost.com/politics/as-clinton-makes-history-some-already-take-it-for-granted/2016/07/26/793d6fd0-534b-11e6-b7de-dfe509430c39_story.html (accessed December 12, 2016).

Tyre, Peg. 2016. "Why Women Rejected Hillary." *Politico*, November 14. www.politico.com/magazine/story/2016/11/hillary-clinton-2016-women-214454 (accessed December 12, 2016).

Wagner, John. 2015. "Sanders Makes His Pitch to A Group That Wants More Women in Office." *Washington Post*, November 7. www.washingtonpost.com/news/post-politics/wp/2015/11/07/sanders-makes-his-economic-pitch-to-a-group-that-wants-more-women-in-office/?utm_term=.6ec5f8fe422c (accessed December 12, 2016).

Wilhelm, Heather. 2016. "Hillary Clinton Lost Because She's Hillary Clinton." *National Review*, November 11. www.nationalreview.com/article/442063/hillary-clinton-lost-2016-presidential-election-sexism-glass-ceiling (accessed December 12, 2016).

Williams, Vanessa. 2016a. "Black Women—Hillary Clinton's Most Reliable Voting Bloc—Look Beyond Defeat." *Washington Post*, November 12. www.washingtonpost.com/politics/black-women—Hillary-clintons-most-reliable-voting-bloc—look-beyond-defeat/2016/11/12/86d9182a-a845-11e6-ba59-a7d93165c6d4_story.html (accessed December 12, 2016).

———. 2016b. "Sanders Campaign Says It Has More Women Donors Than Clinton." *Washington Post*, November 25. www.washingtonpost.com/news/post-politics/wp/2015/11/25/sanders-campaign-says-it-has-more-women-donors-than-clinton/?utm_term=.ddebf3df64ce (accessed December 12, 2016).

Zablit, Jocelyne. 2016. "Trump Fares Well With Women Voters Despite Sex Assault Claims." *Agence France Presse*, November 10.

# 7

# NAVIGATING THROUGH TURBULENCE AND TROUBLESOME TIMES

Latinos, Election 2016, Partisan Politics, and Salient Public Policies

*John A. Garcia*

> *The road toward equality of freedom is not easy and great cost and danger march alongside us. We are committed to peaceful and non-violent change, and that is important for all to understand—though all change is unsettling. Still, even in the turbulence of protest and struggle is greater hope for the future, as men learn to claim and achieve for themselves the rights formerly petitioned from others.*
> — Robert Kennedy, "Day of Affirmation" speech on June 6, 1966, University of Cape Town, South Africa

> *In a world that I have known through family and close friends, it has given me a foundation of home and vision for a better world. Yet living in times with very strong emotions that is dominated with fear, anger, hatred, suspicion and unfriendliness toward me, my family and close friends; then I am challenged to not be a stranger in my own land.*
> — John A. Garcia, for this volume

An apt description for the 2016 election cycle can be characterized as "an election unlike any other." Some unlikely features included the least positive view of the major party's candidates from previous elections; starkness of rhetoric and statements directed to the immigrants, non-Christians, members of communities of color, women, LGBTQ and disability communities; and heightened emotions (i.e. anger, fear, anxiety, etc.). This chapter provides an analytical narrative how Latinos, in their continued efforts to expand their political impact and influence to the 2016 election outcomes, navigated an emotionally charged election period in which this community was the "target" of policy changes and castigated aspersions about their character and value to this nation. This analysis will include four parts: a) critical political dynamics affecting this election; b) update of the Latino electorate with its strengths and challenges; c) the partisan domains and Latino fit; and d) Latinos' views and assessments of about Hillary Clinton and Donald Trump and critical issues. Then I will end with the outcomes for Latinos in this election cycle, with a view toward the near future.

The 2016 elections were marked by a campaign tenor filled with charged emotions, heightened polarization, and a presidential upset victory for Donald Trump and Mike Pence. At the same time, the Latino community was engaged in another series of presidential year elections in which they were trying expand their political influence via supporting Latino/a candidates, engaging in partisan politics (especially the Democratic party), advocating policy priorities and preferences, and mobilizing support for the election of Hillary Clinton. Latinos have faced, for some time, the improvement of registration and turnout levels comparable to other groups. In addition, Latinos continue to seek effective political mobilization and outreach efforts, and to ensure greater responsiveness by the major political parties and their candidates by being responsive to issues important to this community. Finally, contemporary political dynamics and the choices Latinos make operated in more turbulent and rancorous times.

Thus, this chapter places emphasis on Latino communities, their leadership and behaviors working through a turbulent political world and analyzing their political attitudes and behaviors. More specifically, the organization of this chapter will include a short discussion of the major developments occurring in American politics and elections. Secondly, we will look at the developments among the Latino electorate in terms of growth, advancements, and challenges. Then we shall continue with an extensive discussion of changes occurring in the major political parties and their intersection with Latinos (i.e. affiliation, assessments and support). Then, we will examine Latinos' views about Hillary Clinton and Donald Trump and their choices for the presidency. Finally, we will discuss the short- and long-term implications of this "round" of Latino political engagement for its political future and the American political system.

## Some Major Political Developments in America's Landscape

Presidential campaigns have become a much longer extended period of activities such as announcements, campaigning, and fundraising beginning more than a year in advance of the election date. The major political parties (i.e. Democrats and Republicans) still provide the dominant candidates, with minor parties like the Green party and Libertarian party making attempts to expand their electoral bases. The crowded field of Republican presidential aspirants provided a full spectrum of ideological emphases, active segments of the party, two Latino candidates (Marco Rubio and Ted Cruz), and relative political newcomers (i.e. Ben Carson, Carly Fiorina, and Donald Trump). The primary battle in the Democratic primary centered on Bernie Sanders and Hillary Clinton. For Latina/os, early support lined up with the familiar and connected ties with the Clinton candidacy. At the same time, several Latino progressives announced their support for Bernie Sanders, which made for a more contested primary contest.

Latino/as continue to be an expanding segment of the U.S. population and electorate. The 2016 elections represented another opportunity to increase their representation at all levels of government, affect presidential campaigns and policy directions, and influence the presidential and other office outcomes. Before pursuing Latino political engagement, it is noteworthy to highlight key developments occurring in this election cycle. That is, demographic changes happening in this country and political undercurrents in terms of polarization and ideological divides are dynamics that are affecting this election and Latinos' mix in the 2016 electoral arena.

The first major development (or continuing pattern) is the racial/ethnic composition of the United States, which is becoming more of a majority-minority nation. For example, the states of California, Hawaii, New Mexico, and Texas are already majority-minority states; with New York, New Jersey, Nevada, Mississippi, Maryland, Georgia, and Arizona expected to follow suit in the next 5–10 years. This trend is reflected by the groups that are the major contributors to this country's population growth (Ortman and Guarneri 2009). For example, the Census Bureau projects that Latinos represent over 50 percent of the nation's population growth through 2060 (Ortman and Guarneri 2009); while whites represent a 17 percent decline from 2015–2060 (Table 7.1). The realities of a more diverse racial and ethnic population (also diverse religiously) mark some significant changes that have created a range of emotions and assessments about the future uncertainties, anxieties, and fears about national identities, power relations, and policy priorities.

This general population pattern is reflected in the changing composition of the American electorate. The portion of whites has fallen from 87 percent in 1992 to 69 percent in 2015 (Pew Research Center 2015a). At the same time, the minority proportion has increased from 13 percent in 1992 to 31 percent in 2016 with Latinos having the largest gain (8 percent to 13 percent). This trend will continue into future elections and has some of the following implications: conversion of an expanding eligible electoral minorities' bases into a larger share of the registered and voting electorate, partisan alignments of racial and ethnic groups into the major political parties, redistribution of partisan and political leadership, and potential for polarization along racial and ethnic "lines." In the case of the latter, a racial divide can be manifested in policy priorities and preferences,

**TABLE 7.1** Hispanics Will Continue to Account for Over 50% of Future U.S. Population Growth

| Year | 2015 | 2020 | Change 2015 to 2020 | 2040 | Change 2015 to 2040 | 2060 | Change 2015 to 2060 |
|---|---|---|---|---|---|---|---|
| Race/Ethnic Group | Pop. Proj. | Pop. Proj. | % Increase/Decrease in Total Growth | Pop. Proj. | % Increase/Decrease in Total Growth | Pop. Proj. | % Increase/Decrease in Total Growth |
| Other | 6,593 | 7,678 | 8% | 13,089 | 11% | 20,376 | 14% |
| Asian-American | 16,978 | 19,225 | 17% | 28,756 | 20% | 37,879 | 22% |
| African-American | 39,782 | 41,594 | 14% | 48,162 | 14% | 54,028 | 15% |
| Hispanic | 56,754 | 63,551 | 52% | 91,626 | 59% | 119,044 | 65% |
| Non-Hispanic White | 198,354 | 199,400 | 8% | 195,197 | -5% | 181,930 | -17% |

*Note*: All figures are in thousands.

*Source*: Data from U.S. Census Bureau, 2014. Compiled by author.

further demarcation of inside vs. outside groups, and increased cynicism and alienation from the political system.

Another significant development in the American political landscape is the rise of polarization among the electorate along ideological and partisan lines. Ideological "polar" positions are evident in the content of party platforms (Layman 1999), ratings of interest groups of legislators (Stonecash, Brewer and Mariani 2003), and surveys of partisan activists (Layman, Carsey and Horowitz 2006). One of the consequences is that policy making takes on the character of one party imposing its will on the other and the opposition party engaged in persistent "delegitimization" (Mann and Ornstein 2013). Political trust in the institutions and processes has declined to record lows. Another manifestation of this polarization is the expansion of ideological "echo chambers" (Pew Research Center 2014a). That is, 28 percent of respondents overall indicated that it is important to live in a place where most people share similar political views, and 30 percent of close friends share their political views. This pattern is more the case among consistently conservatives (50 percent and 63 percent, respectively) in comparison to consistently liberals (35 percent and 46 percent, respectively).

The literature on polarization focuses on both ideological and partisan divisions as well as elite vs. mass polarization (Bartels 2016; Yphtach 2016). The partisan divide is clearly evident over the past two decades such that there have been dramatic shifts to the farther right and left by Republicans and Democrats. From 1994–2014, 92 percent of Republicans are more conservative than the median Democrat; while 94 percent of Democrats are more liberal than the median Republican (Pew Research Center 2014a). This partisan gap has reinforced perceptions of polarization being driven by partisanship and creating a more pronounced "hostility" between one another (Levendusky and Malhotra 2016). When it comes to presidential trait portrayals, partisans perceive the other party's candidate as extreme and very negative (Hetherington, Long and Rudolph 2016). Racial attitudes among Republications have become more conservative and moral values among Democrats have become more liberal; while Republicans' moral views are a more influential predictor of trait evaluations (Hetherington, Long and Rudolph 2016; Mangum 2013). Finally, there is the role of elite party polarization serving as a primary cue to expedite mass partisanship (Davis and Dunaway 2016), which can activate segments of the electorate to heighten their motivation to vote.

This brief discussion about the demographic changes and growing polarization in the American political system has a direct bearing on Latinos in this election cycle. Perceptions about this community (i.e. their authenticity as true Americans, primarily immigration status and as disproportionately undocumented, more partisan Democrats, etc.) have affected their partisan preferences, presidential candidate support, and emotional stimuli of anger, threat, and fear as contributing to motivations about their political engagement. The remainder of this chapter will discuss the developments regarding the Latino electorate, their relationships with the major political parties, and then the presidential race between Hillary Clinton and Donald Trump.

## The Latino Electorate: Developments and Challenges

In 2016, characterizations about the Latino electorate could include a growing electoral share, long term prospects of an even greater proportion of voters, continuing challenges of converting a growing voter eligible base into active registered voters, expanding and increasing the efficiency of voter outreach and mobilization, and navigating limited options among the major political parties. In 2016, Latinos represented about 13 percent of the total electorate, which was a 62.5 percent increase since 1992. At the same time, approximately one-half of the eligible Latino electorate is registered (i.e. 27.5 million total vs. 13.5 registered) which leaves an even greater share of the electorate with higher registration levels. The main source of Latino voter growth lies with its youthful segment (or millennials) and potential naturalized citizens. For example, from 2012 to 2016, 3.2 million Latinos became eligible to vote as they turned 18 years old and another 3.2 Latino immigrants became citizens (Pew Research Center 2016b). The former contributor is quite significant for Latinos as 44 percent of Latino adults are millennials (Pew Research Center 2016a), which is 13 percent higher the national figure.

The "track " record for the Latino electorate is one of a 15–18 percent turnout gap with African American and Anglo voters over the past three decades (Alvarez and Bedolla 2003). The slippage occurs in achieving higher registration rates as over 85 percent of Latino registered voters do cast their ballots. An examination of presidential elections since 1980 shows that Latino voter turnout for the Democratic candidate increased from 56 percent (Carter) to 71 percent (Obama) (Figure 7.1). Only Republicans Reagan and George W. Bush exceeded 35 percent of the Latino vote. This pattern of voting for the Democratic candidate is also reflected in their partisan affiliation. Pew Research Center (2014b) reported that in 2012, 63 percent of Latinos affiliated with the Democratic party, while 27 percent identified as Republicans. The percentages of Latino Republicans have been declining since 2000; yet the shift has been more in the independent category or in those leaning Democratic.

Even though Latinos have regularly supported Democrats, there are indications that increased access to leadership positions and advocacy of Latinos' policy priorities remain an important concern. For example,

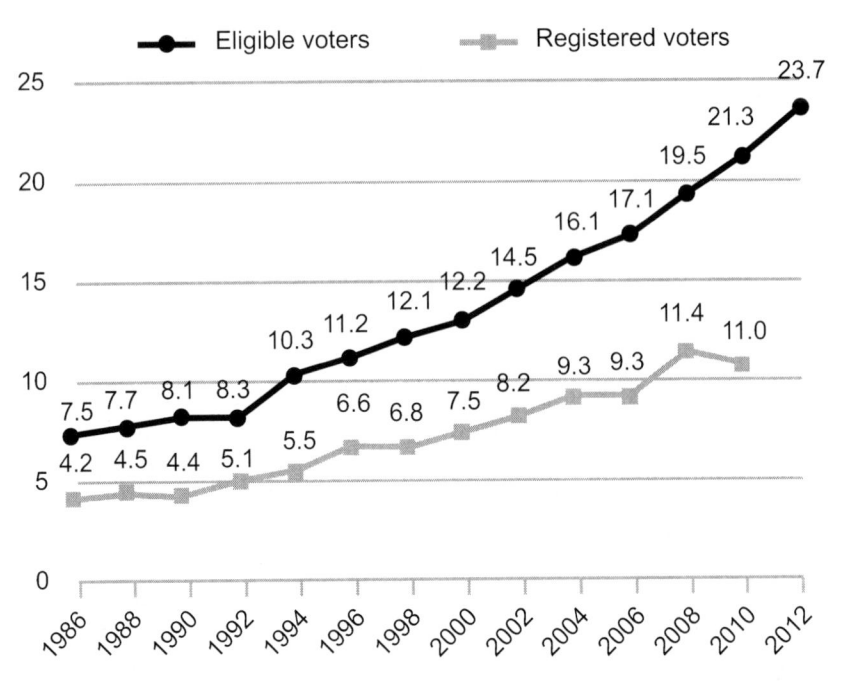

**FIGURE 7.1** Turnout Levels Among Eligible Latino Voters, 1986–2012

*Source:* For 1988–2010, Pew Hispanic Center tabulations of the Current Population Survey November Supplements; for 2012, Pew Hispanic Center tabulations of the August Current Population Survey.

when Latino respondents were asked which party is more concerned about Latinos (2000–2014), the percentage indicating the Republican party remained at 10 percent over this period; while the range for Democrats was 45 percent to 50 percent (Pew Research Center 2016c). It should be noted that a range from 40 percent to 35 percent (from 2000–2014) indicated no difference between the two parties. Similarly when Latinos were asked about the outreach efforts by the major parties, the modal responses about the Republican party (from 2012–2016) were from 46 percent to 27 percent, respectively, as not caring about Latinos; and moving from 19 percent to 43 percent as characterizing the Republican party as hostile toward Latinos (Latino Decisions 2016c). Concomitantly, the responses went from 55 percent to 59 percent for the Democratic party doing a good job and from 23 percent to 21 percent as not caring. Finally, when asked whether both parties should be doing more to be responsive to Latinos, they indicated 71 percent and 59 percent, respectively, for Republican and Democratic parties that such efforts are needed (Figure 7.2).

This relationship between Latinos and the major political parties serves as an important backdrop for Latinos' engagement in the 2016 national

## Figure 7.2

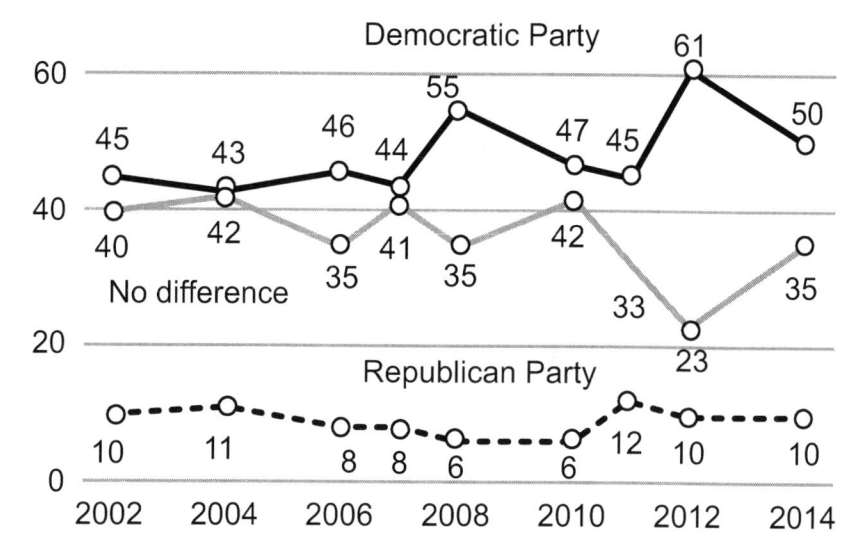

**FIGURE 7.2** Latinos' Views of Major Parties and Their Concerns for Latinos

*Notes:* Voters were asked, "Which party do you think has more concern for Hispanic/Latino: the Republican Party, the Democratic Party, or is there no difference?" Responses of "Don't know/Refused" are not shown.

*Source:* Adapted from Pew Research Center 2002–2014 National Surveys of Latinos.

and local elections. Following the 2012 presidential election, the Republican party national committee assessed its strength and liabilities among segments of the electorate. As a result, the Growth and Opportunity Project (GOP) report (2014) outlines a detailed plan to reach out to African Americans, Asian Americans and Latinos. Strident political stances, elite and mass rhetoric had the "de facto" effect of halting serious attempts to implement aspects of the GOP report. With longstanding and established engagement in the Democratic party, the matter of which party's candidate to support was less in question; but the extent of voter enthusiasm and active and effective mobilization would be a central partisan question for this round of the 2016 presidential election (Table 7.2).

## Election 2016: Interplay of Candidates, Parties and Issues

The road to the major parties' nominations was filled with surprises, a rise of vocal and strong emotions among the electorate, strong personalities as a paramount element, heightened identity politics, targeted population segments, and a push for change from the "established" political elites. Bernie Sanders represented the progressive segment of the Democratic party and promoted issues of reducing income inequality, immediate comprehensive

TABLE 7.2 Party Affiliation, by Group (Percentage of each group that identifies with each political party)

| | Democrat/Lean Democrat | Republican/Lean Republican | Advantage Republican | Advantage Democrat |
|---|---|---|---|---|
| **Groups That Tilt Republican** | | | | |
| Mormon | 22 | 70 | +48 | |
| White evangelical Protestant | 22 | 68 | +46 | |
| White southerners | 34 | 55 | +21 | |
| White men, some college or less | 33 | 54 | +21 | |
| White | 40 | 40 | +9 | |
| Silent generation (ages 69–86) | 43 | 47 | +4 | |
| **Groups That Tilt Democratic** | | | | |
| Black | 80 | 11 | | +69 |
| Asian | 65 | 23 | | +42 |
| Religiously unaffiliated | 61 | 25 | | +36 |
| Post-graduate women | 64 | 29 | | +35 |
| Jewish | 61 | 31 | | +30 |
| Hispanic | 56 | 26 | | +30 |
| Millennial generation (ages 18–33) | 51 | 35 | | +16 |
| TOTAL | 48 | 39 | | +9 |

*Note:* Whites and blacks include only those who are not Hispanic; Hispanics are of any race; Asians are non-Hispanic and English-speaking only [SW1].

*Source:* Data from Pew Research Center (2015b).

immigration reform, higher living wage levels, workers' rights, empowerment of under-represented communities, health care access and affordability, etc. Over the course of his primary campaign, Bernie Sanders gained Latino support and endorsements. On the other hand, Hillary Clinton (and Bill Clinton) had established long standing connections with Latino leaders, especially congressional elected officials and Hillary Clinton's resources built upon her past and policy preferences. Despite almost a two to one lead over Sanders, the enthusiasm and policy positions were more on the Sanders side. Once Hillary Clinton's nomination was secured, she did shift some of her policy stances more in line with Bernie Sanders' campaign themes, especially economic issues.

The Republican primary had over 15 aspirants and represented a full spectrum of party sub-groups, ideological camps, and political newcomers like Ben Carson, Carly Fiorina and Donald Trump. Strong personalities, partisan polarizing rhetoric and counter-Obama policies (i.e. repealing the Affordable Care Act, heightening border security and removal of undocumented immigrants, challenging climate change, etc.) made the partisan "divide" more widened. The eventual nominations of Hillary Clinton and Donald Trump marked a clear delineation for a very significant portion of the Latino electorate. The remainder of this analysis will center on the Latino community's engagement in the 2016 election.

From the offset, Latinos indicated a clear level of support for Hillary Clinton, whereas the issues centered on enthusiasm, motivation to vote, interest, organizational mobilization effectiveness, and assessment of policy congruence of Latinos and the Clinton agenda. Latino Decisions' polls (2016a, 2016b) in the summer and fall of 2016 indicated that Latinos were more enthusiastic about participating in this election (51 percent vs. 37 percent in 2012). In addition, Pew Research Center (2016c) shows that 68 percent of registered Latino voters were more attentive; 67 percent indicated it mattered who won the election; 63 expressed more interest than the previous election; and 67 percent were following this election via the news media. The saliency of this election for Latinos was the result of their continuing efforts to expand their political influence, partisan investment in the Democratic party, a prioritized policy agenda, and operating in a heightened polarized environment along party, racial, cultural, and nativism divides.

The top issues for Latinos (in rank order) are: education (45 percent extremely important—*EI*, and 49 percent very important—*VI*), jobs/economy (39 percent EI and 51 percent VI); health care (35 percent EI and 52 percent VI), and immigration (29 percent EI and 45 percent VI) (Pew Research Center 2014b). In contrast, there are some variations in prioritization with Latinos and the general electorate, but a greater difference is apparent in the policy preferences. That is, jobs and the economy among Latinos meant workers' rights and protection, unionization, and job benefits to include health care access. For the immigration area, reform needed to include pathways to citizenship, human rights for undocumented immigrants, continuation of the immigration policies Deferred Action for Childhood Arrivals (DACA) and Deferred Actions for Parents of Americans (DAPA), and greater recognition of the value that immigrants add to this country. So the intersection of identified issues and the kinds of policies preferences played a key role for Latino engagement. In 2014, Latinos acknowledged that the main reason to vote was support the Latino community (46 percent) followed by supporting the Democratic candidate (39 percent) (Latino Decisions 2016d).

While immigration was ranked fourth, the combined responses of extremely and very important were 75 percent, and the Trump campaign emphasis on immigration placed this area at the forefront. The Trump immigration solutions included greater border security and added personnel, building a wall across the entire southern U.S. border, and mass deportation of undocumented immigrants. The saliency of this policy area was magnified by candidate Trump's characterization of "illegals" as murderers, rapists, drug dealers, and gang members (Oliver and Rahn 2016). A Pew Center survey (2014b) differentiated the Latino community by nativity, gender, language, generational status, and education. Overall, 73 percent of all Latino adults viewed immigration as an important issue. Variation by segments was minor, as 86 percent of the foreign-born, 80 percent of Latinas, 72 percent of registered voters, and 61 percent of second generation Latinos designated immigration as an important issue. Again, Latinos' policy preference critically advocated for a pathway to citizenship, as 75 percent indicated this aspect as central to immigration reform (Latino Decisions 2016c). This sentiment had strengthened over time (from 2013 to 2016) for increased support for a pathway to citizenship (71 percent to 75 percent) and opposition to the "wall" was at 83 percent. When asked about the saliency of immigration reform as a basis to vote, 67 percent indicated it was the most important factor or one of the most key considerations. Another key element playing out this policy dynamic is the "minimal degrees of separation within the Latino community." That is, 62 percent of Latino adults know at least someone who is undocumented and 32 percent know someone who has been deported. Of the 62 percent who know undocumented persons, over 90 percent were either friends or family members (Latino Decisions 2016c).

A transition to the partisan aspect of this election was the kind of immigration reform policy that might be passed. The Republican party would be blamed by 45 percent of Latinos but the Democratic party would be blamed by 34 percent of Latinos (Latino Decisions 2016c) if no immigration legislation is passed with a pathway to citizenship (Hajnal and Rivera

2014). As indicated earlier in this chapter, Latinos are primarily affiliated with the Democratic party with some internal variation so that Latinas have higher Democratic affiliation (70 percent vs. 54 percent of males), as well as 71 percent Spanish-speakers and bilinguals, and 60 percent of Latinos over 30 years old. At the same time, the relatively stagnant level for the percentage of Latino Republicans does mark a shift toward more independent leanings. A majority (46 percent to 62 percent) of Latinos who identify as independent tend to lean to the Democratic party (i.e. across language groups) (Harris Polls 2016; Hajnal and Lee 2004).

The partisan preference among Latinos is affected by their views of the Republican party, which is unfavorable. A Latino Decisions poll (2015b) had Latinos characterizing the Republican party as not caring about Latinos (39 percent) or as hostile to this community (45 percent), and only 16 percent as caring about Latinos. This evaluative dimension will be examined further with the presidential candidates' impact on both who they support and views about the major parties. As described earlier, this partisan divide has not only been exacerbated by ideological and elite rhetoric and policy stances, but by increasingly racial/ethnic aggregation in the two parties. A Pew Research Center study (2015c) identified racial/ ethnic affiliation, religious affiliation, and regional origins of party affiliation. The analysis showed that 68 percent of white evangelical Protestants, 55 percent of white Southerners and 54 percent of white males with some college or less identified with or leaned Republican; while 80 percent of African Americans, 65 percent of Asian Americans, 61 percent of unaffiliated religious persons, and 64 percent of post-graduate women tilted Democratic. The combination of these developments placed Latinos with limited choices of candidate and party. An old cliché—"a house is not a home"—might be one way to portrayed Latinos' electoral options such that the Democratic party remains is partisan "house" to live in; yet expectations of policy advocacy and leadership initiative fall short of identified Latinos' interests. We will return to this analysis at the summary and future implications of this chapter.

## Hillary Clinton, Donald Trump and Latinos

The 2016 Presidential race had placed Hillary Clinton as the clear choice among Latinos. The choice was the combination of her established connections with this community, their Democratic party affiliation, generally congruent policy directions, and the Trump candidacy. In the case of the later, Trump's rhetoric and policy positions served more to distance any Latino support. His emphasis on "illegal immigration" and the accentuated negative impacts placed immigration at the head of Latinos' radar. Ironically, in previous presidential elections, immigration was submerged

**162** Chapter 7

as a major campaign focus due to its volatility among the general electorate and anticipated polarization as to policy solutions. It was the Trump campaign that made this a central issue concomitantly targeting immigrants and refugees, Muslims and, to some degree, raising authenticity as to who are the "real Americans," which served to drive many Latinos away from supporting his candidacy.

A Latino Decisions poll (2016c) asked Latinos how Donald Trump's statement affected their impression of the Republican party (Figure 7.3). Sixty-eight percent indicated an unfavorable view of the Republican party and another 12 percent responded somewhat unfavorably (totaling four-fifths of Latino respondents). There was a net –60 percent unfavorable difference from the smaller percentages that had favorable views. By the summer of 2016, the Latino voters' preference ran 70 percent for Hillary Clinton and 19 percent for Donald Trump. There was little variation among Latino/a segments. For example: Latinas, 73 percent; English speakers, 65 percent; foreign-born naturalized, 77 percent; native-born, 68 percent; over 40 years old, 74 percent; and under 40 years, 68 percent (Latino Decisions 2016e).

A Gallup poll (2016) reported favorability ratings for all Latinos and Latino Republicans. In the case of the former, Clinton had a 59 percent

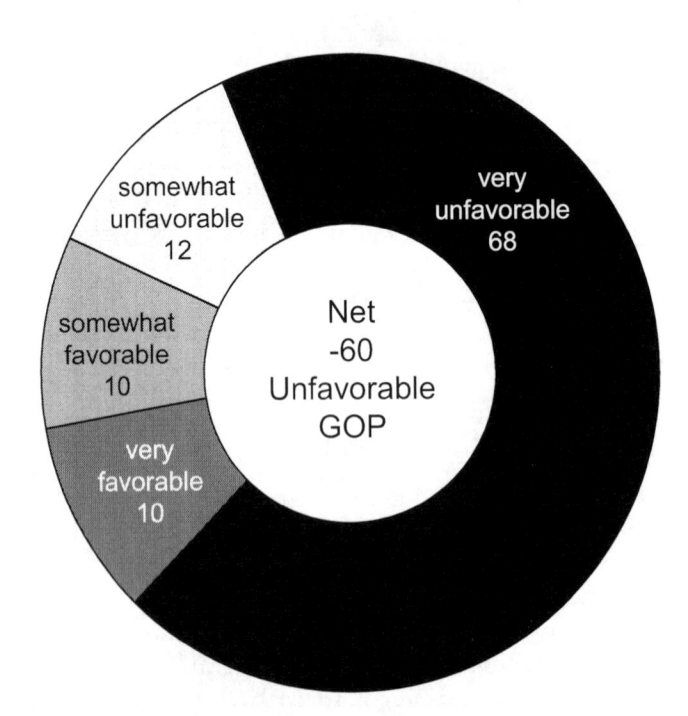

**FIGURE 7.3** Trump's Impact on Latinos' Views of Republican Party

*Source:* Data from Latino Decisions-impre Media Battleground Poll of Latino voters, November 2015.

vs. 26 percent favorability-unfavorability breakdown in comparison to Trump's 12 percent vs. 77 percent breakdown. Among Latino Republicans, the breakdown was 39 percent vs. 50 percent for Clinton (favorable-unfavorable) in comparison to Trump's 31 percent vs. 60 percent. As a result, Latino voters had dual motivations to vote for Hillary Clinton. That is, they had a preference for her candidacy and an eagerness to vote against Donald Trump. A Latino Decisions poll (August 2016) indicated that the Trump unfavorability rating had risen to 87 percent and his favorability declined to 9 percent. Similarly, Latinos' enthusiasm for Clinton and to vote went from 37 percent in 2012 to 51 percent in 2016 (Latino Decisions 2016b). So when Donald Trump was declared the winner of the 2016 presidential election (306–232 in electoral votes), Latinos were on the losing side. Yet an integral part of this discussion of the election and Latinos' electoral engagement requires examination of the patterns of their participation and choices in 2016, as well as continual impacts into the next election cycles.

## Latinos, 2016 Elections and Post-Obama Politics

As indicated from the previous discussion, Latinos' preference for Hillary Clinton's candidacy was not in doubt, but more so was their enthusiasm, levels of voter turnout, and impact on vote totals in both key battleground states and in red states. The post-election exit polls reintroduced both the predictability and accuracy of poll outcome estimates. In the case of Latinos, the difference in Latinos' vote for the major candidates varies by 11 percent. The National Election Pool (consortium of the major networks) analysis conducted by Edison Research reported that 29 percent of Latinos cast their votes for Trump. On the other hand, Latino Decisions reported an 18 percent vote for Trump. This raises persistent issues of exit polling sampling designs, collection of early and Election Day votes, and coverage of sufficient diverse voters to make projections by sociodemographic groups.

Works in 2012 by Nate Silver (2012) and more recently, Barreto and Segura (2016) discuss the significance of exit polls in the context of tracking voters over a period of time prior to the election date, "tapping" early voters, and sufficient sample size and selection of precincts to represent the voting groups reported. Latino Decisions, which specializes in polling this community, polled 5,600 high-propensity Latino voters, which represents a much larger sample than Edison Research. In addition, other exits polls had the following results of Latino vote for Trump: Univision/Washington Post, 18 percent; NBC/Telemundo, 17 percent; NALEO/Telemundo tracking poll, 14 percent; and Florida International University/New Latino voice, 13 percent. Previous discussion about exit polls and minority communities has included the degree of reliable estimates for minority samples and necessary sample size and selection. For example, among the Edison Research sample, 44 percent of non-white voters had college degrees in comparison to 15 percent Latino college graduates nationally (Chavez 2016).

The tracking polls can provide some additional insight into the exit poll estimates of the Latino presidential vote. For example, the tracking results from Latino Decisions (2016d) from September to November 6 indicated a range of 71–73 percent intent to vote for Clinton and a range of 16–18 percent for Trump. Ancillary information in these polls indicated a rising degree of enthusiasm for Clinton, and higher unfavorability for Donald Trump. Based upon multiple sources of exit polls and relative strengths and shortcoming of the exit polls firms, the higher level of Latino vote for Trump—27 percent—seems to be inconsistent with pre-election levels. If so, Trump support represents a lower percentage of Latino support than that of previous Republican nominees in the last half-century. The question at hand is how both the Republican party and President Trump go forward with their relationship with the Latino community (Latino Decisions 2016f).

The impact of Latinos in the 2016 elections had broader implications beyond their presidential vote. The demographic imperative of population growth being fueled in the United States by minorities is best illustrated by the Latino community. With their rise as a proportion of the electorate, the 2016 election also evidences an increase in turnout—a persistent challenge for this community—so that 5–12 percent voter turnout increase has been projected (Latino Decisions and Gross 2016). Other indicators of greater Latino voter engagement is reflected in their early voting turnout rates in states like Florida, Nevada, Arizona, and Colorado.

These turnout increases also played a role in the increase in numbers of Latinos in Congress with a gain of five more in the House (from 29 to 34) and a Latina (Catherine Cortez Masto of Nevada) to the U.S. Senate. Some new members of Congress include Darren Soto of Florida as the first Puerto Rican elected outside of the northeast, Adraino Espaillat of New York as the first Dominican elected, three new Latino/as from California—Salud Carbajal, Nanette Barragan, and Lou Correa—Vicente Gonzalez of Texas, and Ruben Kihuen of Nevada. Actually, there are seven new Latina/os in the House of Representatives, where a couple replaced incumbent Latinos. At the state level, four newly elected Latinos joined state senates (from 73 to 77), with Arizona adding three state senators. Ten more Latinos were elected to state houses of representatives (from 234 to 244), of which 194 are Democrats and 50 are Republicans. The biggest gains were in California (plus-4), Arizona, Colorado, Florida and Texas (plus-2 each). States traditionally with little Latino population like

Rhode Island, Oklahoma, and West Virginia also elected Latino state legislators (NALEO 2016). Thus, Latino electoral engagement continues to make progress in terms of greater rates of electoral participation, increasing political representation, and advocating on behalf of Latino saliency issues and policy preferences.

Another implication of the intersection of demographic trend and political partisan voter support is the current configuration of red and blue states. The increase in Latino population and their location throughout the United States—especially recent locations in the South and Rocky Mountain and Midwest regions—has a direct partisan consequence. The Latino vote either continued the pattern of deepening the blueness of a state (i.e. Virginia and Colorado) or altering the state's red hue to more purple. Examples of the latter are the more competitive partisan nature of Arizona, Texas, Florida, and Nevada. The significant influx of Puerto Ricans into central Florida, along with more Mexican origin and Central Americans into the state, has made it more Democratic. The difference in the margin of victory for Romney against Trump in Texas, Arizona, and Georgia diminished. This pattern could continue as these states become more majority-minority populations. This demographic shift, along with the continued tendency of Latinos to support Democratic candidates, has a serious consequence for party politics and representatives.

The Growth Opportunity Project (2013)—the Republican party's blueprint to expand its base into communities of color written in 2012—was not implemented to any significant degree, and the actions of party elites/leaders, policy stances, and rise of nativism and nationalism has placed greater distance between the Republican party and communities of color. By making illegal immigration a keystone issue and placing emphasis on the "negative effects" of undocumented persons and the sharp and negative rhetoric directed toward immigrants—especially Latinos—the Trump campaign created the perception by Latinos of a more hostile and less caring Republican party. The future of Latinos and the major political parties will require serious assessment of the Latino community's interests and the extent of discernible responses by either or both of the major parties.

In the case of the Republican party, moving to enact policies like mass deportations, building a wall along the southern border, dismantling the Affordable Care Act, moving away from climate change initiatives, and tax reform with minimal benefits to working and middle class segments run counter to Latinos' policy preferences and desired actions. The additional policy areas of voting rights (i.e. voter identification laws, shorter early voting periods, greater state discretion on voting changes) and forthcoming redistricting processes accent the growing disconnect to a closer working relationship between elements of the Latino community and the Republican party.

How the Republican party responds to this community as a more congruent partner in the party will depend on the actions of its leadership and the Trump administration, as well as any changes to the hostility directed at immigrants, minorities and non-mainline Christian religious groups, and the like by vocal rhetoric and in-vs.-out-group attitudes. An earlier research finding indicated that Latinos' political support for candidates and their parties will be driven more by positions and actions that support and advance Latino interests. Demographically, it has been suggested that if the Republican party can garner 35–48 percent of the Latino vote in national elections, it provides them a working "majority" along with its current core base (Latino Decisions 2015a). The shift of white working-class voters voting for Donald Trump can become more enduring and may reduce the need to actively seek out segments of the Latino community and other communities of color by the Republican party. In any event, the Republican party side of the partisan configuration will—in—part, factor in the Latino community's assessment of this party as a viable option in light of its policy and political interests.

Historically and continued partisan affiliation with the Democratic party is unlikely to result in a shift to the Republican party. At the same time, the shift has been to independent leanings with weaker ties for the Democratic party. Primary issues for Latinos have been Democratic party responsiveness to policy advocacy and wider access to party engagement in leadership roles and Latino candidate support. Again the theme in this part of the chapter lies with Latinos' partisan strategies and, in this case, long established "investment" with the Democratic party. As the Democratic party assesses its post-2016 election strategies, how much further outreach it makes with communities of color—as they are clearly a significant part of the party base—will be an issue. At the same time, "mending" fences with the white working class could result in "perceived trade-offs" of solidifying Latino partisan support with outreach themes to the "white working class." Ironically this perceived tension reflects the intersection of race and class. That is, on the whole, the majority of Latinos fall into the working and lower middle class strata; yet policy referents do not appear to incorporate race and ethnicity in dealing with the working class.

Continued Democratic engagement among Latinos has been linked to a present and salient identity as Latinos (Huddy et al. 2016). Latinos who identify strongly as Latinos and see pervasive discrimination against Latinos are the strongest Democrats. This dynamic was further deepened during the course of the 2012 election (Huddy et al. 2016). Partisan preference evidences an increased in political campaign activity, although the level was modest overall. Relatively few Latinos had worked on a campaign or given money to a candidate; somewhat larger numbers had tried to convince others about a candidate or worn a button or displayed a sticker. Finally, some support was evident for an instrumental account. Latino support for government-provided health insurance in 2012 consistently increased support for the Democratic party (Sanchez and Medeiros 2016). There was substantiation of that during the 2016 presidential election. Latinos were energized and compared this election as more important than recent Presidential elections. The dual responses of support for Hillary Clinton and similar policy positions and the heightened emotional antagonism toward Donald Trump were almost equally motivating to the Latino vote (Latino Decisions 2016e).

The relationship between Latinos and political parties following the 2016 national elections represents an opportunity for some deliberative and strategic discussions regarding prioritization of a Latino policy and political agenda and where to direct resources, activities, and organizational targeting. Given the stated policy directions of the Trump administration, immigration and health care polices have a direct bearing on this community. The saliency of immigration reform (i.e. more so in terms of human rights, normalization of the undocumented, pathway to citizenship, etc.) during the 2016 elections has even greater relevance to Latinos. The DACA and DAPA executive orders may be "undone" in early 2017 and its impact extends beyond the "Dreamers" and their parents to a wider circle of family and friends. Potential policies implementing massive deportation efforts will, again, not only affect undocumented persons, but the neighborhoods and work places where many Latino households reside. Some local institutions (i.e. municipalities, counties, universities and colleges, religious organizations) have implemented alternative actions and policies regarding immigrants such as sanctuary designations, protecting DACA students, limiting law enforcement working relations with U.S. Immigration and Customs Enforcement (ICE) and other immigration-related law enforcement agencies.

Latino organizations and leaders have already begun to work at the state and local levels to continue or enact policies that are consistent with Latino policy preferences in the area of immigration. Recently, a coalition of universities and colleges in states like New Mexico, Pennsylvania, Michigan, Minnesota, and Texas have begun to explore ways to provide sanctuary to their undocumented students. For example, college administrators in New Mexico—the state with the highest percentage of Latino residents—are looking into proposals that would grant protections to immigrant students living in the country illegally while they pursue their studies (*Arizona Daily Star* 2016). In addition, supporters in California, Georgia, Illinois, Minnesota, and Texas are pressing their state and private universities to provide sanctuary to these immigrant students (i.e. Dreamers).

The earlier reporting of the most salient issues and policy domains also included health care. Under the more general category of health care, matters of access, health insurance coverage and affordability, and dealing with addressing health disparities between Latinos and other populations comprise significant areas of concern (Sanchez and Medeiros 2016). With the ACA targeted for elimination, Latinos' health policy vulnerability becomes even more pronounced. Latino engagement in this policy area could take place at both the federal and state levels.

One other policy area of importance is that of voters' rights and protection. The recent court ruling of *Holder vs. Shelby County* and upswing voter identification and other limiting state actions (Garcia 2016; Ybarra, L. Sanchez and G. Sanchez 2015) has placed greater vigilance and legal actions by Latino advocacy organizations—Mexican American Legal Defense and Educational Fund (MALDEF), American Civil Liberties Union (ACLU), National Association of Latino Elected and Appointed Officials (NALEO), etc.—to challenge disparate effects on Latinos, other minority group members and lower income persons. Under the rationale of eliminating or reducing voter fraud, the Republican party has been actively engaged in passing voting reform laws that are more restrictive in nature. With the recent campaign rhetoric and divisive national mood, voting rights and protection from discrimination will remain a very prominent area of policy activity. Strategically, where do Latinos direct their resources and attention (i.e. the courts, legislative bodies, local jurisdictions) to continued their impact on electoral politics?

This discussion of the political future of the Latino community in these "turbulent times" would suggest multiple political arenas, working within political and civic institutions, and building up its internal political base. As our focus has been the electoral arena, the continued growth of Latinos as a proportion of the electorate will occur due to their continued population growth. At the same time, natural growth (i.e. annual contribution of Latinos turning age 18) can be substantially augmented through two major segments. Millennials are becoming a sizeable portion of America. Millennials make up a greater share of Latino eligible voters than any other racial-ethnic group. That is, 44 percent of Latino eligible voters are millennials, in comparison to 27 percent of whites, 35 percent of African Americans and 30 percent of Asian Americans (Pew Research Center 2016a). From 2012 to 2016, Hispanic eligible population growth increased from 23.3 million to 27.3 million (Pew Research Center 2016a). Slightly less than three-fourths of that increase was Latino citizens turning 18.

Thus the challenge for Latino leaders and organizations is not only to increase the proportion of millennials registered to vote, but once registered, to be actively, engaged voters. Mobilization has been a growing activity by the Democratic party and Latino groups (Bedolla and Michelson 2012;

Michelson 2005). Targeted efforts at millennials have both promise and some uncertainty. That is, among those millennials who did vote, the Democratic party was the greater benefactor, especially with their involvement in the Sanders campaign. At the same time, more millennials are not as strongly partisan, even though Democrats hold an edge over Republicans. Overall this age grouping has the lower turnout rate compared to older age groupings. Yet, Latinos working to expand their electoral base would benefit significantly with better efficiency and success of adding more millennials to its electoral base (Bedolla and Michelson 2012).

The second largest contributor to the growth of the Latino electorate is naturalized citizens (Table 7.3). Almost one-fourth of the Latino electorate growth is immigrants who become U.S. citizens. Since the 1980s, Latino organizations (i.e. NALEO and National Council of La Raza, or NCLR) have prioritized efforts to facilitate and encourage Latino "permanent resident aliens" toward naturalization. While there has been a steady increase among Latino origin immigrants, conversion to more naturalized citizens can close the gap between potential and actual numbers of Latino voters. During the 1990s, the anti-immigrant mood, especially in California, served as a catalyst for some Latinos to pursue naturalization to "elevate" their legal protections and rights. Thus a combination of a rising threat of nativism and xenophobia and expanding political impact by Latinos can serve as the mobilizing dynamics to expand the millennial and immigrant segments to register and vote in the near future.

**TABLE 7.3** Youth and Naturalizations Are the Main Sources of Eligible Hispanic Voter Growth

*Hispanic Eligible Voter Growth 2012–2016*

| Year | | |
|---|---|---|
| 2012 | Hispanic Eligible Voters | 23.3 mil. |
| | U.S. Citizens/Hispanics Turning Age 18 | 3.2 mil. |
| | Immigrant Hispanics Who Will Become U.S. Citizens | 1.2 mil. |
| | Increase Due to Out-Migration from Puerto Rico | 130,000 |
| | Hispanic Eligible Voters Who Pass Away | −537,000 |
| 2016 | Projected Hispanic Eligible Voters | 27.3 ml. |

*Note*: Those born in Puerto Rico are U.S. citizens at birth.

*Source*: Data from Pew Research Center [SW1]. For 2012, Pew Research tabulations from the November Current Population Survey [SW2]. Compiled by author.

## Conclusion

In this collection of *Winning the Presidency 2016*, this chapter examines the Latino community's participation in a most unique election cycle, in which the candidacy of Donald Trump and the levels of negative and antagonistic rhetoric polarized the American electorate along ideological, racial—ethnic, religious, and gender divides in very overt and direct manner. The candidacy of Hillary Clinton as the first female nominee of a major political party and the gender effect was more nuanced, at times, although the level of support from Latinas and other women of color was more evident in terms of women voters in contrast to white women. The turbulence and emotional levels of this election accorded Latinos challenges as to how they could be an important factor in Presidential politics. With the final nominees, there was a clear preference for Hillary Clinton that went beyond traditional Democratic party support. The issues, rhetoric, and policy directions of Donald Trump and a nativist and hostile mood placed Latinos squarely in the Democrats' camp, but concerns about enthusiasm, saliency of the election, and extent of voter turnout were more their focus.

Evidence to date indicates an increase in the numbers of registered Latino voters and greater numbers of votes cast. Latinos participated at higher rates in early voting states and on Election Day. The major of Latino support is estimated to have exceeded that of President Obama in 2012, and Donald Trump received the lowest Latino voting percentage of Republican presidential candidate over the last half-century. There are clearly partisan implications beyond 2016 which have been discussed in this chapter. Yet the discussion of this round of American elections and Latinos is still grounded in the objectives of weightier influence in the American political system. Goals of empowerment, influencing public policy, more responsiveness to salient concerns and issues to this community, and better political representation continue to motivate Latinos to engage politically. The election outcome will pose serious challenges for the Latino community in terms of directing their political energies and strategies in what is perceived to be a hostile and restrictive environment.

## Bibliography

Alvarez, R. Michael and Lisa Garcia Bedolla. 2003. "The Foundations of Latino Voter Partisanship: Evidence From the 2000 Election." *The Journal of Politics* 65:1. February. Pp. 31–49.

*Arizona Daily Star*. 2016. "Universities Exploring 'Sanctuary' Status for Immigrants." *The Associated Press*, December 4.

Barreto, Matt and Gary Segura. 2016. "Lies, Damn Lies, and Exit Polls." Latino Decisions: Seattle, Washington, DC, November 10.

Bartels, Larry M. 2016. "Converge: Presidential Candidates, Core Partisans, and the Missing Middle in American Electoral Politics." *ANNALS, AAPSS 667*. September. Pp. 143–165.

Bedolla, Lisa Garcia and Melissa R. Michelson. 2012. *Mobilizing Inclusion: Transforming the Electorate Through Get-Out-the-Vote Campaigns*. New Haven, CT: Yale University Press.

Colby, Sandra L. and Jennifer M. Ortman, Projections of the Size and Composition of the U.S. Population: 2014 to 2060, Current Population Reports, P25-1143, U.S. Census Bureau, Washington, DC, 2014.

Chavez, Linda. 2016. "Why Exit Polls Were Wrong About Latino Voters." *Townhall News Media*, November 18.

Davis, Nicholas T. and Johanna L. Dunaway. 2016. "Party Polarization, Media Choice, and Mass Partisan-Ideological Sorting." *Public Opinion Quarterly* 80:Special Issue. Pp. 272–297.

File, Thom. 2013. "The Diversifying Electorate—Voting Rates by Race and Hispanic Origin in 2012 (and Other Recent Elections)." Current Population Survey Reports, P20-569. U.S. Census Bureau, Washington, DC.

Gallup Polls. 2016. "Presidential Election 2016: Key Indicators." Gallup World Headquarters. Washington, DC, January–November.

Garcia, John A. 2016. *Latino Politics in America: Community, Culture, and Interests*, 3rd ed. Lanham, MD: Rowman & Littlefield.

Hajnal, Zoltan and Taeku Lee. 2004. "Latino Independents and Identity Formation Under Uncertainty." *The Center for Comparative Immigration Studies*. Working Paper No. 89. January.

Hajnal, Zoltan and Michael U. Rivera. 2014. "Immigration, Latinos, and White Partisan Politics: The New Democratic Defection." *American Journal of Political Science* 58:4. October. Pp. 773–789.

Harris Polls. 2016. "Harris Political Polls July–November, 2016." Louis Harris Poll: Rochester, NY.

Hetherington, Marc J., Merit T. Long and Thomas J. Rudolph. 2016. "Revisiting the Myth: New Evidence of a Polarized Electorate." *Public Opinion Quarterly* 80:Special Issue. Pp. 321–350.

Huddy, Leonie, Lilliana Mason and S. Nechama Horwitz. 2016. "Political Identity Convergence: On Being Latino, Becoming a Democrat, and Getting Active." *RSF: The Russell Sage Foundation Journal of the Social Sciences* 2:3. Pp. 205–228.

Latino Decisions (David Damore and Matt Barreto). 2015a. "The Latino Threshold to Win in 2016." Latino Decisions: Seattle, WA, July.

———. 2015b. "ImpreMedia/Latino Decisions Battleground States Survey." Latino Decisions: Seattle, WA, November 16.

———. 2016a. "America's Voice/LD 2016 National Latino Vote Tracking Poll, Wave 1." Latino Decisions: Seattle, WA, April 21.

———. 2016b. "America's Voice/LD 2016 National Latino Vote Tracking Poll, Wave 2." Latino Decisions: Seattle, WA, September 2.

———. 2016c. "America's Voice/LD Trump Immigration Poll." Latino Decisions: Seattle, WA, September 8.

———. 2016d. "NALEO Educational Fund/Noticias Telemundo/LD Tracking Poll." Latino Decisions: Seattle, WA, September 19–November 6.

———. 2016e. "2016 Election Eve Poll." Latino Decisions: Seattle, WA.
Latino Decisions (David Damore and Matt Barreto) and Gross, Justin. 2016. "Latino Electorate on Track for Historic Turnout in 2016." Latino Decisions: Seattle, WA, November 3.
Layman, Geoffrey C. 1999. "'Culture Wars' in the American Party System." *American Politics Research* 27:89. P. 121.
Layman, Geoffrey C., Thomas M. Carsey and Juliana Menasce Horowitz. 2006. "Party Polarization in American Politics: Characteristics, Causes, and Consequences." *Annual Review of Political Science* 9:83. P. 110.
Levendusky, Matthews S. and Neil Malhotra. 2016. "(Mis)Perceptions of Partisan Polarization in the American Public." *Public Opinion Quarterly* 80:Special Issue. Pp. 378–391.
Mangum, Maurice. 2013. "The Racial Underpinnings of Party Identification and Political Ideology." *Social Science Quarterly* 94:5. December. Pp. 1222–1244.
Mann, Thomas E. and Norman J. Ornstein. 2013. "Finding the Common Good in an Era of Dysfunctional Governance." *Daedalus* 142:2. Pp. 15–24.
Michelson, Melissa R. 2005. "Does Ethnicity Trump Party? Competing Vote Cues and Latino Voting Behavior." *Journal of Political Marketing* 4:4. Pp. 1–25.
NALEO. 2016. "Half of Latinos Have Already Voted." News Release. NALEO Educational Fund: Washington, DC, November 7.
Oliver, J. Eric and Wendy M. Rahn. 2016. "Rise of the Trumpenvolk: Populism in the 2016 Election." *ANNALS, AAPSS* 667, September. Pp. 189–206.
Ortman, Jennifer M. and Christine E. Guarneri. 2009. "United States Population Projections: 2000 to 2050." U. S. Bureau of the Census. USGPO, Washington, DC.
Pew Research Center. 2010. Lopez, Mark Hugo. "The Latino Vote in the 2010 Elections." Pew Research Center, Washington, DC. November.
———. 2014a. Dimock, Michael, Carroll Doherty, Jocelyn Kiley and Russ Oates. "Political Polarization in the American Public: How Increasing Ideological Uniformity and Partisan Antipathy Affect Politics, Compromise and Everyday Life." Pew Research Center: Washington, D.C., June.
———. 2014b. Lopez, Mark Hugo, Ana Gonzalez-Barrera and Jens Manuel Krogstad. "Latino Support for Democrats Falls, But Democratic Advantage Remains." Pew Research Center, Washington, DC, October.
———. 2015a. Lopez, Mark Hugo, Jeffrey Passel and Molly Rohal. "Modern Immigration Wave Brings 59 Million to U.S., Driving Population Growth and Change Through 2065: Views of Immigration's Impact on U.S. Society Mixed." Pew Research Center, Washington, DC, September.
———. 2015b. "Strong Groups for Democratic and Republican Parties." April 6. www.people-press.org/2015/04/07/a-deep-dive-into-party-affiliation/4-6-2015_lede/
———. 2015c. Doherty, Carol and Rachel Weisel. "A Deep Dive into Party Affiliation: Sharp Differences by Race, Gender, Generation and Education." Pew Research Center, April.
———. 2016a. Krogstad, Jens, Manuel, Mark Hugo Lopez, Gustavo Lopez, Jeffrey S. Passel and Eileen Patten. "2016 Millennials Make up Almost One-Half of Latino Eligible Voters in 2016: Youth Naturalizations Drive Number of Eligible Voters to Number 27.3 Million." Pew Research Center, Washington, DC, January.

———. 2016b. Doherty, Carroll, Jocelyn Kiley and Bridget Johnson. "A Divided and Pessimistic Electorate: Voters Skeptical of Progress in Many Areas—Even Jobs—Since 2008." Pew Research Center, Washington, DC, November.

———. 2016c. Lopez, Mark Hugo, Ana Gonzalez-Barrera, Jens Manuel Krogstad and Gustavo López. "Democrats Maintain Edge as Party 'More Concerned' for Latinos, But Views Similar to 2012." Pew Research Center, Washington, DC, October.

"Polarization in the American Public: How Increasing Ideological Uniformity and Partisan Antipathy Affect Politics, Compromise and Everyday Life." Pew Research Center, Washington, DC, June.

Republican National Committee. 2013. "Growth and Opportunity Project—Republican Party Plan." Washington, DC.

Sanchez, Gabriel R. and Jillian Medeiros. 2016. "Linked Fate and Latino Attitudes Regarding Health-Care Reform Policy. *Social Science Quarterly* 97:3. September. Pp. 525–539.

Silver, Nate. 2012. "Which Polls Fared Best (and Worst) in the 20–012 Presidential Race." *New York Times*, November 10.

Stonecash, Jeffrey M., Mark D. Brewer and Mack D. Mariani. 2003. *Diverging Parties: Social Change, Realignment, and Party Polarization*. Boulder, CO: Westview.

Ybarra, Vickie D., Lisa M. Sanchez and Gabriel R. Sanchez. 2015. "Anti-Immigrant Anxieties in State Policy: The Great Recession and Punitive Immigration Policy in the American States, 2005–2012." *State Politics & Policy Quarterly* 15:3. September. Pp. 1–27.

Yphtach, Lelkes. 2016. "The Polls—Review Mass Polarization: Manifestations and Measurements." *Public Opinion Quarterly* 80:Special Issue. Pp. 392–410.

# 8

# THE ELECTION IN PERSPECTIVE

*John Kenneth White*

> *I'm sorry the show didn't have a happier ending.*
> — Frank Skeffington, *The Last Hurrah* (1958)

It wasn't supposed to end this way. Nearly every poll, pundit, and political scientist believed a Democratic victory was inevitable against a first-time, inexperienced, and personally flawed Republican (Campbell 2016, 649–695). Much had gone in Hillary Clinton's favor: her party had an on-message nominating convention; polls showed she convincingly won the three presidential debates; Barack Obama, Michelle Obama, and Bill Clinton vigorously campaigned on her behalf, while the two George Bushes, John McCain, and Mitt Romney shunned Donald Trump; the political demography favored Clinton; and Barack Obama's job approval stood at 53 percent on Election Day (Edison Research 2016). In addition, Trump was viewed as temperamentally unfit to hold the nation's highest office; and the final pre-election polls showed Hillary Clinton with a small, but seemingly durable, lead. Of course, Clinton had deficiencies: her use of a private email server sent her favorable ratings plunging; most saw her as dishonest; there was a profound restlessness despite improving economic conditions; and there was a strong desire to try something new after Democrats held the presidency for eight years. Of those who voted, 39 percent cited "can bring change" as the most important quality they were seeking in the next President and, of these, *83 percent* supported Donald Trump (Edison Research 2016).

There are many lessons from the 2016 election. This chapter will focus on five important ones:

- The establishments of both political parties are dead;
- Politics and culture have merged into one;
- Demography is destiny—until it isn't;
- The Democratic party is in disarray;
- Republicans are the party of Donald Trump.

## The Death of the Establishment

### Democrats: Bye-Bye, Super-delegates; Hello, Bernie

In killing two political dynasties named Bush and Clinton, Donald Trump's rise to the presidency signaled the death knell of once-powerful establishments that controlled both political parties. On the Democratic side, Hillary Clinton faced a formidable challenge from Bernie Sanders who is quickly emerging as one of the party's most powerful spokespersons. Sanders' rise was completely unexpected. Back in 2015, the Democratic contest was anticipated to be a foregone conclusion in Clinton's favor. Instead, it turned into a slugfest that lasted right into the party's mid-summer convention. Sanders captured the imagination of restless Democrats who "felt the Bern," agreed that the system was rigged in favor of Wall Street, and that more government intervention was required to restore economic justice. That message had such a powerful resonance that the Vermont senator came close to winning the Democratic nomination against a former First Lady, U.S. Senator, Secretary of State, and two-time presidential candidate. That fact alone points to the profound weakness of the Democratic establishment. Consider: until 2016, Sanders had *never* run for office as a Democrat, having been listed on the Vermont ballots as an independent and calling himself a "democratic socialist" (Qiu 2016).

That diffidence won Sanders considerable support from a restless electorate. This happened *despite* the fact that Barack Obama remained hugely popular with his fellow Democrats, and that both Obama and the party establishment did all they could to make sure that Hillary Clinton would be the party's nominee. Thanks to Clinton's support from older voters—especially African-Americans in southern states—she was able to eke out a win. Yet the close contest forced Clinton to make several concessions, including sacrificing any prominent role for the so-called "super-delegates" at future conventions. Beginning in 1984, Democrats sought to restore their party leaders to a degree of prominence by creating the super-delegates.

Of the 716 super-delegates attending the 2016 Democratic Convention, Hillary Clinton had the support of 609, while Bernie Sanders garnered a mere 47. Such overwhelming support said much about the judgment of party elders as to whether Clinton could be a capable president (and also pronounced their negative assessment about a potential Sanders administration). Thanks to Clinton's concessions, super-delegates will be vastly reduced at the next Democratic conclave, and they will be bound hereafter to support the winner in their individual state primaries and caucuses. In short, the super-delegates are relegated to the history books.

In the wake of Clinton's defeat, Bernie Sanders is promising to play a much more substantial role in Democratic affairs. Senate Minority Leader Chuck Schumer has given Sanders a seat at the leadership table. Even more important, Sanders wants his progressive supporters to engineer wholesale takeovers of the state Democratic parties—a task that shouldn't prove difficult given the sad state of party affairs. In Maine and Wisconsin, challenges are under way to eliminate those party chairs who supported Clinton. And in Hawaii and Nebraska, Sanders supporters have already been installed in leadership positions (Strauss 2016).

### *Republicans: An Abject Surrender*

Whereas the Democratic establishment barely managed to confer its nomination upon its chosen candidate, Donald Trump forced the Republican establishment into an unconditional surrender. Establishment Republicans held Trump in near-universal contempt—a stance that many believed would all but deny him the nomination given the party's long-standing preference for establishment-backed candidates. Steve Schmidt, John McCain's 2008 campaign manager, expressed the anti-Trump sentiments of most GOP leaders:

> You see someone who is manifestly unprepared for the duties of the office of President of the United States, who has no idea what he's talking about from a policy perspective, who lacks the requisite dignity required of someone who wishes to be the Head of State of the government of the United States, and someone who lacks the capacity to be the Commander-in-Chief of the most powerful military and the world's most potent nuclear arsenal.
>
> *(Schmidt 2016)*

Schmidt was not alone in his assessment. Ohio governor John Kasich refused to endorse Trump, even boycotting the party's convention held in his home state. George H. W. Bush let it slip that he voted for Hillary

Clinton, while both George W. and Laura Bush left their presidential ballots blank. Mitt Romney was especially contemptuous, describing the New York billionaire as "a phony [and] a fraud," adding:

> [T]his is an individual who mocked a disabled reporter, who attributed a reporter's questions to her menstrual cycle, who mocked a brilliant rival who happened to be a woman due to her appearance, who bragged about his marital affairs, and who laces his public speeches with vulgarity. . . . Now, imagine your children and your grandchildren acting the way [Donald Trump] does. Would you welcome that? Haven't we seen before what happens when people in prominent positions fail the basic responsibility of honorable conduct?
> *(Romney 2016)*

The contempt the Republican establishment had for Donald Trump was returned in kind. In an unprecedented attack on his adopted party, Trump called George W. Bush's Iraq War "a big fat mistake" (Trump 2016); pictured John McCain's heroism as a tortured prisoner of the Vietnam War as a badge of dishonor, saying, "I like people who weren't captured" (Schreckinger 2015); and described Mitt Romney as someone who "choked like a dog" for having lost to Obama (Sherfinski 2015). Trump's message found a receptive audience, as former Mississippi governor and Republican National Chairman, Haley Barbour, graphically conceded: "Trump is the manifestation of people's anger. People all around the country want to send Washington the bird, and they see him as the gigantic middle finger" (Caldwell 2016).

The role party leaders once so powerfully exercised as mediators between the governors and the governed has been relegated to the ash heap of history. Replacing them are candidates who ask, "Why not me?" and are driven, as Alan Ehrenhalt points out, by a "politics of ambition" (Ehrenhalt 1991). Historically, presidential candidates have been preternaturally ambitious—after all, it was once said of Abraham Lincoln that "his ambition was a little engine that never quit" (Ambrose 1987, 71). But the peer review which party leaders once exercised has faded away as base partisans cast their leaders aside and decide who should lead their party—often without regard to the institution that person would inhabit. Today's partisans want to send the establishment a message, not a President. As one Trump backer put it: "The more he riles up the establishment, the better I like it. I think the establishment is in cahoots to bring this country down" (McCutcheon 2016, 723).

The result has been an increased inability of establishment leaders to have much of a say in awarding the highest prize any party can give: its nomination for the presidency of the United States. In an *Atlantic Monthly* article, Jonathan Rauch deplored the passing of the political establishments whose presence once managed conflicts behind closed doors, and whose collapse became a victim of populist-inspired reforms:

> Our intricate, informal system of political intermediation, which took many decades to build, did not commit suicide or die of old age; we reformed it to death. For decades, well-meaning political reformers have attacked intermediaries as corrupt, undemocratic, unnecessary, or (usually) all of the above. Americans have been subtly demonizing and disempowering political professionals and parties, which is like spending decades abusing and attacking your own immune system. Eventually, you will get sick.
>
> (Rauch 2016)

## The Merging of Politics and Culture

In the 1958 movie, *The Last Hurrah*, the late Spencer Tracy memorably portrays Frank Skeffington, mayor of a large New England metropolis, who invites his young nephew, Adam Caufield, to watch what will be his last campaign for reelection—the "last hurrah." Caufield, a sportswriter, has little interest in politics, but is intrigued by the offer for a ringside seat. In making his pitch, the quintessential Irishman and his young protégée engage in a bit of banter:

*Skeffington:* "Tell me this. What would you consider the greatest spectator sport in the country today? Would you say it's baseball, basketball, football?"
*Caufield:* "I think basketball is the largest paid attendance."
*Skeffington:* "It's politics. That's right. Politics. Millions and millions of people following it every day in the newspapers, over the TV, and the radio. Now, mind you, they wouldn't get mixed up in it themselves for all the tea in China. But they know the names and the numbers of all the players. And what they can tell the coaches about strategy! Oh, you should see some of the letters I get."
*Caufield:* "I can imagine."
*Skeffington:* "I doubt that. I doubt that. But, nevertheless, politics is an exciting game to watch."

(*The Last Hurrah* 1958)

Watching presidential politics has been a perennial pastime for millions of Americans. But the audience for it grew larger in 2016 (even as it became more disillusioned), as what once were civil disagreements between staid candidates became the latest television reality show. Its contestants included a former reality star who, incredibly, became the nominee of a major party for the presidency of the United States despite having no prior political experience. Also featured was the first woman to receive a major party nomination, and cast by her opponent as the reincarnation of Cruella de Vil. Dozens of other contestants added their own sound bites to the tawdry dialogue.

While some candidates emerged as full-fledged, interesting personas whose reputations were enhanced by the ongoing series (Bernie Sanders and John Kasich come to mind), the real star of 2016 was the Republican nominee, Donald Trump. He received so much air time that his GOP rivals could hardly break through, except when the self-proclaimed billionaire singled them out for scorn (think Jeb "Low Energy" Bush, or "Little Marco" Rubio, or "Lyin' Ted" Cruz). In the general election, the Trump-Clinton matchup had all the drama of a daytime soap opera. Eighty-four million watched the first presidential debate, and many watched to see whether the ever-unpredictable Trump would implode on stage and call Clinton's husband a rapist, while accusing his wife ("Crooked Hillary") of covering up for his alleged crimes. Americans were drawn to their television sets in much the same way that a car crash attracts the attention of fellow motorists. We watch, all the while thinking we shouldn't.

And what we watched reflected the coarsening of our culture led by Donald Trump. His perverse characterizations of women, references to the size of the male anatomy and female menstrual periods, boasts about his predatory sexual behavior in a videotape made by *Access Hollywood*, vulgarities expressed in handmade signs at his rallies, conspiracy allegations made against his fellow rivals and others (accusing Ted Cruz's father of involvement in the John F. Kennedy assassination), and even his mention of actress Rosie O'Donnell in a presidential debate spoke volumes about the derogation of American politics and made parents want to cover their children's ears. The Trump victory marks a final blurring of any remaining lines between reality television and politics. In the former, there are no boundaries with its "anything goes" formula. Now the same is true of politics. It is not libertarianism, but a libertine approach that now prevails where bubbles never burst and old rules about decorum are tossed out the window.

In 1998, the National Commission on Civic Renewal, co-chaired by former Democratic senator Sam Nunn and former Reagan education secretary William Bennett, sounded an alarm:

> Compared with previous generations, Americans today place less value on what we owe others as a matter of moral obligation and common citizenship; less value on personal sacrifice as a moral good;

less value on the social importance of respectability and observing the rules; less value on restraint in matters of pleasure and sexuality; and correspondingly greater value on self-expression, self-realization, and personal choice. . . . We must ask ourselves some hard questions about this new understanding of individual liberty. Dare we continue to place adult self-gratification above the wellbeing of our children? Can we relentlessly pursue individual choice at the expense of mutual obligation without corroding vital social bonds? Will we remain secure in the enjoyment of our individual rights if we fail to accept and discharge our responsibilities? Is there a civic invisible hand that will preserve our democratic institutions in the absence of informed and engaged citizens?

*(National Commission on Civic Renewal 1998)*

The search for a "civic invisible hand" has often pointed to a political establishment that viewed itself as a necessary arbiter between citizens and their government. The presidency has been the premier institution where, historically, established party leaders sought someone worthy of inhabiting that sacred office. Thus, Republicans nominated Abraham Lincoln, Dwight D. Eisenhower, and Ronald Reagan to fulfill the role. Democrats, too, elevated candidates who would best serve the national interest, including Franklin D. Roosevelt, Harry S. Truman, John F. Kennedy, and Lyndon B. Johnson. More than merely finding nominees who would advocate mutually agreed upon policies, party leaders searched for candidates who could inhabit the presidency and serve as the nation's chief of state. As Franklin D. Roosevelt once said, the presidency must be "a place of moral leadership" (Friedel 1990, 94). This theme was eloquently echoed decades later by George W. Bush: "After power vanishes and pride passes, this is what remains: The promises we kept. The oath we fulfilled. The example we set. The honor we earned. We are united in a common task: to give our children a spirit of moral courage" (Bush 1999).

The role party leaders once so powerfully exercised as mediators between the governors and the governed has been relegated to the ash heap of history. Instead, a coarsened culture has promoted one of its stars, Donald Trump, into the Oval Office. Trump's persona, forged in a series of best-selling books and successful television shows, created a "can-do" image that easily crossed whatever boundaries remained between popular culture and politics. Trump's purported $10 billion wealth only enhanced his cultivated persona. Trump's self-written biography is illustrative of the image he seeks to project: "Donald J. Trump is the very definition of the American success story, continually setting the standards of excellence while expanding his interests in real estate, sports, and entertainment. He is the archetypal businessman—a deal-maker without peer" (Trump

2015, 177). It was this image that managed to overthrow a party establishment. Simply put, Donald Trump's victory was no mere aberration. It came thanks to a fusion of politics and culture that allowed both Trump and future nominees to remake the Republican and Democratic parties into Hertz-Rent-A-Cars to be used for their own purposes and traded in whenever necessary.

## Demography Is Destiny—Until It Isn't

In 1998, President Bill Clinton gave a commencement address at Portland State University in which he hailed the coming of a "third great revolution"—one as powerful as the American Revolution and as formidable as the civil rights and women's rights revolutions. According to Clinton, this gathering revolution was being manned by an army of immigrants:

> Today, nearly one-in-ten people in America was born in another country; one-in-five schoolchildren are from immigrant families. Today, largely because of immigration, there is no majority race in Hawaii, or Houston, or New York City. Within five years, there will be no majority race in our largest state, California. In a little more than fifty years, there will be no majority race in the United States.
> *(Clinton 1998)*

When Bill Clinton told the Portland State University students that immigrants would alter the country they knew, he spoke an important truth. The face of the typical—mostly white—American was being recast into a twenty-first century shade of bronze. Today, the Pew Hispanic Research Center estimates that there are 41.7 million immigrants residing in the United States. Of these, 11.7 million are *undocumented*, 1.7 million are *temporary legal residents*, and 28.3 million are *legal residents* (Passel, Cohn and Gonzalez-Barrera 2013). Estimates are that by 2050 (or sooner) the entire United States will become a majority-minority nation (Passel and Cohn 2008, 1). That trend became clear in 2011 when, for the first time in history, Hispanics outnumbered African-Americans as the nation's leading minority group (U.S. Census Bureau 2012). Moreover, with every passing month an additional 50,000 Hispanics turn eighteen years of age and are legally eligible to vote (Selby 2011).

Hispanics are not alone in coming to America. Asians have substantially increased their presence starting in 1965 with an immigration reform bill signed into law by Lyndon B. Johnson. More came after his failed Vietnam War. Today, there are 17.3 million Asians residing in the United States, with 10.5 million being immigrants. Recent census figures show Asians have surpassed Hispanics as the largest group of new immigrants

(Hoeffel, Rastogi, Kim and Shahid 2012, 4). And Indian migrants are yet one more growing racial minority, with 1.9 million living in the United States (Whatley and Batalova 2013).

A racial revolution has been accompanied by a transformation of family structures. Since the election of Ronald Reagan in 1980, the so-called "nuclear family" consisting of a mom, dad, and kids no longer determines election outcomes. Consider:

- In 1980, 60.8 percent of households were headed by married couples; today, 48.7 percent (Vespa, Lewis and Kreider 2013, 5);
- In 1980, 22.6 percent of households consisted of people living alone; today, 27.5 percent. And more than half of these households consist of single women (55 percent) (Vespa, Lewis and Kreider 2013, 5, 6);
- In 1980, nearly one in five children were born to an unmarried mother; today, more than four in ten (Child Trends Data Bank 2014).

Another rising group is millennials. Although initially attracted to Bernie Sanders, Hillary Clinton captured a majority of the youth vote. Young people matter. As political scientists attest, if a party can capture first-time voters in successive elections, they will retain many of these same voters over the course of their lifetimes. Franklin D. Roosevelt did just that in the 1930s, and Ronald Reagan accomplished a similar feat in the 1980s. The Roosevelt and Reagan generations constituted an electoral bubble that remained loyal to their respective political parties. Today's millennials have cast majorities for Democratic presidential candidates in three straight elections: 66 percent in 2008 (Edison Media Research and Mitofsky International 2008); 60 percent in 2012 (Edison Research 2012); and 55 percent in 2016 (Edison Research 2016). While millennials are not yet firmly in the Democrats' grasp, if the Republican party of Donald Trump violates a sacrosanct millennial value of tolerance, one can expect millennial majorities will gravitate to future Democratic candidates.

Taken together, the rising electorate—i.e. racial minorities, single women, and young people—constituted a majority of 2016 voters for the first time in history. Voters ages 18–29 outnumbered seniors 19 percent to 15 percent; racial minorities totaled 30 percent; and unmarried women totaled 23 percent (Edison Research 2016). For the second time in sixteen years, the popular vote winner did not receive an Electoral College majority. Hillary Clinton out-polled Donald Trump by more than 2.5 million votes—nearly five times the margin Al Gore received over George W. Bush. States populated by the rising electorate saw an increase in Democratic votes: Florida, Georgia, Arizona, Colorado, Nevada, and Texas each gave Hillary Clinton more support than Barack Obama received in 2012.

These demographic changes have been noted by many political scientists, including me (White 2009, 2016). And they have led many to believe that there was an emerging Democratic majority (Judis and Teixeira 2002). That was an error. Instead, it is more accurate to say that there was an *Obama coalition, not a Democratic one.* As Table 8.1 shows, Hillary Clinton's share of the vote was down in virtually every key demographic group that formed the Obama coalition. The only exceptions were gays, where Clinton added two points; and those who never attend religious services, where she held her own.

A decline in turnout hit Democrats hard in important battleground states. In Detroit, Clinton received roughly 70,000 fewer votes than Obama in 2012 (she lost Michigan by just 12,000 votes). In Milwaukee County, Wisconsin, Clinton got 40,000 fewer votes than Obama and lost the state by 27,000. In Cuyahoga County, Ohio, turnout in majority African-American precincts was down 11 percent from four years before (Plouffe 2016). In key states, Clinton fell below Obama's 2012 totals—including North Carolina, Pennsylvania, Ohio, Wisconsin, and Minnesota.

Donald Trump won the presidency based on superlative performances in predominantly white, rural, and exurban counties. Overall, Trump won 58 percent of the white vote (Edison Research 2016). That alone would not have been enough to win. Recall that Mitt Romney captured 59 percent of this important demographic in the previous presidential election (Edison Research 2012). But it was Trump's historic edge in rural and exurban counties, where significant numbers of whites who had never attended college, that made the difference. For example, in Madison County, an exurban area outside Columbus, Ohio, Romney's margin of victory in 2012 was 20.4 percentage points; in 2016, Trump beat Clinton by an astounding 39.8 points. In Buchanan County, Iowa, just outside Cedar Rapids, Obama prevailed by 13.9 percentage points; in 2016, Trump beat Clinton

**TABLE 8.1** A Rising American Electorate: Obama and Clinton Compared

| *Demographic* | *Obama's Percentage* | *Clinton's Percentage* |
|---|---|---|
| 18–29-year-olds | 60 | 55 |
| African-Americans | 93 | 88 |
| Latinos | 71 | 65 |
| Asians | 73 | 65 |
| Unmarried voters | 62 | 55 |
| Unmarried women | 67 | 62 |
| Gays | 76 | 78 |
| Democrats | 92 | 89 |
| Never attend religious services | 62 | 62 |
| Not born-again | 60 | 59 |

*Sources*: Data from Edison Research (2012, 2016).

by 14.2 points (Plouffe 2016). This happened despite the fact that the percentage of white voters without college degrees fell from 83 percent in 1960 to just 34 percent in 2016. But Trump's 39-point lead among this group far surpassed Mitt Romney's 25-point margin in 2012. At the same time, Trump's mere 4-point margin among college-educated whites was far below the 14-point lead amassed by Romney (Edsall 2016).

In an influential book titled *Coming Apart: The State of White America, 1960–2010*, Charles Murray describes two distinctive communities that epitomize the political and cultural divides that characterized the Clinton-Trump contest:

- *Belmont*: Everybody has a bachelor's or graduate degree and works in the high-prestige professions or management, or is married to such a person;
- *Fishtown*: Nobody has more than a high school diploma. Everybody who has an occupation is in a blue-collar job, mid- or low-level service job, or a low-level white-collar job.

*(Murray 2012, 146)*

In many respects, the 2016 presidential election can be characterized as the revenge of Fishtown over Belmont—a triumph of a populism defined by resentments against dominant east coast elites in the media, culture, and politics—not to mention profound grievances against a rising electorate that is more inclined to live in the metropolises that resemble the growing populations of Belmont than in the gritty, rural communities that characterize the declining Fishtowns. At the same time, Fishtown's revenge should not be overstated: Trump won narrow victories in states that have an outsized role in the electoral college: Florida by 1.2 percentage points; Pennsylvania, 1.09 points; Wisconsin, 0.81 points; Michigan, 0.27 points.

Political scientist Matthew R. Kerbel writes that the Republican party of 2017 will be "at the peak of its formal power at the same time it is self-destructing" (Kerbel 2016). Like many analysts, Kerbel sees a rising electorate that remains distant from the Republican party of Donald Trump. In 2016, 55 percent had an unfavorable view of the GOP, and just 40 percent were favorably disposed. This was in sharp contrast to opinions held about the Democrats: 49 percent unfavorable, 47 percent favorable (Edison Research 2016). Noting these trends, Kerbel writes:

> How does the right approach governance if it emerges as the dominant voice in a regime supported by a plurality segment of the electorate that does not represent the populace at large? Would questions arise about the regime's legitimacy, and to what degree might this

constrain its ability to implement its agenda? In power, would it be able to avoid awakening voters whose disinterest enabled its ascendancy, or could it find a way to win over a large segment of the electorate? Would it tear itself apart trying to broaden its appeal or trying to broker differences between elites and the rank and file? Radicals generally do not support moderation; would they be able to temper their ideology in order to govern? If not, would their ascendancy be a false start?

*(Kerbel 2016)*

No-one should misread the results of the 2016 election, nor ignore the demography that will shape future twenty-first century presidential contests. Trump's victory certainly signals an end to a Reagan-like Republican party. But it does not herald an emerging Republican coalition that can hold onto the presidency without winning ever-larger numbers of white, rural voters. This time, Donald Trump proved it could be done. But with every passing quadrennial, the number of these available voters to the Republican party gets smaller. Ruy Teixeira notes that as we approach 2032, political scientists are "far more likely to view the 2016 election as the last stand of America's white working class, dreaming of a past that no longer exists, than as a fundamental transformation of the political system" (Teixeira 2016). In 2016, Republicans found themselves winning congressional races based on gerrymandering and a lack of split-ticket voting. But it is also worth noting that in every contested Senate race, the Republican candidates *out-polled* Trump. Trump's coattails, such as they were, *did not* permit Republicans to keep their congressional majorities; rather, Republicans won *in spite of* Trump. While the GOP should recognize that it is not a majority party in the truest sense of that term, the challenges posed to the Democratic party by Hillary Clinton's unexpected loss cannot be overstated either.

## Democratic Disarray

Just forty-eight hours after Hillary Clinton's surprising defeat, Massachusetts senator Elizabeth Warren delivered a speech before the AFL-CIO labor organization, saying: "This wasn't a pretty election. In fact, it was ugly" (Warren 2016). For Democrats, the "ugliness" of the contest is clear: today, the party is in the worst shape since *1922*. Consider: when Obama won the White House in 2008, Democrats controlled 62 of the nation's 98 partisan legislative chambers; today, Republicans have majorities in 67 (Podhoretz and Rothman 2016; Hollingsworth 2016). Between Obama's election in 2008 and his exiting the presidency in 2017, more than 1,100 Democratic officials have lost their jobs (Podhoretz and Rothman 2016).

These include eleven U.S. Senate seats, sixty House seats, fourteen governorships, and *nine hundred* state legislative seats.

The latter is especially important since state legislators are a party's talent base. One only need to be reminded that in 2004, Barack Obama was an Illinois state senator who, just four years later, was elected President of the United States. Today, Republicans hold 4,170 state legislative seats, while Democrats occupy just 3,129 (Wilson 2016). In 2016, Republicans won majorities in the Minnesota and Iowa legislatures, while Republicans will have a majority in Kentucky for the first time in a century (Podhoretz and Rothman 2016). In twenty-four states, Republicans control both the state legislatures *and* the governorships, while Democrats have complete control in just six states (Wilson 2016). David Avella, head of GOPAC, a group that grooms young legislative candidates, says: "Republicans have been working for this moment for years, to have a federal government with Republican majorities and now at the state level" (Wilson 2016). These enhanced Republican majorities have long-term implications. As another census looms in 2020, Republicans are in an ever-stronger position to redraw congressional boundaries to protect their already engorged congressional majorities and even add more recruits to their ranks.

The decimation of the Democratic party at the state level has hurt the party's standing in Congress. Only two Democratic Senate seats were added to the party's ranks in 2016 (Maggie Hassan in New Hampshire and Tammy Baldwin in Illinois), a startling development given that Republicans had to defend twenty-four seats while Democrats had just ten to protect. Come 2018, Democrats face a daunting task: in ten states won by Donald Trump, incumbent Democratic senators must defend their seats against presumably strong Republican challengers. Likewise, House Democrats must continue to compete in districts gerrymandered by the GOP. While Republicans may face contentious primaries from challengers prepared to defend their new President against any whisper of defections, the normal impulse of a midterm election—namely, to put the brakes on an incumbent President—may be forestalled for an indefinite future.

At the same time, a note of caution should be struck. Shortly after Lyndon B. Johnson overwhelmed Barry Goldwater in 1964, political scientist Nelson Polsby declared that the much-heralded U.S. two-party system had morphed into a "one-and-a-half party system," with Republicans serving in the unenviable role of being the nation's "half-party" (White 2016, 2). Yet a mere four years after Goldwater's landslide loss, Republican Richard Nixon was walking triumphantly into the White House. Today, Washington Post columnist Eugene Robinson has taken up Polsby's cry, noting that the "two-party system is, at best, one-and-a-half," with the Republican party controlling the White House, Congress, and the Supreme Court, adding: "As far as the federal government is concerned, that's the whole trifecta" (Robinson 2016, A-27). But Barack Obama has reminded his fellow Democrats that after George W. Bush's 2004 win, Republicans had control of the federal trifecta, and just four years later surrendered two of these—the presidency and the Congress—to the Democrats (Remnick 2016). As the foregoing attests, predicting a party's future is hazardous business.

## The Party of Trump

Founded in the advent of a bloody Civil War, the Grand Old Party has historically viewed itself as a *preserver* of the Union. Abraham Lincoln, the first Republican President, saw his primary duty to preserve the Union. In a letter dated August 22, 1862, Lincoln made his policy clear:

> My paramount object in this struggle *is* to save the Union, and is *not* either to save or destroy slavery. If I could save the Union without freeing *any* slave I would do it, and if I could save it by freeing *all* the slaves I would do it; and if I could save it by freeing some and leaving others alone I would also do that. What I do about slavery, and the colored race, I do because I believe it helps to save the Union; and what I forbear, I forbear because I do *not* believe it would help save the Union.
>
> *(Donald 1995, 368)*

Later, Lincoln embraced the radical idea of freeing the slaves and endowing African-Americans with the dual responsibilities of citizenship and casting a ballot. Other Republican presidents in less crisis-driven times saw themselves as conservationists of policies enacted by their predecessors. In 1956, Dwight D. Eisenhower proclaimed the GOP to be a "one interest party; and that one interest is the interest of every man, woman, and child in America" (Eisenhower 1956). Privately, Eisenhower derided those who sought to erase the memory of Franklin D. Roosevelt:

> Should any political party attempt to abolish social security and eliminate labor laws and farm programs, you would not hear of that party again in our political history. . . . There is a tiny splinter group that believes you can do these things. . . . [But] their number is negligible and they are stupid.
>
> *(Greenstein 1982, 50)*

Similarly, Richard M. Nixon and Ronald Reagan preserved (and even expanded) the social safety net—despite cries from fellow partisans that they had gone too far. Even some of his fellow ideologues criticized Reagan for betraying conservative principles with their cry of "Let Reagan Be Reagan"—a tacit admission that a docile Reagan had become a tool of the political establishment. George H. W. Bush signed the Americans with Disabilities Act, and his son, George W., won congressional approval for a major education reform: No Child Left Behind. Eisenhower, Nixon, Reagan, and both Bushes acted according to the historic principles of the Grand Old Party as both preservers of an accepted past and a reform party that sought to build upon it.

Donald Trump has cast that tradition aside. In his hostile takeover of the Republican party, Trump argued that the federal government is run by corrupt politicians who allow illegal immigrants easy entry, sign bad trade deals that undermine manufacturing jobs, refuse to stand up for America overseas, and allow "radical Muslim extremists" to run free in the Middle East and, eventually, find their way into the United States. These sentiments found favor with the party's base:

- 71 percent of Republicans agreed with Trump's proposed ban on Muslim immigration (Wong 2016);
- 67 percent wanted a wall constructed on the U.S.-Mexican border (Pfeiffer 2016);
- 69 percent thought immigrants were a "burden" on the United States (Pfeiffer 2016);
- 67 percent thought free trade had been bad for the United States (Pfeiffer 2016);
- 51 percent believed that Trump's view of what the Republican party stands for best matches their own; only 33 percent chose House Speaker Paul Ryan as the better spokesperson (Selzer and Company 2016).

Several post-election analyses concluded that the Republican party had become the party of Donald Trump. Truth be told, Trump was always the GOP's sole proprietor. Trump prevailed in a seventeen-candidate primary field because he best represented the attitudes of Republican voters. Many believed that the America they once knew had been lost with the election of the first African-American President. Donald Trump tapped into these sentiments with his dogged pursuit of the claim that Barack Obama was born in Kenya, forcing a visibly annoyed Obama to release a long form of his Hawaiian birth certificate. Trump also knew that many Republicans falsely believed Obama to be a Muslim, and he sought to capitalize on that by banning Muslim immigration to the United States. Simply put, Trump's supporters saw Obama as the subversive "other" whose presidency was fraudulent and whose purpose was to undermine the United States. Also fueling Republican anger was *not* simply hatred of Barack Obama, but a widespread feeling that he had been *successful*. To this point, Obama signed into law the Patient Protection and Affordable Care Act—a measure Republicans pejoratively referred to as "Obamacare" (a term Obama embraced). In the view of many Republicans, Obama was rewarding his loyal supporters by giving them something for nothing—be it a stimulus bill, Obamacare, an auto bailout, banking reform, or sanctuary from prosecution for being in the country illegally—and doing so unilaterally. As one Tea party sympathizer put it: "When Congress is gone. . . he just does an Executive Order. He's going to get anything he wants. And there's nobody there that will have the guts enough to stand up to him" (Greenberg and Carville 2014, 23).

Donald Trump played up to these sentiments by promising to be a President of *action*: undo Obamacare, appoint conservative justices to the U.S. Supreme Court, give jobs to workers undercut by trade deals Obama supported, end the something-for-nothing programs designed to benefit Obama's minority supporters, build a wall on the Mexican border and deport 11 million illegal immigrants, bring "law and order" to minority neighborhoods, ban Muslims from entering the United States, "bomb the shit" out of ISIS, take the oil from Iraq, enact term limits, negate Obama's executive orders, reform the tax code, teach Republican officeholders how to win, and "make America great again." In short, a President Trump would expunge Obama from the history books and reduce the 44th President to a consequential asterisk. That erasure is exactly what Republican partisans wanted, and 90 percent of them cast their ballots for Trump (Edison Research 2016). GOP dissenters completely ignored Trump's dominance of the party base, and at its core the "#Never Trump" movement represented an infinitesimally small intellectual wing of the Republican party, along with some former Bush administration officials, a few elected Republicans in Congress, and editorial writers in heretofore rock-ribbed Republican newspapers. All earned the disdain—if not wrath—of the Republican party in the electorate.

## Conclusion: Can We Do Better?

At the end of the film, *The Last Hurrah*, Frank Skeffington, the aforementioned character earlier in this chapter, loses his bid for reelection. Lying on his deathbed, Skeffington summons his nephew, Adam Caufield, to his side and says, "I'm sorry the show didn't have a happier ending" (*The Last Hurrah* 1958). Much the same can be said about the 2016 election. Voters were unhappy with their choices and dubious of the result. A CBS News/New York Times poll taken on the eve of the election found an astonishing *82 percent* saying the Clinton-Trump race left them disgusted about the state of American politics (CBS News/*New York Times* 2016). Similarly, 64 percent told pollsters that the campaign polarized the country, and 62 percent said the contest made them "less proud" of the United States (NBC News/*Wall Street Journal* 2016). Only 30 percent gave Trump marks of "A" or "B" for the manner in which he conducted his campaign, the lowest grade given to any winning candidate since 1988 (Pew Research Center 2016). Following the proclamation that Donald Trump would become the 45th President of the United States, many Americans (especially high school students too young to vote) took to the streets to protest. None of this was surprising, as Trump's campaign of hate would have its price.

Adding to this is the increased isolation of country's Belmonts and Fishtowns. According to one post-election survey, 76 percent of voters who lived in counties with a Cracker Barrel Restaurant cast ballots for Donald Trump, while only 22 percent who resided in counties with a Whole Foods Supermarket did so (Powers 2016). That is just one indicator among many that our motto, "E Pluribus Unum"—"out of many, one"—is now more aptly described as "E Pluribus Duo"—"out of many, two"—two very different Americas, each standing separate and apart. Americans were angry in 2016, and angry voters vote. But this was anger with a difference: in 1980, Americans were *angry at* Washington, D.C., and they voted in landslide proportions for Ronald Reagan. In 2016, Americans were *angry with* each other. Whites were angry with non-whites whom they blamed for an economy that was eroding the American Dream by taking away their jobs; minorities were angry with police officers who seemed hellbent on incarcerating them and taking their lives in an unprovoked manner; Republicans were angry with Democrats who represented cultural values that were antithetical to their beliefs; Democrats were angry with Republicans who reflexively opposed a Democratic President regardless of the merits of his proposals; gays were mad with those heterosexuals who wanted to deny them their rights; some heterosexuals were angry at a Supreme Court that legalized gay marriage; and millennials were angry at seniors who benefitted from Social Security and Medicare (programs they believe they will never see), while seniors thought millennials were too quick to overturn centuries of traditional values, especially when it came to same-sex marriage. In 2016, there was no middle, no center, and virtually no swing constituencies. Landslides for either party were impossible to attain, even though Republicans won control of the federal government.

When the late Earl Weaver was leading the Baltimore Orioles and a baseball umpire would make a controversial call, the furious manager would go charging onto the ballfield and demand, "Are you going to get any better, or is this it?" (Will 1987). We have become a nation of Earl Weavers. In 2016, both parties nominated unpopular candidates whose deficiencies were readily apparent. Americans did not trust Hillary Clinton following disclosures that she kept an email server at her home where classified government secrets were housed while she was Secretary of State. The fact that Clinton was not charged by the FBI—coupled with criticism by its Director James Comey that she was "extremely careless" in handling national security information—did nothing to ameliorate concerns about her veracity and penchant for secretiveness. These doubts were brought into sharp relief when FBI Director Comey, on the very eve of the election, announced that the Clinton investigation was being reopened after emails between the former Secretary of State and a loyal staffer were found on the computer of that staffer's estranged husband. Although the Director further clarified his findings just forty-eight hours before the polls closed and announced no change to his initial finding not to prosecute Clinton, voters were hardly assuaged: 45 percent said Clinton's use of a private email server bothered them "a lot;" 61 percent said she was "not honest and trustworthy;" and 54 percent had an unfavorable view of her (Edison Research 2016).

But Donald Trump hardly fared any better: 60 percent said he was "not qualified" to serve as President; 63 percent believed he did not have the right temperament to be Commander-in-Chief; 63 percent thought he was "not honest and trustworthy;" 60 percent had an unfavorable view of him; and 50 percent said his treatment of women bothers them "a lot" (Edison Research 2016). Not surprisingly, just 13 percent were "excited" about the prospect of a Trump presidency; 27 percent were "optimistic;" 20 percent were "concerned;" and 36 percent said they were "scared" (Edison Research 2016). In sum, an exhausted electorate—willing to dispense with politics and dismayed by the spectacle it witnessed—collectively said to both parties, "Can't you do better than this?" Given a choice between a dishonest candidate and an unqualified one, it is not surprising that 59 percent of voters pronounced themselves to be unhappy with the whole process (NBC News/*Wall Street Journal* 2016).

In sum, the major parties are under siege. In 1971, journalist David S. Broder wrote an important book titled *The Party's Over*. Broder's view that the major parties had been upended by a combination of ambitious candidates and party reforms that undermined their establishments was nearly a half a century ahead of its time (Broder 1971). Whether the parties can rebound is in doubt, a fact has potentially grave consequences. In 1951, Harry S. Truman wrote to Bertram M. Gross, executive secretary to his Council of Economic Advisers, inviting members of the just-published

American Political Science Association report, *Toward a More Responsible Two-Party System*, to visit him at the White House (Committee on Political Parties 1950). In his letter, Truman expressed his interest in "maintaining our two-party system," and warned that "unless we are very careful it can become obsolete and that we don't want" (Truman 1951).

But even more important than the tests facing both major parties are the challenges posed by the 2016 election to our democracy itself. Donald Trump's victory demonstrates democracy's descent into a kind of netherworld of tawdry reality television that reduces our politics to shouting matches which, in turn, undermines the very nature of citizenship. On the eve of U.S. participation in World War Two, First Lady Eleanor Roosevelt authored a book titled *The Moral Basis of Democracy*. In it, she argued that "we must acknowledge that the life of Christ was based on principles which are necessary to the development of a democratic state" (Roosevelt 1940, 42). Roosevelt's call for a "Christ-like way of living," she believed, would "give us a sense of obligation about living with a deeper interest in the welfare of our neighbors" that would, in turn, create "a sense of brotherhood, a sense that we strive together toward a common objective" (Roosevelt 1940, 43, 48, 79). Democracy, the First Lady concluded, is not about keeping "some particular group that is stronger than other groups in power. It is a method of government conceived for the development of human beings as a whole" (Roosevelt 1940, 56).

The Greatest Generation passed the various tests to democracy that the First Lady foretold were coming. The rise of Hitler's Nazism and Soviet communism were met with stiff resistance from Roosevelt's fellow Americans who paid heed to her admonishments, despite occasional deviations from the country's established norms and values. The internment of Japanese Americans during World War Two, the blacklisting of American citizens during the Cold War, and the ongoing struggles to ensure civil rights for *all* Americans despite the many infringements upon them were among such lapses. But there came a reckoning, and eventual apologies were made for those unfortunate digressions. Today, Roosevelt's contention that democracy be based on "Christ-like" principles of cooperation and mutual respect faces its most important test. As Donald Trump prepares to assume the presidency, a nagging question remains: "Are we going to get any better, or is this it?"

## Bibliography

Ambrose, Stephen. 1987. *Nixon: The Education of a Politician, 1913–1962*. New York: Simon and Schuster.

Broder, David S. 1971. *The Party's Over: The Failure of Politics in America*. New York: Harper and Row.

Bush, George W. 1999. "The True Goal of Education." Gorham, New Hampshire, November 2.

Caldwell, Leigh Ann. 2016. "A Party Divided: How Donald Trump Emerged From Decades of GOP Tension." *NBC News*, July 7.

Campbell, James E. 2016. "Politics Symposium: Forecasting the 2016 American Elections." *PS*, 49:4. October. Pp. 649–654.

CBS News/New York Times. 2016. Poll, October 28–November 1.

Child Trends Data Bank. 2014. "Births to Unmarried Women," Child Trends Data Bank. www.childtrends.org/?indicators=births-to-unmarried-women (accessed August 3, 2014).

Clinton, Bill. 1998. Commencement Address. Portland State University, Portland, Oregon, June 13.

Committee on Political Parties. 1950. *Toward a More Responsible Two-Party System*. New York: Rinehart.

Donald, David Herbert. 1995. *Lincoln*. New York: Simon and Schuster.

Edison Media Research and Mitofsky International. 2008. Exit poll, November 4.

Edison Research. 2012. Exit poll, November 6.

———. 2016. Exit poll, November 8.

Edsall, Thomas B. 2016. "The Not So-Silent White Majority." *New York Times*, November 17.

Ehrenhalt, Alan. 1991. *The United States of Ambition: Politicians, Power, and the Pursuit of Office*. New York: Times Books.

Eisenhower, Dwight D. 1956. Acceptance Speech. Republican National Convention, San Francisco. August 23.

Friedel, Frank. 1990. *A Rendezvous With Destiny*. Boston, MA: Little Brown and Company.

Greenberg, Stanley B. and James Carville. 2014. "Inside the GOP: Report on the Republican Party Project." June 12.

Greenstein, Fred W. 1982. *The Hidden-Hand Presidency: Eisenhower as Leader*. New York: Basic Books.

Hoeffel, Elizabeth, Sonya Rastogi, Myoung Oak Kim and Hassan Shahid. 2012. "The Asian Population, 2010." U.S. Census Bureau, Washington, DC, March 12.

Hollingsworth, Barbara. 2016. "Republicans Now Control Record Number of State Legislative Chambers." *CNSNews.com*, November 16.

Judis, John B. and Ruy Teixeira. 2002. *The Emerging Democratic Majority*. New York: Scribner.

Kerbel, Matthew R. 2016. "Sorting It Out (1 of 5)." *Wolves and Sheep*, blog, November 12.

*The Last Hurrah*. 1958. Movie.

McCutcheon, Chuck. 2016. "Populism and Party Politics." *CQ Researcher* 26:31. September 9. Pp. 721–744.

Murray, Charles. 2012. *Coming Apart: The State of White America, 1960–2010*. New York: Crown Forum.

National Commission on Civic Renewal. 1998. "A Nation of Spectators: How Civic Disengagement Weakens America and What We Can Do About It." University of Maryland, College Park, June.

NBC News/Wall Street Journal. 2016. Poll, November 3–5.

Passel, Jeffery S. and D'Vera Cohn. 2008. *U.S. Population Projections: 2005–2050.* Pew Research Center Report, February 11.

Passel, Jeffrey S., D'Vera Cohn, and Ana Gonzalez-Berrera. 2013. "Population Decline of Unauthorized Immigrants Stalls, May Be Reversed." Pew Research Center, Hispanic Trends Project. Press Release, September 23.

Pew Research Center. 2016. "Low Marks for Major Players in 2016 Election—Including the Winner." Press Release, November 21.

Pfeiffer, Alex. 2016. "Poll Shows Where Trump Supporters and Other Republicans Agree." *Daily Caller*, May 12.

Plouffe, David. 2016. "What I Got Wrong About the Election." *New York Times*, November 11.

Podhoretz, John and Noah Rothman. 2016. "How Obama Wrecked the Democratic Party." *Commentary Magazine*, November 17.

Powers, Kirsten. 2016. "Trumping the Liberal Elite." *USA Today*, November 10.

Qiu, Linda. 2016. "Is Bernie Sanders a Democrat?" *Politifact*, February 23.

Rauch, Jonathan. 2016. "How American Politics Went Insane." *The Atlantic*, July/August.

Remnick, David. 2016. "Obama Reckons With a Trump Presidency." *The New Yorker*, November 28.

Robinson, Eugene. 2016. "Learn from the GOP and Rebuild From the Ground Up." *Washington Post*, November 18.

Romney, Mitt. 2016. Remarks on Donald Trump. Salt Lake City, Utah, March 3.

Roosevelt, Eleanor. 1940. *The Moral Basis of Democracy.* New York: Howell, Soskin and Company.

Schmidt, Steve. 2016. *Meet the Press.* NBC News Broadcast, October 9.

Schreckinger, Ben. 2015. "Trump Attacks McCain: 'I Like People Who Weren't Captured.'" *Politico*, July 15.

Selby, W. Gardner. "Pundit Says 50,000 Hispanics Turn 18 and Are Eligible to Vote Every Month." *Politifact*, October 7, 2011.

Selzer and Company. 2016. Poll, October 14–17.

Sherfinski, David. 2015. "Donald Trump: Mitt Romney Choked Like a Dog in 2012." *Washington Times*, November 11.

Strauss, Daniel. 2016. "Bernie's Empire Strikes Back." *Politico*, November 12.

Teixeira, Ruy. 2016. "Trump's Coalition Won the Demographic Battle. It'll Still Lose the War." *Vox*, November 15.

Truman, Harry S. 1951. Letter to Bertram M. Gross, September 14.

Trump, Donald J. 2015. *Crippled America: How to Make America Great Again.* New York: Threshold Editions, Simon and Schuster.

———. 2016. Republican Debate. Greenville, South Carolina, February 13.

U.S. Census Bureau. 2012. "Most Children Younger than Age One Are Minorities: Census Bureau Reports." Press Release, May 17.

Vespa, Jonathan, Jamie M. Lewis and Rose M. Kreider. 2013. "America's Families and Living Arrangements 2012." U.S. Census Bureau Report, August.

Warren, Elizabeth. 2016. Remarks to the AFL-CIO. Washington, DC, November 10.

Whatley, Monica and Jeanne Batalova. 2013. "Indian Immigrants in the United States." Migration Policy Institute. Press Release, August 21.

White, John Kenneth. 2009. *Barack Obama's America: How New Conceptions of Race, Family, and Religion Ended the Reagan Era.* Ann Arbor, MI: University of Michigan Press.

———. 2016. *What Happened to the Republican Party? And What It Means for American Presidential Elections*. New York: Routledge.

Will, George. 1987. *This Week With David Brinkley*. ABC News Broadcast, October 18.

Wilson, Reid. 2016. "Democrats Hit New Low in State Legislatures." *The Hill*, November 18.

Wong, Kristina. 2016. "Half American Voters Back Trump's Muslim Ban." *The Hill*, March 29.

# INDEX

Note: Page numbers in italic format indicate figures and tables.

advertising/advertisements: Clinton's style of 34; imbalance in 75; Super PAC's 40; Trump's style of 34, 38, 76
Affordable Care Act 20, 39, 123, 124, 189
African Americans 157, 161, 168, 175, *183*
amateur candidates 109, 110, 113, 119, 123
American dream 82, 190
American elections and electorate 30, 152, 164, 170, *183*
AP-GfK poll 93, *94, 96, 97, 98*
Arizona primary *45, 46, 49*
Ayotte, Senator Kelly 122, 123

"basket of deplorables" remarks 20, 78–9
battleground states 24, 28, 62, 163, 183
Biden, Joe 7, 38, 52
"blue firewall" 58, 62
border security 159, 160
Boxer, Barbara 123, 137
Bush, George H. W. 58, 90, 91, 176, 188
Bush, George W. 80, 90, 155, 180, 187
Bush, Jeb 8, 37, 40, 76, 103

California primary *45, 49, 51*
campaign: astonishing 69–76; of Bernie Sanders 7, 39, 51–2; for congressional elections 116–17; controversies related to 18, 19; debates and 15–21; of Donald Trump 2–3, 38, 74, 160, 162, 165; effect of 77–8; of Hillary Clinton 3–5, 27–8, 39; negative 75; odd development in 20–1, 74; potential impact of 108; qualities of 74–6; for resources 111–13, 115; shifting pattern in *70*; for votes 116–23; *see also* fundraising
candidates: acceptance speech of 71–2; amateur 109, 110, 113, 119, 123; campaign style of 2–7; character of 92, 95–8; congressional 106; endorsements for 42–3, 73, 112, 117, 159; female 103, 109–10, 113, 136–9; interplay of 157, 159–61; introduction to 2; lack of trust in 5; liabilities of 14–15; polls about 34, 41, 42, 53, 92, 100; primaries and 37–9; public opinion assessment and 107; sorting through so many 37; vote percentages and delegates *44–5, 48–9*; voters' perception of 92–3; *see also* primaries

Carson, Dr. Ben 9
caucuses: Democratic 36, *48–9*; procedure of 36; purpose of 35; Republican 36, *44–5*
character traits 95–8
Christie, Chris 7, 37
class *see* ethnic minorities; working-class whites
classified information 14, 70
climate change issues 92, *94*, 159, 165
Clinton, Bill 4, 6–7, 28, 181
Clinton, Chelsea 14, 130
Clinton, Hillary: acceptance speech of 72, 133, 140, 141; advertising style of 34; "basket of deplorables" remarks by 20, 78–9; Bernie Sanders and 175–6; campaign of 3–5, 27–8, 39; concession speech 29–30, 146; continuation of Obama's policies and 140–1; controversies related to 4, 39, 52; dampened excitement for 108; debate style of 15; election loss of 28–9, 77–8; electoral votes and 14, 22; endorsements for 42, 73; FBI investigation issues 14, 20–1, 52, 117, 130; final look at 145–6; as a First Lady 4; fundraising by 74; gender as the reason to vote for 134–5; introduction to 3; lack of trust in 5; Latino community and 159–63; likability problem of 139–40; making-history reason for supporting 133–4; media coverage of 42; party identification issues 89; popular vote and 22, 59–63, 100, 182; presidential vote for *59–61*; primaries and caucuses 47–52; public policy issues 91–5; as a senator 4; share of the vote for *183*; support for 16, 67–8; voter turnout for 65–7; woman's issues and 141–2
Clinton Foundation 4, 14, 96
Clinton supporters 63, 89, 92, 135–6, 138
Comey, James 21, 39, 70, 77–8, 191

*Coming Apart: The State of White America* (Murray) 184
Congress: Democratic party and 186; email investigation and 20, 39; increase in numbers of Latinos in 164–5
congressional elections: campaign for 116–17; candidate emergence and 108–11; conclusion about 123–5; fundraising for 107, 111–13, *115*; House races 117–20; incumbents and 111, 116; introduction to 103–4; outsiders and 109; run up to 105–6; Senate races 120–3; spending in *113–14*; strategic context 106–8; types of 104–5
congressional votes 23, 24, 43
Cruz, Ted 8, 34, 37, 71, 179

debates: campaign and 15–21; in democracy 74–5; final 18–19, 72–4; first 16, 72–3; introduction to 15; media coverage and 41–2; presidential election 15–21; primary 7, 15; range of issues in 19–20; second 18, 73
Decisions poll 162, 163
Deferred Action for Childhood Arrivals (DACA) 160, 167
Deferred Actions for Parents of Americans (DAPA) 160, 167
delegates: controversial 7; convention 35, 51, 133; Democratic 35, 36, 48–50; for nomination 12; Republican 35, 36, 44–6; selection of 35
democracy 29, 36, 74–6
Democratic caucuses 36, *48–9*
Democratic National Committee 11, 30, 53, 74
Democratic party/Democrats: congressional vote 23, 24; defection rates for 89–90; in disarray 185–7; Latino community and *157*, 166; national convention 11–12, 16, 52–4, 70–1, 133, 140; nomination 5–7, 34, 38–9, 108–9, 130, 175; Sanders' message with 6–7; state

legislatures 24; *see also* Electoral College/votes
Democratic primaries 44–5, 47–52, 108, 132, 152
demographic groups: population growth of 164; of presidential vote 22–3, 66–7; as "third great revolution" 181–5
deportation, mass 160, 165, 167
double standards for female candidates 136–9
Duckworth, Tammy 122, 123

economic development 4, 27, 28
economic policies 12, 28, 75
education: demography of vote and 66; female voters and 143, *144*; gender and *144*; by race 23
election cycles 37, 38, 104, 150–2, 163
Election Day 21, 51, 77, 87, 131
Electoral College/votes: changing or replacing 22; design of 13; disparity between popular vote and 88; Donald Trump 14, 21–2; effect of 62–4; Hillary Clinton 14, 22; introduction to 12–13; presidential vote and 57–60; recount issue 30
electoral map 13, 21, 58, 62
eligible voters 65, *156*, 168, *169*
email investigation *see* private e-mail server
endorsements: for candidates 40, 42–3, 73, 112, 117, 159; for congressional leaders 112; public opinion poll and 42–3
establishment, death of 175–8
ethnic minorities 68–9, 143, *144*, 158

family structures, transformation of 182
FBI investigation 14, 20–1, 52, 117, 130
federal courts 112, 125
federal government: dissatisfaction with 91, 99; size and efficiency of 93, *94*; as too large and intrusive 38
female candidates 103, 109–10, 113, 136–9

female solidarity, overestimating 131–2
female voters 129, 130, 133, 134, 143
financing *see* fundraising
Fiorina, Carly 9, 130
Fox News 8–10, 16, 41
Freedom Partners Action Fund 112, 113
fundraising: by Clinton 74; for congressional elections *115*; by congressional leaders 107, 111–13; for the House *115*; introduction to 2, 4; during preseason 40–1; by Sanders 7, 39, 54

Gallup polls 5, 90, *94*, 162
gender gap issues 67–8, 138
general election 12–15, 103, 104, 112, 113
generational divide in presidential election 142–3
glass ceiling, shattering xvii, 103, 109, 130, 146
GOP voting and voters 65, 106
governorships 24, 25, 186
Graham, Senator Lindsay 9
Great Recession 90, 107
Green party 45, 54, 65, 130, 131
Growth Opportunity Project 165
gun control 39, 92
gun rights 118, 123

Hassan, Maggie 122, 123
Heck, Joe 121, 122
Hillary Clinton presidency 26, 27
*Holder vs. Shelby County* 168
Hollen, Chris Van 123
House candidates 109, *110*, *111*, 113
House races 117–20
Huckabee, Mike 8

illegal immigrants 161, 165, 188, 189
immigration issues: candidates' position on 43, 91; exit polls for 95; Latino community and 160; presidential vote and 80; voter breakdown and 23; working-class voters and 38, 82

income inequality 100, 157
incumbent party 77, 79, 80, 108, 109
incumbent President 57, 88, 90, 91, 186
incumbents, congressional 111, 116
independent spending 112, 113
independent voters 51, 88, 117, 9099
industrial states 13, 21, 30, 62, 63
international trade agreements 6, 12, 17
Iowa caucuses 36, 39, 41, 43–4, 47–8
ISIS organization 14, 76, 189

Jindal, Bobby 9

Kasich, John 8, 34, 71, 176, 179
Kelly, Megyn 16, 41
Kirkpatrick, Ann 123
Koch Brothers 10, 112

*Last Hurrah, The* 178, 189
Latino community: Clinton and Trump and 159–63; conclusion about 170; Decisions poll 162, 163; Democratic party and 157, 166; Donald Trump and 159–63; immigration issues 160; introduction to xviii–xix; Latino electorate and 155–7; millennials 168; naturalized citizens 169; partisan consequences and 165; partisan preference among 161; political developments and 154–5; population growth of 151–3, 164; post-Obama politics and 163–9; presidential election and 68–9, 150–1; Republican party and 157, 162, 166; top issues for 159–60
Latino Republicans 155, 161, 162, 163
leadership trait 97–8
Libertarian party 8, 54, 65, 143, 151
Libya, attack on 7, 14, 39

majority-minority nation 152, 165, 181
"Make America Great Again" slogan 17, 38, 71, 80, 189
mass deportation 160, 165, 167
Masto, Catherine Cortez 121, 122, 123

media coverage: of Clinton 42; debates and 41–2; of Sanders 42; of Trump 10–11, 41
men, voter breakdown by 22–3
Mexican border, wall across 15, 188
middle class voters 24, 54, 82, 98, 165
millennials: connecting with 132; gender as the reason to vote and 134–5; Latino community 168; as a rising group 182; Sanders' message with 6–7
*Moral Basis of Democracy, The* (Roosevelt) 192

national conventions: contested 46; delegates 36; Democratic 11–12, 16, 52–4, 70–1, 133, 140; introduction to 7, 8; nominee selection at 35; opinion polls after 72; Republican 12, 52–4, 70–1
National Election Pool 89, 91, 93, 95, 163
national exit polls: for character traits 97; for immigration issues 95; Latino proportion of electorate and 68; for party identification 89–90; voters' message and 79; voting patterns and 142–5
nationalized elections 104, 105
Nevada caucuses 44, 47, 48
New Deal 6, 68, 81
New Hampshire primary 8, 43, 44, 48
nomination/nominees: conclusion about 54–5; conventional versus unconventional 34–55; delegates for 12; Democratic 5–7, 34, 38–9, 108–9, 130, 175; national conventions and 52–4; preseason phase 40–3; primaries and caucuses and 35–7, 43–52; Republican 7–11, 37–8, 40, 54, 68; rules for 35; selection of 35; unpopularity of 5, 29, 116, 138, 191
North American Free Trade Agreement (NAFTA) 17, 68

Obama, Barack: approval ratings 90–1; introduction to 4; share of the

vote for *183*; vote pattern shifting away from 62
Obama, Michelle 12, 53, 71, 133, 174
Obamacare 91, 92, 124, 141, 189
opinion polls *see* public opinion polls
outsider(s): congressional elections and 109; House candidates 109, *110*, *111*, 113; success rates for 117–18; support for 108; Trump as an 91, 99, 109

partisanship 66, 67, 105, 154
partisan voting 107, 116, 165
party affiliation 132, 143–5, *158*, 161
party identification 88–90, 98–9
party ideology 88–90, 99
party leaders, role of 180–1
*Party's Over, The* (Broder) 191
Pataki, George 9
Paul, Senator Rand 8
Pence, Mike 10, 53, 71, 151
Perry, Rick 8
Pew Research Center poll 93, *94*, 96–8, 154–61, 168–9
polarization, rise of 154
political action committees (PACs) 40, 107
political financing *see* fundraising
political glass ceiling xvii, 103, 109, 130, 146
politics and culture, merging of 178–81
polls: about candidates 34, 41, 42, 53, 92, 100; opinion 72; pre-election 51, 96, 98, 142, 174; public opinion 34, 41–3, 53, 92
popular vote: direct 22; disparity between Electoral College and 88; Donald Trump 22, 59–63, 99, 182; Hillary Clinton 22, 59–63, 100, 182; introduction to 13; patterns in 65–9
post-Obama politics 163–9
pre-election polls 51, 96, 98, 142, 174
preseason phase 35, 40–3
presidential election: broad outlines of 26–7; campaign style during 2–5; conclusion about 21–5, 82–4, 170, 189–92; critical markers in 67–9; death of establishment and 175–8; debates 15–21; democracy issues and 57–84; economic issues during 27; electoral map and 58, 62; general elections and 12–15; generational divide in 142–3; introduction to 1–2; Latino community and 68–9, 150–1; lessons learnt from 175–89; national conventions 11–12; nomination phase 5–11; recount of 30–1; results of *13*; as revenge of Fishtown over Belmont 184, 190; Russia's role in 74; style-versus-substance problem in 137; summary about 25–30; ten firsts in 130; Trump as a star of 179; very strange 87–8; vote count of 19, 30, 31, 51; voter turnout for 65, 155, 163, 164, 170; women and 129–46
presidential performance, evaluations of 90–1
presidential vote: for Clinton and Trump 59–61; conclusion about 98–101; demographics of 22–3, 66–7; electoral map 58, 62; electoral votes and 57–60; immigration issues and 80; influences on 80, 87–8
primaries: candidates and 37–9; closed 36; common calendar 37; Democratic side *44–5*, 47–52, 108, 132, 152; open 37; purpose of 35; Republican side 36, 43–6, 72, 103, 159; rules for 36; semi-closed 36–7; *see also specific states*
primary debates 7, 15
private e-mail server: criticism for use of 14, 39; FBI investigation about 14, 20–1, 52, 117, 130; introduction to 11
public dissatisfaction 91, 100, 107–9, 119
public opinion polls 34, 41–3, 53, 92
public policy issues 91–5

race: eduction by 23; gender and 143, *144*; voter breakdown by 22–3, 66–7
racism 78, 79
Republican caucuses 36, *44–5*
Republican delegates 35, 36, 44–6

Republican party/Republicans:
  Congressional vote 23, 24; debates
  restriction by 41; defection rates for
  89–90; introduction to 2, 3; Latino
  community and 157, 162, 166;
  national conventions 12, 35, 52–4,
  70–1; never-Trump faction and
  52, 189; nomination 7–11, 37–8,
  40, 54, 68; state legislatures 24–5;
  unconditional surrender of 176–8;
  see also Electoral College/votes
Republican primaries 36, 43–6, 72,
  103, 159
rigged system 19, 36, 63, 73, 125
Romney, Mitt 8, 90, 174, 177, 183–4
Rubio, Senator Marco 9, 38, 40
Russia: computer hacking issues and
  74; leaked emails and 11, 14, 30
Rust Belt states 13, 21, 28, 116, 131
Ryan, Paul 10, 117, 188

Sanders, Bernie: campaign of 7, 39,
  51–2; feminist supporters of 135;
  fundraising by 7, 39, 54; Hillary
  Clinton and 175–6; introduction to
  6; Latino support for 159; media
  coverage of 42; primaries and
  caucuses 47–52
Santorum, Rick 9
Senate races 116, 120–3, 185
sexism 72, 79, 136, 138
social media 34, 39, 43, 76, 116
South Carolina primary 46, 47
spending in congressional elections
  113–14
state legislative elections 24–5, 123,
  124, 186
status quo election 104, 116, 120, 124
"Stronger Together" slogan 24, 82
super delegates 7, 48–51, 175, 176
Super Political Action Committees
  (Super PACs) 2, 5, 40, 74, 119
Super Tuesday 35, 38, 46, 47, 50

tax return issues 17, 72
Tea Party 8, 9, 38, 104, 189
televised debates see debates
television time, paid 15, 75
"third great revolution" 181–5
"tidal wave" elections 104

Toomey, Patrick 122
tracking polls 163, 164
trade agreements 6, 12, 17, 82
Trump, Donald: acceptance speech
  of 71; accusations of being a
  misogynist 16; advertising style of
  34, 38, 76; appeal of 81, 99, 116;
  business interests 10, 18; campaign
  of 2–3, 38, 74, 160, 162, 165;
  comparison with Julius Caesar
  82–3; controversies related to 18,
  19, 105–6; debate style of 15, 72;
  delegates' support for 46; democratic
  discussion and 75–6; electoral votes
  and 14, 21–2; endorsements for 42;
  introduction to 2; lack of trust in
  5; Latino community and 159–63;
  media coverage of 10–11, 41; as
  an outsider 91, 99, 109; party of
  187–9; personal money spent by 40,
  41; popular vote and 22, 59–63, 99,
  182; presidential vote for 59–61;
  public policy issues 91–5; tax return
  issues 17, 72; see also presidential
  election; voters
Trump, Ivanka 12, 130
Trump, Melania 12, 53
Trump presidency 12, 26, 30, 53, 191
Trump supporters 15, 89, 92,
  136, 138
Twitter platform 20, 34, 38, 75, 137
two-party system 35, 36, 186, 192
two-party vote 59–61, 62

undocumented immigrants 159,
  160, 167

vote percentages 44–5, 47, 48–9
vote rationales 132–42
voters: appealing to 2, 3, 28; behavior
  of 87–9, 101; breakdown 22–3;
  eligible 65, 156, 168, 169; hostility
  of 75; independent 51, 88, 90, 99,
  108, 117; marital status of 145;
  message of 79–82; middle class 24,
  54, 82, 98, 165; minority 47, 81;
  perception of 92–3; religious 43, 46;
  Republican candidates and 37, 38;
  Trump as voice of their grievances
  81–2; turnout 65, 155, 156, 163,

164, 170; working-class 28, 38, 46, 82, 116, 121
vote(s): campaign for 116–23; meaning of 77–9
voting patterns 62, *132*, 142–5
voting rights 165, 168

Walker, Scott 9
war in Iraq 14, 16, 39
Warren, Elizabeth 52, 53, 185
WikiLeaks 11, 14, 30, 74, 117
winner-take-all provision 36

Wisconsin primary *45*, 46, *49*, 51
women: House candidates 110, *111*; House elections *118*; introduction to 3, 4; presidential election and 129–46; Senate campaign 121; success rates for 117–18; support for Clinton 16, 67–8; Trump's statements about 16, 72–3, 97; vote rationales 132–42; voter breakdown by *22–3*; voting patterns *132*
working-class whites 25, 69, 122, 139, 142